THE SUPERNATURAL POWER OF LOVE
ISBN 13: 978-1-946467-00-3
ISBN 10: 1-946467-00-6
Copyright © 2016 by Jack Shoup
4514 Briar Hill Rd.
Lexington, KY 40516

Published by:
Piercing Light Publishing
4514 Briar Hill Rd.
Lexington, KY 40516
859-299-0664
Printed in the United States of America.
All rights reserved under International Copyright Law. Contents and/or cover may not be reproduced in whole or in part in any form without the express written consent of the Publisher.
All Scripture quotations are taken from the *King James Version* of the Bible.

Cover design by Troy D. Ledford www.bluewhaleinnovation.com.

THE SUPERNATURAL POWER OF LOVE

by
Pastor Jack Shoup

TABLE OF CONTENTS

                                                            Page

Acknowledgments
Introduction   *i*

Chapter 1   ***The Need For Love***   *01*

    The Focus of this Book
    The Problem is ...
    Love Fulfills the Law
    Love is the High Calling for Every Believer
    Pleasing God
    Love is not Wimpy
    Disciples of Love
    Love Never Fails
    The Attitude of Love

Chapter 2   ***Supernatural Love***   *21*

    Close Encounters of the God Kind
    Love is:
    The Nature of God and Born-Again Man
    The Inner Motivation to Live in a Benevolent, Forgiving, and
                                        Unoffendable Manner
    The Fruit of the Spirit
    The Bonding Force that Produces Church Unity
    The Giving Nature and Motivational Force
    The Atmosphere of Heaven
    The Evangelistic Anointing
    The Anointing that Eradicates Strife and Removes Offense
    An Anointing that Causes the Demonic to Manifest and Flee
    An Anointing that Delivers from Fear and Fear of Death
    An Anointing that Disperses Darkness and Brings Light
    An Anointing that Charges, Motivates, and Directs our Faith
    An Anointing that is to be Developed and Poured out unto
                                             the Glory

Chapter 3   ***God's Recipe For Love***   *45*

    Embracing New Revelation
    Targeting Genuine Love
    A Pure Heart
    A Good Conscience

TABLE OF CONTENTS

Page

Chapter 4   ***The Seed of Love***   *65*
Genuine Faith
Five Steps of Faith
Speaking Love
Acting in Love
The Fight of Faith
Living as a Blessing
Greater Love
Giving Love

Chapter 5   ***Rooted in Love***   *101*
The Key to Success
The Rooted Remnant
Converting Love to Fruit
Roots of Faith
Balanced Roots
Attracting the Harvest

Chapter 6   ***The Glory of Love***   *123*
A Glory Revival
Tabernacles of Glory
New Testament Temples
Exceeding Glory
The Mirror of the Word
Lively Stones
United Unto Glory

Chapter 7   ***Covenant Love***   *153*
The Difficulty of Acting in Love
Defining Covenant
The Church Covenant
The Commitment of Covenant
The Rules of Covenant

TABLE OF CONTENTS

Page

Chapter 8   God's Stairway to Agape   *175*
   Mandatory Steps to Love
   Step 1: Faith
   Step 2: Virtue
   Step 3: Knowledge
   Step 4: Temperance
   Step 5: Patience
   Step 6: Godliness
   Step 7: Brotherly Kindness
   Step 8: Love
   The Stairmaster

Chapter 9   Abiding in Love   *205*
   Connected to the Vine
   Obedient Branches
   Knowing Love
   A Note on Hyper-Grace
   Revelation by Love

Chapter 10   Perfect Love   *223*
   Bold Love
   Addressing Fear
   Rejecting the World

Chapter 11   The Truth of Love   *241*
   What is Truth?
   Loving Truth
   The Alternate Recipe for Love

Chapter 12   Forgiving Love   *253*
   The Love Limiter
   Forgiveness Seed
   Forgiveness Intercession
   Blessing Our Enemies
   The Process of Forgiving
   Forgiving Versus Enabling

Chapter 13   The End of Love   *271*
   All-In
   A Love Checklist

Acknowledgments

I dedicate this book to my wife Patty. Her extreme compassion enabled her to tolerate me as I learned the principles outlined within this book.

As well, I want to thank my mother, Geneva Wallace, who always encouraged me to pursue and choose truth.

I give special thanks to Apostle Ron Callahan who mentored me through so many years of ignorance.

I also want to thank Dr. Bobbie Jean Merck, Dr. John Bullock, and Pastor Kim Roth whose support furthered my pursuit in completing this writing.

Thank you

Introduction

I was raised an agnostic and growing up never knew of a Christian in my family. The first time that I went to church I was seventeen years old and became so bored that I couldn't wait to get out of the place. I went again when 20 at the invitation of a girlfriend and was equally bored. I didn't go back to another church service for nearly ten years. I had been raised under a mindset that Christianity was *a crutch for weak-minded people* and that all this stuff about God was *a bunch of malarkey.* I am sure some of you have heard these same things. Therefore, I was already predisposed to question the reality of God.

My parents however were somewhat open-minded. Even though they didn't personally believe in God or believe that the Bible was the Word of God, they told me I should study it for myself. So, in my twenties I decided to do just that after someone had given me a Gideon pocket Bible. As my coworker who had given me the Bible instructed me to do, I opened to the book of Mark and began reading. I don't remember if I got through two verses or two chapters, *but the power of God came on me, and I knew that I knew that every word in that Bible was true and that Jesus was the son of God!* I didn't even know anything about Jesus but from what I had only just read, I knew that what the Bible said of Him was true.

I tell you this because, not having been raised in religion, I was never trained that the power of God portrayed in the Scriptures had passed away. I had not been programmed to believe that God was powerless and that His working of miracles had died away with the first disciples. It would be several years later before I actually gave my life to the Lord but after salvation, I began reading my Bible voraciously. With little outside influence to teach me other than the Holy Spirit, as I read about the power of God and of miracles, I had no reason to believe that it was not for today.

My salvation had been somewhat miraculous in itself. Called out through a *word of knowledge*, my wife and I ended up getting born again the same evening. We had only been married for a few months so once saved, we immediately started looking for a church. However, everywhere we went, the churches lacked power. We were waiting for the dead to be raised, for limbs to grow out, and for blind eyes to see. We wondered where the miracles were. As we continued to visit churches, we eventually did start finding some that were operating in the power of God and we ended up connecting with a whole group of believers who also were seeking after this same power.

I had been saved for seven years and had been working as an engineer for fourteen when God told me to start a Bible study out of my home. I consulted with my pastor about this and he encouraged me to do it. During the week prior to my second class, I was seeking to hear the voice of God and to get direction on what to teach. As I laid on my face for an extended time, I heard Him very clearly say "love." I knew from this that He wanted me to study and teach on the love of God. However, that was about the last thing I wanted to teach.

Let me explain a little more about my background. As many my age can attest, during the time frame when I grew up, if a male showed any resemblance to softness he was immediately labeled and certainly persecuted. Nobody would want to come around him. Love was something men didn't even speak of, much less pursue. Furthermore, I have an analytical mind. Engineers think; they calculate a lot. I love the subjects of math and science and grew up with that focus. When I was a teenager, my favorite television show was Star Trek and my favorite character was Mr. Spock. I liked Mr. Spock because everything he did was logical - he had no emotions. I decided then that emotions were for weak people and I didn't want them. So I attempted to live emotion free. Therefore the thought of focusing on love, even after being saved for seven years, was not my preferred topic.

However, once I started teaching on love, God wouldn't let me off of that subject. I wanted to teach about healing, or miracles, or faith, but God started showing me how He wanted to focus the ministry I had on this Love.

As I got into the scriptures, I found that Love is more than just a feeling, it is a supernatural force. For over twenty five years now I have been doing intense study and teaching on the subject of love. From this, I believe that God has given me quite a bit of revelation on how to access this supernatural force – a force that the majority of the church has never experienced.

Much of the church of today has explained away the miracle power of God leaving their congregations with no expectation of the supernatural. In the same way, the supernatural components of the love of God have been nullified and replaced with philosophical reasonings. Without an awareness that the genuine love of God is supernatural in content, no one walks with an anticipation of love's true capabilities operating in and through them.

Love is the most powerful force in the universe yet its full potential lies dormant and untapped within most of Christianity. This book targets teaching the serious student how to take the lid off of this infinite power supply.

Many of you have been in church all your lives and have been told all along that there is no power remaining in the church. I'm a believer in the infinite power of God. So when I begin describing the Love of God, I'm going to describe it as an empowerment that is way beyond what most people have ever comprehended. Understanding how to access the power of the Love of God may require you to understand some new concepts. I'm asking you right now to not mentally short circuit when you read something new. Ask the Holy Spirit to expand your comprehension of the genuine love of God. I encourage you to just keep reading to the end because, I promise you, if you read and apply the concepts in this book, *you will be changed.* I'm convinced of that. I know what it has done in my life and what it has done in my household. And I'm convinced it will do the same things in anyone's life who will apply what I am going to teach in the following chapters.

This is an intense book. In these chapters you will find out the importance of Love and what it does for us. We will cover what I call the *Recipe for Agape*, where you will start finding out how to access the Love of God. You will find instruction on *forgiveness intercession* and see how aspects of the Love of God can supercharge your prayers and see people set free. You will learn about the Fruit of the Spirit in a whole new light and find out how to get your roots planted so deeply in the Love of God that you can never be uprooted. You will learn about covenant and explore the connection between walking in covenant and manifesting love. You will discover that the level that you manifest the love of God is directly proportional to your relationship with Him. And you will find that this means more than just being born-again. You will see that truly walking in the Love of God requires that you be led of the Spirit.

As you put into practice the concepts of this book and start walking in the empowerment of the genuine love of God, it will act as a magnet to bring in the harvest of God. Pastors will no longer have to pound people over the head and condemn them to get them into the church. They will be drawn in magnetically by the force of love that you carry - representative of the image and nature of God Himself.

You are going to need your Bible. Because of religious training, we've skimmed over and passed by truths that are in there and as a result have not been able to access the power in the Word. We will cover several passages of scripture repeatedly to extract every bit of revelation on love that we can. These will be the same scriptures that God started challenging me with in my pursuit to understand *agape*. I want you to see that I am not just taking one verse out of context. Instructions to walk in love are embedded throughout the Word of God and in particular elaborated on within our New Testament. I want you to see that I'm not making these things up.

The Bible tells us that we are to walk in love; that love fulfills everything God has called us to do and become. If you will apply the Biblical principles explored in this book, you will experience a fulfillment you may previously not have realized. You will learn how to access and operate in the genuine Love of God, versus merely attempt to perform a series of good deeds out of your own strength.

You'll find out before we're done that you can burn yourself out merely attempting to do good works. Yet, we will see that the Love of God will never burn you out. It will bring you into a relationship with God where you can really enjoy your walk with Him and experience true contentment in it. Not only that, but as you learn to access this empowerment, it can deliver you personally from past emotional strain or hurts.

This book contains instructions of how to restore any damaged relationships in your life, including those with any family members whom you have previously been unable to associate.

This book will challenge and train the serious believer to enhance their Christian experience to whole new levels. I pray that it blesses you.

Jack Shoup

Chapter 1

The Need For Love

Congratulations! You've made the most important decision you will ever make outside of that to be born again. In reading this book, you're demonstrating a desire to pursue the most powerful force in the universe - the *agape* love of God. *Agape*, the Greek word for the *love of God*, represents God's highest calling for the Christian since repeatedly The Bible declares that love fulfills all the commandments of God.

Hosea 4:6 informs us that God's people are destroyed for lack of knowledge. Jesus declared in Mark 7:13 that the traditions of men nullify the power of the Word of God. This book is intended to strip away misunderstandings regarding the love of God, and to impart revelation of this supernatural empowerment that will enable us to genuinely love with the God kind of love.

THE FOCUS OF THIS BOOK

The purpose of this book is to teach in a logical, orderly, and scriptural manner:

1) **What the genuine *agape* of God is in reality, exploring its supernatural qualities,**
2) **What the *agape* of God will accomplish in the life of the believer,**
3) **How can we access and manifest this supernatural force, and**
4) **How *agape* ties to the manifestation of God's glory.**

When we talk about love, we naturally think about an emotional feeling or we think about love in terms of affection, endearment, or some type of attractive power (i.e., *"I love her,"* or *"He loves me."*). While the true love of God affects the emotions, it is a supernatural empowerment that far surpasses human emotions. It is a release of power from the Kingdom of God itself.

THE GENUINE LOVE OF GOD IS MULTIFACETED:

First - The love of God is imprinted within our born-again nature when we are saved. It's who we are. Love is the program that we have on the inside of us once we become God's child. We are made in the image of love.

Second - The love of God is a force, it's an anointing that will alter natural events. It will even charge the realm of the soul and drive demonic forces out of people's lives.

Third - The love of God is a fruit - an outward manifestation of our inner reborn spirit.

All three represent the love of God in some form, in the form of our nature, in the form of an anointing, and in the form of His fruit manifested through us. This book will unveil greater depths of understanding regarding each of these, and the impact they may have upon our lives once accessed.

THE PROBLEM IS ...

The problem is, that in our pursuit of love, so few know what *agape* actually is, and even fewer know how to manifest and develop it. **The biggest challenge to a Christian's being able to walk in love is that we confuse *agape* with 'natural' human love. However, natural man is incapable of walking in *agape*; a love that originates only from God Himself.** As we shall see, The Bible lets us know that it is a love that can only manifest through the born-again child of God.

If we do not comprehend what the love of God actually is then we will be tempted to pursue a watered-down counterfeit philosophical version of love. If we do not know what genuine love will produce in our lives then we will not be adequately motivated to pursue it at all.

This first chapter is intended to provide scriptural reasons to desire love to flow in our lives. Chapter two will relate many of the supernatural benefits of love.

In the Greek language of the first century, there were three words commonly used for love, each with different meanings. The first of those words is *eros*. You've probably heard of *eros*. It's where we get the word *erotic*. *Eros* is flesh-oriented love. It represents natural, physical attraction which is usually sexual in nature.

The second word that's frequently used in scripture for love is *phileo*. *Phileo* represents the love of friends or family. It's the love that human beings are normally able to express toward one another. Usually it's a reciprocal love (i.e., *"I'll bless you because you bless me."*). *Phileo* actually becomes the highest level of love people can regularly walk in without knowing Christ.

The focus of this book is on the third type of love - the *agape* of God.

Regarding *agape*, an amazing statement is made in First John that may potentially anger those not born-again and even some that are.

> *1John 4:7-8 - "Beloved, let us love one another: for love is of God; and every one that loveth is born of God, and knoweth God. He that loveth not, knoweth not God; for God is love."*

Here we see that the level that we personally know God is directly proportional to the level that we can walk in love. **If we don't know God and have not developed a relationship with Him, we cannot walk in love.** God is the initial source of all agape love that we are assigned to demonstrate.

The word *agape* in classical Greek literature was never used except with regard to God's supernatural love. It is not found in any ancient writings regarding the actions of men until after the resurrection of Jesus. **And, it says that the love of God is only available for those who are born-again.** If we look at Verse 7, it clearly states, *"He that loveth is born of God."*

A person may experience the love of God when they're not born again; they may receive a taste of it, but they cannot manifest it nor walk in it. Only a born again Christian has access to the supernatural love of God; that is to live and abide in it and to carry it themselves. And this is really what we are supposed to do. For the Christian to not manifest a higher level of love than the world demonstrates is the epitome of hypocrisy. Many saved individuals may say that they love God with all of their heart yet never spend any time in prayer or the Word to allow them to know Him. Consequently, they never get to manifest genuine agape.

When we tap into supernatural love, it will often come upon us as an anointing. The word *anointing* means *to rub on*. And the Bible tells us in Isaiah 10:27 that the anointing is the power of God which *removes burdens and destroys yokes*. The anointing of God is a visitation of the power of God in our life that produces supernatural results. This is true of all the anointings of God. They produce results beyond the natural.

For example, God has gifts that heal through an anointing. And if we learn how to access the healing power of God, then a supernatural force that transcends our ability comes upon us and allows us to overcome sickness and disease.

The love of God functions in the same way. Just as divine healing is supernatural in content, the true love of God is also. It has the ability to heal our relationships, to take scars from off of our hearts, and to pull inappropriate walls down. These walls represent mental strongholds that have caused us to resist allowing people to interact in our lives or have hindered us from acting as a blessing to others. Anointed love will take us onto a whole other plane of walking in relationship with God and experiencing His supernatural power.

Did you know that Jesus didn't have any hindering walls erected in his life? The love that Jesus walked in kept all limiting walls pulled down allowing Him to love without restraint. There exist what I call ***landmines*** of the soul – **personal soul defense reactions**. The enemy has buried these landmines within people by causing them to meditate on perceived past rejection or abuse, thus creating sensitive areas in their thinking that make them prone to offense. With many people, if you say or do the wrong thing, a hair trigger is touched within them and 'boom' they explode. Without love, many walls and landmines that exist within us cannot be deactivated, thus hindering us from walking in the full image of Jesus.

One (now) humorous example of this occurred when my wife and I were first married. We had gone to Dairy Queen where she ordered a chocolate dip cone. Before I handed it to her, I erroneously bit the little curly-Q off the top only to watch a shadow fall across her beautiful face. Little did I know but that was a landmine that would set off a nuclear explosion in our car as we headed home! I relate this, not to demean my bride but to let you know that even the most seemingly perfect angel on earth may indeed have some of these hidden mindsets. I would have cheerfully purchased her another dip cone but in her mind this was an egregious transgression. Praise God, it is good to know that the love of God can deliver us from even the most catastrophic of events.

It's hard to convince people that we properly represent Jesus when, if the wrong thing happens in traffic, if the wrong thing happens at work, or if someone cuts in line in front of us at the mall, we go off and manifest something that may not represent godliness. The love of God has the potential to set us free from all of these triggers of the enemy.

As well, before we proceed any further, I want you to know that there is no more depression under the influence of the love of God; we'll be smiling all the time when under love's influence! We will discuss this more in the next chapter.

Most people misunderstand the love of God. They perceive the love of God to be an emotion or an emotional reaction when in fact the Love of God totally transcends the realm of emotion. They think the Love of God is fully expressed through performing a good deed such as mowing someone's lawn or visiting those in the hospital. These are actions that supernatural love may inspire us to do, but that's a very limited comprehension of this most powerful force.

When God interacts with this natural realm, He interacts primarily in the form of releasing some type of empowerment – doing something beyond the level of human ability. So when we're referencing the genuine love of God, it must be something that allows us to transcend our own emotional capacity or our personal ability to do good deeds. The truth is, we can only do good deeds as long as we feel like doing them. As long as we're in the right mood and have the right opportunity we may do some nice things. However, the love of God is a force that will take us far beyond human limitation and into a realm that we can't imagine.

For the remainder of this book unless otherwise indicated, when we use the term *love*, we are referring to *agape* or one of its forms.

LOVE FULFILLS THE LAW

The supernatural quality of love is demonstrated in it's ability to fulfill the intent of the Old Testament Law, which no man of himself could keep.

> *Rom 13:8-10 -"Owe no man anything, but to love one another: for he that loveth another hath fulfilled the law. For this, Thou shalt not commit adultery, Thou shalt not kill, Thou shalt not steal, Thou shalt not bear false witness, Thou shalt not covet; and if there be any other commandment, it is briefly comprehended in this saying, namely, Thou shalt love thy neighbor as thyself. Love worketh no ill to his neighbor: therefore love is the fulfilling of the law."*

When Paul is writing that the love of God fulfills The Law, the law that he's referring to is the Old Testament. The Word that God gave to Moses and the children of Israel became the constitution in which they were supposed to walk to fulfill His plans for them. If Israel could have fulfilled the law, they would have satisfied God's purpose for them in every area of their lives.

Here Paul informs us that when we walk in the Love of God, we fulfill the entire Old Testament's intention and thus fulfill

God's entire purpose for man. So from this we can deduce that if the law satisfied God's desire for man and love fulfills that law, then **if we can walk in love we will fulfill every desire that God has for our lives.** It becomes the utmost calling, plan, and purpose of God for man.

When first saved, my original thoughts were that *"As a man, I didn't need love"* and that *"Love is for women."* How silly that must have sounded to God. You can imagine how it must sound to tell God, Who is love, that we don't need the very essence of Him in Whose image we were created. This is equivalent to saying that we don't need Him or His plans and purposes; that we don't want to please Him and that we are going to live in the same limited fashion as we always have. And we'll hit the same walls that we've always hit. Men need the love of God as much as women, and may need to focus on it even more. Because men tend to put up more barriers and walls against love in their lives, they need an empowerment that will tear down these obstacles to their walk with God.

Additional revelation of how love fulfills The Law is provided in the Book of Galatians.

> *Gal 5:14 - "For all the law is fulfilled in one word, even in this; Thou shalt love thy neighbour as thyself."*

Many people say they love God, but God didn't say that loving Him alone fulfilled all of The Law. He said that loving our neighbor did. And who's our neighbor? It is not just the one who has the address right next door to us. In general, it is whomever we're coming in contact with. In particular, it's certainly those within our church. Here again Paul says that we must love our neighbor and that this fulfills all of the purpose and intent of The Law.

In other words, our Bible was given to us as God's plan for man. And when we walk in love, we fulfill the Word and therefore we fulfill everything that God has in mind for us. In fact, the Old Testament describes man's effort to walk in love through obeying a written set of laws - and of course that didn't work. The truth is, it won't work for us either. We cannot walk in the love of God by merely having a structured and organized life; a life where we have certain dos and don'ts in how we always interact with God, within the church, and with each other. We must develop a relationship with God to activate God's plan for our lives. The New Testament relates God's instructions on how to really walk in that Love. So when we walk in the Love of God, we are fulfilling all of the instruction of both the Old and New Testaments for us. Reading further in Galatians we find:

> *Gal 5:15-16 - "But if ye bite and devour one another, take heed that ye be not consumed one of another. This I say then, Walk in the Spirit, and ye shall not fulfill the lust of the flesh."*

Here Paul declares that if we don't walk in love, we will *"bite"* and *"devour"* one another. Without love, we'll get caught up in cannibalism - specifically church cannibalism. If we look at the average church, it's full of gossip and backbiting, jockeying for position, and politicking. In God's eyes, all of that is biting and devouring one another within His church body. If we don't learn to access the true love of God, we'll get suckered into this kind of activity. Thankfully, the love of God contains power to deliver us from all of these ungodly actions.

LOVE IS THE "HIGH CALLING" FOR EVERY BELIEVER

> *Mark 12:28-31 – "And one of the scribes came, and having heard them reasoning together, and perceiving that he had answered them well, asked him, "Which is the first commandment of all?" And Jesus answered him, "The first of all the commandments is, Hear, O Israel; The Lord our God is one Lord: And thou shalt love the Lord thy God with all thy heart, and with all thy soul, and with all thy mind, and with all thy strength: this is the first commandment. And the second is like, namely this, Thou shalt love thy neighbour as thyself. There is none other commandment greater than these.""*

These scriptures tell us that love is the greatest of the

commandments – loving God and loving those around us. Here God is letting us know that we had better learn how to love. For several years I tried to do this in my own strength and I would fail at it every time. I couldn't seem to love with the kind of love that Jesus commanded us to carry.

> *John 15:12 – "This is my commandment, that ye love one another, as I have loved you."*

Did you see that? Jesus said to *"love one another as I have loved you"*. Wow! Most of you reading this know that Jesus is God. And He here says that we should walk in the same type and level of love that He walked in. Jesus went to the cross for people who hated, mocked, and spit on Him. They beat him, pulled out His beard, and put a crown of thorns on His head. He went to the cross for all of us while we were yet sinners. That to the natural man is an unattainable level of love. And here Jesus is instructing us to walk in that same fashion.

If you are anything like me, you learned to build the previously mentioned walls in your life. We proclaimed sayings like: *"No one will ever get close to me again"* and *"You can hurt me once but never twice."* In fact, my wife was the recipient of a horrendous set of walls that I had put up. Before I was born again, as with many people, I had been burnt in a romantic relationship or two. As a result of this, I said that I would never let a girl get close to me like that again. When I met my future wife, as we began dating we really cared for each other and she wanted me to open up to her. But I had erected numerous walls of resistance and treated her terribly. I treated her like I didn't care whether she stayed in the relationship or not. This was a result of the past cuts to my heart. I looked at those scars and, realizing that I never wanted to allow myself to be hurt like that again, put up walls to keep out her and anyone else. It had to be the intervention of God to keep her with me until I could get my head on straight.

James, the brother of Jesus, proclaimed love as the royal law:

> *Jas 2:8 - "If ye fulfil the **royal law** according to the scripture, Thou shalt love thy neighbour as thyself, ye do well."*

The royal law is fulfilled through loving our neighbor. I knew that I had much to learn when I finally came to the realization that I couldn't do this of myself.

PLEASING GOD

As a calculating person I was aware even before I was born again that I am only on this earth for a limited period of time. It was my intent to maximize these years. Prior to being saved, I tried to project how much I could drink, how much I could do drugs, and how much I could party on a level that would let me live the longest amount of time and yet maximize this opportunity. I was an alcoholic for twelve years. The longest I went sober during that period was for two weeks when I had tried to quit. But I calculated that if I stayed drunk all the time I wouldn't live past 40 and that would reduce the time I could spend partying. So I figured that if I just limited the time I spent drunk to two or three times a week, I could live to 60 or 70 and then go on to wherever.

After I became saved, I realized that I still only had a limited amount of time here on Earth. I realized also that I was going to be in Heaven for a lot longer time than I was going to be here. It also occurred to me that God is going to be the one to determine what I do in Heaven and what the rewards will be. My logical conclusion became that it would be beneficial for me to focus on doing God's will while on earth rather than my own.

In these verses that we just read it says that love fulfills the commandments. Therefore, love must be what God is looking for. I believe 'love' is what truly pleases God. Therefore, **God's highest rewards will surely be set aside for those who walk in love.** It only makes sense that the Christian should maximize his effort to target walking in this power.

LOVE IS NOT WIMPY

Many people refer to Hebrews 11:6, teaching that *faith* pleases God, but that's not what the verse actually says. Let's look at the whole verse:

> *Heb 11:6 - "But without faith it is impossible to please him: for he that cometh to God must believe that he is, and that he is a rewarder of them that diligently seek him."*

It says that **without** faith we can't please God. One thing that this book is going to reveal is that the number one thing we can use faith for is to access love. Love fulfills God's plan for us. Love pleases God! As I started seeing that love is what God is going to reward me for, I realized that I needed to find out more about it. And if there is anything within me that is too macho or that thinks love is unmanly, then I had better retrain myself to realize that that's not how God looks at it. If you think that love is soft, recall that the Bible says that Jesus went into the temple and made a whip then started beating the moneychangers and turning over their tables. So love is not soft; love is all-powerful.

One of the first challenges we have when targeting love is to get out of our minds the mistaken notion that love is some mushy, emotional type of thing. It's the most powerful force in the universe because it's the very essence and nature of God Himself. Ephesians 5 provides even more dimension to this:

> *Eph 5:1-2 - "Be ye therefore followers of God, as dear children; and walk in love, as Christ also hath loved us, and hath given himself for us an offering and a sacrifice to God for a sweet-smelling savor."*

Here it says that when we walk in love we are walking as followers of God; that we are walking as Christ walked. You may already know that we are supposed to reflect Christ's image on the earth, and it says in the Bible that walking in love accomplishes just that. However, it also says that He gave Himself for a sacrifice. We will have to learn to live our lives as a blessing to other people versus being self-centered. Selfishness and self-centeredness reflect the nature of satan.

Many people including Christians, operate in a 'me' mentality, which asks: *"What can I get out of people?"*; *"What am I going to get out of this situation?"*; *"What am I going to get out of this conversation or this interaction?"* But the truth is, that this is 180 degrees out of phase with operating in the love of God. To truly access the love of God, we will have to develop a mentality that asks: *"What can I impart to this person?"* As we learn to do that, we will demonstrate that we are beginning to learn how to step over into the supernatural force of love.

Looking at Jesus as our example, we see that He was rejected throughout His ministry even to the point that efforts were made to kill Him multiple times. He was ran out of cities and not let into others. He was lied about and had His words twisted. That type of assault would cause most to want to just walk away.

You and I have had people rub us the wrong way and we were tempted to cut them out of our lives. If someone cut us off in traffic, we had to cast down the temptation to call hailstones down upon their car. We have had to continually guard ourselves in those types of situations. **But we see Jesus walking in a level of love that allowed Him to open Himself to people who attacked Him in a way that transcended human ability.** Neither the natural mind nor the natural man can walk in that level of refusing offense yet still keep blessing other people. But the love of God is the supernatural force that allows us to do just that.

It may sound like the love of God is going to make us serve other people all the time, possibly without any thanks from them. It sounds like the love of God may merely remove walls in our lives and possibly position us to be used and abused by others. However, we're going to find out that the love of God is going to bring blessings into our lives far beyond what we've ever thought possible. This holds especially true when we understand that God is not mocked, and that whatsoever we sow we will also reap. God will transform the relationships in our lives as we learn to walk in His love.

DISCIPLES OF LOVE

So far, we have seen that we need the love of God in order to:

- Fulfill all of the intentions of God's commandments;
- Please Him; and
- Enable us to walk in His image.

Now let's look at some additional aspects of walking in agape love.

John 13:34-35 -"A new commandment I give unto you, That ye love one another; as I have loved you, that ye also love one another. By this shall all men know that ye are my disciples, if ye have love one to another."

Here Jesus says that when we operate in love, it allows us to be identified as his disciples. The word disciple infers a people of 'discipline'– the disciplined ones of God. Scripture speaks of three main groups of people: The *unsaved*, and then among those who proclaim Christ, both *multitudes* and *disciples*. The same thing exists in the world today. There are *unsaved* people and there are *multitudes* who come to church merely because they believe it is their duty to do so. The multitudes put in their time with God and punch the church time clock. They say to themselves; *"Well, I made it; I lasted the hour. I went through the bulletin and checked off all of the activities listed."* They survived the session, but they didn't receive a thing; those would be the multitudes.

However, the disciples come to be changed. They come to manifest that which God said they are supposed to produce. They come to reflect the image of Jesus as the Word declares they are to demonstrate. And Jesus says that men will know that we are *students* of the Word of God - we are *disciplined* in what we are endeavoring to do for God, by the love that we walk in. So once again, **love is not something that we are permitted to reject; it's not meant to be optional.** Love is God's commandment for us. It's God's best for our lives.

LOVE NEVER FAILS

Here's a verse that should really capture our attention:

1John 2:10 - "He that loveth his brother abideth in the light, and there is none occasion of stumbling in him."

Now when I first got saved, I was 100% on fire for God. I was in the Word all of the time. I thought, if God is real and this Word is true then I need to learn about God and this drove me to read the

Bible nonstop. I attempted to pray all I knew to pray however this usually only took about five minutes. But I stayed in the Word hours and hours a day. And even with me seeking God with all of my heart and going to church every opportunity that I had, the devil would still come and tell me: *"You're not going to make it. You're going to backslide. You'll go back to being a drunk. Before your life is over, you'll end up falling."*

And, I'd go to the altar repeatedly and say: *"Lord, please don't let me backslide! Please don't let me go to hell!"* Even with all of my hunger for God, it took all of my faith just to hold onto my salvation.

Then I came across First John 2:10 and other similar scriptures that taught me, if we walk in love then there's no *"occasion of stumbling"* in us. I started realizing that if I can do this, backsliding won't be an option; it won't be a concern anymore. And I'll tell you what, I'm so far from being concerned that I'll backslide that I no longer give it a thought! This is because I've learned that the love of God will keep us from stumbling.

The Word says in Second Peter (you can read through the whole passage to get the entire context):

> *2Pet 1:7 -"And to godliness brotherly kindness; and to brotherly kindness charity."*

That word *"charity"* here, in the Greek is the same word *agape* that we recognize as *love*. The Bible is instructing us that we are supposed to be developing in the love of God. In fact, we will later learn that this passage is what I refer to as God's *Stairway to Agape*; our interlocking personal attributes that God will deal with us on in order for us to be able to manifest His love.

The same chapter goes on to say this:

> *2Pet 1:10 -"Wherefore the rather, brethren, give diligence* [kind of sounds like being a disciple, doesn't it?] *to make your calling and election sure: for if ye do these things* [he's talking about staying in this cycle of manifesting the love of God]*, ye shall never fall."*

Now God should really have our attention! **If we walk in love we'll never fall!** You know, I don't preach a lot about hell. I don't think a lot about hell. I'm not concerned about hell, but I would not want to go there. And, when I find out that the love of God keeps us from ever falling – I'm interested! Conversely, if we don't walk in the love of God we probably will stumble. If for no other reason, the fact that love will prevent our fall should fully motivate us to pursue this force.

Are you starting to see the need for the love of God in your life? This isn't something to take lightly; it's of utmost importance to the Christian! Before Jesus returns, we're going to see an increase in the revelation of God's love unfolding in these last days.

Don't you just love the Word? I *love* the Word of God, especially the way that it all hangs together! Now let's look at First Corinthians 13:

> *1Cor 13:1 - "Though I speak with the tongues of men and of angels, and have not charity* [agape love] *I am become as sounding brass, or a tinkling cymbal."*

Here Paul states that we can be filled with the Holy Spirit and pray in our supernatural prayer language, and yet still operate outside of love. So just because we've been born again, just because we think we've reached the epitome of Christianity because we became filled with the Holy Spirit, here it says that we can still be as sounding brass or a tinkling symbol. This infers that we are empty on the inside. Even though we may be manifesting supernatural abilities outwardly, the key ingredient that God is looking for can be missing – love.

Let's keep reading:

> *1Cor 13:2 - "And though I have the gift of prophecy, and understand all mysteries, and all knowledge; and though I have all faith, so that I could remove mountains, and have not charity, I am nothing."*

This verse backs up the point made earlier regarding Hebrews 11:6. This confirms that faith alone does not automatically please

God but rather how our faith is used. Paul says that we can operate in the gifts of the Holy Spirit, we can prophesy, we can have a doctorate in theology and understand all of the Word, yet miss the mark. We may possess spiritual expertise in the things of Scripture, however if we are not actively and forcefully accessing the love of God then we are nothing.

Now we're going to further address the commonly held mentality that love is fully demonstrated through the performance of good deeds:

> *1Cor 13:3 - "And though I bestow all my goods to feed the poor, and though I give my body to be burned, and have not charity* [agape]*, it profiteth me nothing."*

Now God should really have our attention again, because anyone with a speck of wisdom would readily desire His blessings. God built us to be reward-oriented. We like to be rewarded for what we do. And I'd hate to think that I gave away everything that I had to the poor and didn't profit from it. I'd hate to think that I received nothing after I spent all of my efforts ministering. Yet from this passage it is obvious that this is possible.

And so, we can try to do the works of God until we burn out and we may not gain a thing from it. And I've been there – my goodness! Early in my walk with God, I was trying to be a good Christian so I was attempting to minister to everyone with whom I came into contact. I was trying so hard to evangelize – to hand out tracks, to knock on doors and to bring people into church. I was also in an organization geared towards stamping out pornography in our area but I just about burned myself out because I was attempting to do it in my own strength. And the Word says that good deeds profit us nothing if not mixed with love.

See, God wrote the Bible as a love instruction manual, and that's primarily what He's looking for. As on-fire Christians, we often target trying to do great works for God, including attempting to operate in the spiritual gifts. And that's great but what's our motivation, and what force are we trying to accomplish it out of? God's looking for Himself to be released *through* us. See, that's what the manifested love of God is - it's God moving through us.

And that's the only thing that He declares is going to profit us. And anything we are doing out of our own intellect, out of our own cunning, out of our own strength, even out of our own financial ability - if we are not accessing the supernatural motivation and empowerment of love, there's no profit in it.

God has a system in Scripture where He promises whatever we sow, we will reap. And He says that if we sow seed into His system, it will produce up to and above hundredfold return in our lives. But here **Scripture also infers that if we don't walk in the love of God, our seed becomes neutralized.** There are a whole lot of people who have sown a lot of seed and they haven't seen a harvest. The reason they haven't seen a harvest may be because they're skipping the number one fertilizer which will allow their seed to produce, and that's the love of God.

So, we see here that love is the key to pleasing God. It's the key to profiting. It's the key to having purpose for our lives as far as God's concerned. We will also later see that love is the force that is going to bring in God's last day harvest.

THE ATTITUDE OF LOVE

Now let's go back to First Corinthians 13 and continue reading:

> *1Cor 13:4-8 - "Charity* [agape love] *suffereth long, and is kind; charity envieth not; charity vaunteth not itself, is not puffed up, doth not behave itself unseemly, seeketh not her own, is not easily provoked, thinketh no evil; rejoiceth not in iniquity, but rejoiceth in the truth; beareth all things, believeth all things, hopeth all things, endureth all things. Charity never faileth... "*

From the time that I was first saved, God began dealing with me on the topic of *the love of His love.* So, I took these verses and wrote them out. I put them on my refrigerator at home and on my bulletin board at work. I'd then say to myself: *"Today, I'm not going to lose my temper. Today, I'm not going to be unkind. Today, I'm going to do this whole list!"*

And, by about 10:00, I'd broken about half of them. What was going on? In actuality, I was trying to re-establish law in my life.

I was trying to produce actions of godliness through my own strength and ability, and through my own willpower and determination. And being a self-reliant individual, I thought I could do this. But I couldn't do a bit of it! And the more I would try, the more I would mess up at it. Without the power of God manifesting in our lives, none may consistently produce the attributes of love.

If we study these verses and we look up all of these attributes of love, we'll find out that every characteristic described is a verb. These are not adjectives. Usually when we describe something we'll say: *"That is a **red** barn"* or *"There is an **open** door"*. We'll use adjectives to describe the characteristics of something. However, when God describes His love, He always speaks of it using verbs. And verbs are action words. What God began showing me was that these are not things or descriptions of what we can do of ourselves, they are actions that His love in us will produce through us. **And as we start accessing this supernatural force of the love of God, it will enable us to supernaturally fulfill First Corinthians 13:4-8 beyond our own ability.**

Let me give you a quick example of areas where the love of God may have kicked in during the past and you didn't realize it. Have you ever been to a funeral where someone close to you passed away? Your mind may have been battling grief and sorrow that was so heavy that you couldn't control yourself. However, when someone prayed with you for the peace of God, a supernatural force suddenly came upon you. In the midst of a situation where you should have been emotionally in pieces, the peace of God sustained you. Grief no longer emotionally dominated you.

Peace is an attribute of the love of God. It's one of the nine fruit of the Spirit listed in Galatians 5. Peace is a supernatural anointing that can come upon us where there is a need to take us beyond ourselves. And in the same way, the Bible says that the *"fruit of the Spirit is love, joy, peace, longsuffering, gentleness, goodness, faith, meekness and temperance."* Each one of these attributes are aspects of love that when we learn to access them, we will be enabled to walk through situations we normally couldn't.

We can actually have people close to us chew us out, call us names or challenge our sainthood, and we can sit there with a smile on our face. We can continue through love's empowerment to maintain an open attitude toward them, even though everything in our natural selves would say to close down, run away, and build up defenses like Fort Knox.

When a person cuts us off in traffic, the love of God can come upon us and we'll smile and pray for them. It takes us beyond ourselves and produces fruit-filled actions supernaturally. The love of God is not something we do when we feel like it. The love of God is something that comes on us and makes us feel like it. Hallelujah!

Before I close this chapter, I want to cover just a few more things that the supernatural force of love will do for us. It will produce all of the results that we saw in First Corinthians 13:4-8. As well, paralleling the fact that the anointing has been coined as *the burden removing, yoke destroying power of God*, the love of God also manifests as an anointing. I refer to the love of God as *the strife-removing, offense-destroying power of God*. It will take offense from out of our lives! It will remove strife out of our relationships! It will transform the atmosphere around our heads so that we're not mad anymore – and not because we have such great self-control and can count to ten. My goodness, counting to ten never did it for me; "37, 38, 39...209, 210!" I had to have a supernatural force! And the love of God is that force that will take us beyond what we can do of ourselves.

The love of God will produce the fruit of the Spirit in our lives amidst contrary circumstances through a release of joy and peace. We may have everything collapsing in our lives. They may come to us and say: *"We're foreclosing on your house"* or *"You've just been fired."* And if we access the joy of the Lord, which is one of the attributes of manifested love, we'll laugh. We'll be free of sorrow. It will take us beyond our circumstances.

The love of God truly is the manifestation of our newborn nature that God put in us when we were saved. He put in us a born-again, image of God nature; and walking in the love of God represents the outward release of that true nature. That's why there's fulfillment in it! As long as we're hard-hearted, we're selfish and self-focused, as long as we are acting in our old ways, we are battling within ourselves against ourselves. So when we try to withhold or resist the love of God, we're frustrating that reborn, genuine real person on the inside us,. Love allows us to experience full release of who we are. We might think: *"But people will think I'm soft!"* or *"They'll think I'm a sucker!"* However, even if they do, we'll experience life like we've never thought possible.

In the next chapter, we will examine more closely some of the supernatural attributes of the love of God.

CHAPTER 2

SUPERNATURAL LOVE

CLOSE ENCOUNTERS OF THE GOD KIND

In September, 1991, I was instructed of the Lord to begin a Bible study in my home. In preparation for my second weekly lesson, I besought God, lying on my face for what message to minister. After several hours, I heard the Lord whisper to me one word, *"love"*. Taking the assignment seriously, I printed out every verse in scripture containing any form of the word love, spending many more hours assembling the lesson.

Upon teaching this first love lesson, the revelation that love was a supernatural force became overwhelmingly apparent. For the next year, nearly every lesson that I taught was on the subject of the *agape* love of God. Much of what is contained in this book arose from those initial lessons. As my studies continued, God again spoke to me and informed me that the topic of love would become the predominant message of my ministry. Over twenty-five years later, this has been confirmed to be true.

For years I taught of a supernatural love that transcended human love. I saw in the Bible repeated ties between love and the glory of God. I received revelation of how we are to access the supernatural love of God by faith. Yet all of this was proclaimed from a theoretical standpoint, for I had never experienced or even witnessed the fullness of this radical type of love.

However, since those early days I have been visited by this supernatural love on several occasions, some of which are mentioned later on in this book. In about half of the cases, the glorious love that I experienced only stayed with me for a few hours. In the other half of the occurrences, supernatural love remained on me for a few days.

But in one case, this precursor to the glory abode upon me for nearly two weeks. It was during this time that God confirmed to me the phenomenal, paradigm altering, qualities of His genuine love poured out. For those two weeks, my entire life seemed turned totally upside down, however, I completely loved every minute of it.

Being caught up in and overtaken by a cloud of God's love, nothing in my life resembled that of a few days prior. I was so aware of God's love for me that any form of discouragement or oppression disappeared. Faith arose to all new heights knowing that God had my back. I was so cognizant of God's love for mankind, that I knew that He would heal everyone for whom I prayed. And I so loved *everyone,* such that I could not wait to encourage or bless those about me.

However, somewhat of a problem arose. In this cloud of glory, I was nearly as aware of the working of the Spirit realm about me as I was the natural realm. I had not yet learned to function in this level of God's love such that my mind had great difficulty focusing on everyday tasks. Whereas normally I am usually in a rush to get somewhere and rarely drive much below the speed limit, under love's influence I often found myself driving at half of the permitted speed. I was so alert to the presence of God that it became difficult for me to keep up with traffic. And if people cut me off, rather than become frustrated, I sincerely prayed for them.

As an engineer, under normal circumstances I am fairly adept at mathematics. But under the anointing of love it became a challenge to even balance the checkbook. The continual flow of bills that normally come to a church were of no concern to me for that involved activities limited to this world only. In fact, for those two weeks I am not sure if I even was able to focus on the books clearly enough to pay any of the bills.

I became aware that no one can step straight into this anointing and function in a regular job or career for very long without first 'learning how' to operate in this full measure of God's outpoured glory. To walk in the glory will require us to straddle two dissimilar realms. I have heard the testimonies of men who were told of God that: *"if He were to pour the glory upon The Church now, it would destroy it."* I now know why. Men will need to learn to adapt to such power poured out to be able to maintain continuity of life for any extended period of time.

However during that time, I experienced joy, peace, patience, and fulfillment as in no other time in my life. Then after about two weeks, this supernatural visitation of love lifted from me. I was devastated, having seemingly dwelled in the Heavenly realms, I had been now returned to the natural world. As I sought God to discover where I had missed His will to lose such a gift, He assured me that I had not. His comfort to me was not that I had done anything wrong, but that He was giving me a taste of His outpoured love that is to come.

I am convinced that God intends to train up His revivalist church to carry this supernatural love in these end-days. This chapter is intended to reveal many of the powerful attributes that this outpoured *agape* love provides.

All prior efforts to define the love of God have fallen far short of providing full comprehension to what this divine nature and force actually is. Even The Bible does not venture to define love beyond declaring that *"God is Love."* The Scriptures in an effort to describe the love of God, may only do so by listing the results of love operating in the saint's life. Even in First Corinthians 13, rather than provide us with a definition of love we are instead only provided with a short list of some of what love produces in the life of the believer.

> *1Cor 13:4-8 –"Charity suffereth long, and is kind; charity envieth not; charity vaunteth not itself, is not puffed up, Doth not behave itself unseemly, seeketh not her own, is not easily provoked, thinketh no evil; Rejoiceth not in iniquity, but rejoiceth in the truth; Beareth all things, believeth all things, hopeth all things, endureth all things. Charity never faileth..."*

Close examination of this list reveals to us that all of these attributes of love are *verbs*. Even the best efforts of Scripture may only describe the *actions* or *results* of love; for even God Himself could not provide us with a comprehensive definition of His own nature. As well, all of these actions listed are in the continuous tense. Love doesn't just try to be kind with hit and miss results. The power of love enables us to be kind, etc. at all times.

It is interesting to note that in His efforts to reveal to man who He is, God could only describe Himself as *"I Am."* God, in an attempt to provide further clarity to His nature did so by unveiling His attributes through the names He would attribute to Himself. As *"El Shaddai,"* He is revealed as the *"Almighty God.";* as *"Jehovah Rapha,"* He is *"The God Who Heals.";* and so forth. All human language is far too limited to fully capture and define the totality of God and of His love.

If The Bible may only define the love of God through attempts to describe its results, how can we expect to do more? This chapter will focus on examining from the Word many of the supernatural attributes of love. Several of these characteristics of love will be examined in much more detail in later chapters. This chapter is intended to provide only a brief overview of what genuine love will produce in the believer's life once it is fully accessed.

Because past efforts by the church to define love have fallen far short of the fullness of love's supernatural capacity, Christianity has been duped to substitute man's natural, limited love in place of the *agape* love of God. **If we do not comprehend the fullness of *agape's* capacity, we will not expect the supernatural results of love to manifest in our lives. Instead, we will settle for a feel-good, emotionally centered placebo; mistaking it for the real thing.** In doing so, we miss out on the greatest experience available to born-again man; to walk in the most powerful force in the universe - the supernatural love of God. Following is a list of some of the supernatural aspects of God's love that should give us some idea of what He desires to bring into the life of the end-time revivalist saint.

LOVE IS:
THE NATURE OF GOD AND BORN-AGAIN MAN

As we have already discovered, *"God is love."* Love is not merely what God does, but it is the epitome of His very nature. **Because God is love, His supernatural love is as far superior to human love as God Himself is superior to fallen man.** No human effort may bridge the two. Man's failure to be able to uphold the Old Testament law was proof that man of his own efforts could not attain to the righteousness of God. In equal fashion, man's best efforts to be loving cannot even approach the power or holiness of the perfect God of love.

Possibly the most amazing manifested supernatural aspect of love is that which takes place when a man is born-again by the Word of God. Through faith in the incorruptible seed of the Word, man has imparted to him the very nature of God. The same righteous nature that Jesus received when He was conceived by the Holy Ghost is created within us. Our spirit man has been recreated without sin and we are no longer who we used to be. Through the born-again event, fallen man is recreated within to be as righteous as God. Love now becomes our new nature. Love becomes who we now are.

Although initially we may perceive no apparent change to our lives, the most powerful force in the universe has now been imbedded within us. For the rest of our days on earth, we must endeavor to release this power from the inside of us to the outside. Most of the remainder of this book will be focused upon that process. Through implanting the nature of love within us, God has performed the primary step to enable us to walk in His image as the representatives of His kingdom and as members of His body.

We will explore our new righteous nature in more detail in the following chapter. However, of all of the gifts that the God of love could extend to us, none could ever be of more value. Through this new nature of love we have been granted, not just access to God's presence today, but also entry to heaven for eternity should we keep the faith.

THE INNER MOTIVATION TO LIVE IN A BENEVOLENT, FORGIVING, AND UNOFFENDABLE MANNER

The new born-again nature of love that we possess doesn't only give us access to God and His eternal kingdom, it changes who we are at the very heart of our being. **Where prior to salvation we were self-centered and self-serving, afterwards our entire view of life experiences a quantum shift.** Suddenly, our life's focus is directed toward God and the things of God. No longer is life only about us but is redirected toward the fulfillment of His plans for our lives.

Even our thirst for sin has been reversed. Where once involvement in sinful activity was our delight in life, such actions no longer align with our new righteous nature. Our hearts' desire is now to bless rather than to take, to nurture rather than to abuse, to soar in the presence of God rather than to flee from Him. Through the seed of love vested within us, a hunger to know God has been established. As we answer the call to satiate that hunger through time in The Word and prayer, God is able to promote us to higher and higher levels of outwardly walking in His love.

Our new nature is quick to bless, eager to serve, willing to forgive, determined to live above offense, and abhorrent of sin. As a *little leaven* of sin leavens the loaf unto corruption, in like manner, the nature of love deposited within us if acted upon will elevate us over time to walk in the *fullness of the stature of the image of Christ*. What an honor to walk in the same love that represents the character and image of the God of creation!

THE FRUIT OF THE SPIRIT

Once saved, our spirit man has been recreated righteous. However until we are able to manifest love outwardly in a form the world may witness, we may have little impact on our surroundings. The *"fruit of the Spirit"* represent the manifested supernatural results of love operating in our lives. A list of some of the visible displays of love is recorded in Galatians:

> *Gal 5:22-23 – "But the **fruit of the Spirit** is love, joy, peace, longsuffering, gentleness, goodness, faith, meekness, temperance: against such there is no law."*

The Greek word for *"is"* in this verse is a singular verb, therefore, the primary *"fruit of the Spirit"* is 'singularly' love. Thus love becomes the essence of God within us from which all of the other fruit listed flow. *"Joy," "peace," "longsuffering," "gentleness," "goodness," "faith," "meekness,"* and *"temperance"* all are outward products of our new inner nature. Until we begin to produce the tangible fruit of these other eight manifestations of love, no outwardly visible change takes place in our life.

A fruit tree rooted into good ground, brings in the nutrients from the soil and combines them with moisture to produce fruit. The soil in an *unseen* realm is absorbed and converted to produce fruit in the *seen* realm. As *trees of righteousness* we bring in the raw material of love, and by processing it through a mind renewed to the Word of God we thus convert it to the other eight fruit. Love within us is unseen until we manifest it as the other fruit of the Spirit which become visible to all.

Once saved, our primary assignment becomes to develop this fruit. Only extensive time in the Word and prayer truly allows us to supernaturally manifest these attributes. Many might say that these fruit listed may be displayed by anyone whether born-again or not, for all are capable of experiencing joy or showing kindness. However, to produce the *genuine* fruit of the spirit transcends human capacity. Whereas *human* joy, goodness, and temperance are dependent upon circumstances or are displayed for potential reward, the authentic fruit of the spirit arise from within and are independent of one's natural surroundings.

In particular, the fruit of *"faith"* is declared by the Word to be increased or grown primarily by spending time meditating the Scriptures.

> *Rom 10:17 – "So then faith cometh by hearing, and hearing by the Word of God."*

Those Christians who have gained understanding of the real power of faith comprehend its supernatural mountain-moving potential. But equally, all of the other fruit listed are supernatural in content as well. No amount of human will-power or effort may produce them.

The genuine fruit of the spirit is not the result of a Christian *trying* to be like Jesus or walking by *WWJD* (What would Jesus Do?). Walking in the real fruit of the Spirit is the result of the compelling force of love rising up from within us in overflowing fashion and manifesting as these desired qualities.

Again, we have confused human love with the love of God and have attempted to walk in these attributes by will-power. No such man-made efforts even approach acting as a suitable substitute for the most powerful force in the universe flowing from us. Man-generated attempts to walk in this fruit produce a placebo affect which deceive Christians and misdirect them from seeking to abide in the *real thing*.

Further discussion of the fruit of the Spirit will be covered in our chapter *Rooted in Love*.

THE BONDING FORCE THAT PRODUCES CHURCH UNITY

Quantum scientists have discovered that the most powerful force in the universe lies within the heart of the atom and is named the *"Strong Force"*. The Strong Force holds the protons of the atom together in the nucleus despite their inherent characteristic to repel one another because of their like electromagnetic charges. Without this strong force being in operation, the entire universe would disintegrate into oblivion. No known force even approaches the attractive potential of this power.

However, the strong force displays a very interesting phenomenon. The power of the strong force is not activated until the sub-atomic particles venture outside of their assigned nuclear radius. As long as they lie within the boundaries assigned to the nucleus of that atom, the particles have total liberty to move about; for until then the strong force remains untapped. But once the particles move *out of bounds*, the most powerful force in the universe rapidly pulls them back into position.

I am convinced that God has embedded within the building blocks of this universe a perfect picture of what is actually the most powerful force in existence - His love. For those who are in covenant with God, He gives us total liberty to enjoy our lives as we function in our assigned positons. However, should we begin to venture out of bounds through whatever type of offense, the love of God is designed to jerk us back into position. By love, we become unoffendable. By love, we are content to forbear, favor and even elevate those about us. Even the correction that the Lord will at times bring us is rooted in His love for us. In these end-times, God is going to supernaturally unite His church together through this unbreakable force - the power of His love.

The number one destructive force that the enemy has used against revivals of the past has been division. As the power of God is poured out, competition for positions, resources, and control threaten to divide the very people revival is intended to unite. However, in this last-day revival, God is going to supernaturally bond His church together through the force of supernatural love. Paul writes of this power in the book of Colossians:

> *Col 2:1 -"For I would that ye knew what great conflict I have for you, and for them at Laodicea, and for as many as have not seen my face in the flesh; that their hearts might be comforted, being knit together in love, and unto all riches of the full assurance of understanding, to the acknowledgement of the mystery of God, and of the Father, and of Christ."*

Notice that this verse declares that our hearts are to be *"knit together in love."* Here is confirmation that love is the binding force that God has designed to unite His church. Love is the bonding force to hold people in the positions that God has assigned them to fill to accomplish the assignments that He has directed them to fulfill. Paul again declares in Colossians:

> *Col 3:14 - "And above all these things put on charity (agape love), which is the bond of perfectness."*

The love of God is the bonding force that is going to bring the church into perfect unity in these last-days. As the fires of revival increase and His laborers become busier in The Kingdom than they have ever dreamed, only love will be able to keep us together. Love has the ability to put our emotions at ease where normally they would be going *haywire*. The love of God has the power to flood our emotions with supernatural peace and thus cause us to respond in the fruit of the spirit rather than to experience mental meltdowns.

In our chapter on *Covenant Love*, we will examine the bonding power of love in much more detail.

THE GIVING NATURE AND MOTIVATIONAL FORCE

When we were born-again, God transformed our nature from one of selfishness to one of love. In that reversal of natures, God implanted within us His own inclination and motivation to give to others. Suddenly, we are no longer as concerned with amassing worldly goods for ourselves as we are to be able to be a blessing to those about us. We see God's giving nature displayed in the most well-known verse in The Bible.

> *John 3:16 – "For God so loved the world, that he gave his only begotten son, that whosoever believeth in him should not perish, but have everlasting life."*

God so loved mankind that He sowed the most precious seed in the universe for our salvation - His son Jesus. As we learn to progressively step into higher levels of living out of our new nature of love, the manifested result will be reflected in our giving. The full expression of our righteous nature is demonstrated as we live to be a blessing to those about us. Stinginess in the life of a Christian relates that they have not grown beyond *baby* stage and are still bound by a prior worldly, self-focused mentality.

For a Christian to ever really know true fulfillment, they must learn to become a radical giver. Only then will our outside actions match our new reborn nature. A child of God who has not learned to give with abandon, trusting in God's promises to return his seed to him in multiplied fashion is sure to be frustrated to some level. Love always looks for opportunities to give and to bless.

In our chapter *The Seed of Love*, we will look at the giving nature of love in more depth.

THE ATMOSPHERE OF HEAVEN

Christians who have been caught up to Heaven and yet returned often speak of the atmosphere of Heaven being comprised of love. Their testimonies declare that those there actually breathe in the energizing power of the love of God.

As we advance to higher and higher levels of walking in the love of God, we become anointed to manifest an atmosphere of the love of God around us. By the expression the *atmosphere* around us, I am referring to the realm or dimension of the soul about us where thoughts and emotions have expression. As we manifest love in the air around us, the emotions of all about us will likely experience supernatural tranquility. Their thoughts will automatically become focused upon God and His goodness.

We will find in the chapter *The Glory of Love* that God's glory is actually made up of concentrated love. Moses, after he descended from Mount Sinai shined with this love. When the Old Testament Tabernacle was completed, the glorious love of God so filled the atmosphere that Moses could not enter. As Solomon's Temple was finished, the same love manifested so powerfully that the priests could not stand to minister.

This overflowing love that end-time saints are assigned to carry will fill the air about us and become the most powerful tool that we will possess to transform our assigned localities. An atmosphere of love will fill our churches, our homes, and our places of employment. In fact, love will dominate the atmosphere wherever we go. Jesus spoke to His disciples regarding allowing their anointing to fill the homes where they would stay.

Mat 10:12-13 – "And when ye come into an house, salute it. And if the house be worthy, let your peace come upon it: but if it be not worthy, let your peace return to you."

Peace, being one of the fruits of the Spirit, may reside on a home. Those accustomed to genuine praise and worship in a church service understand how the peace of God will fill the sanctuary. At other times, joy may overtake many of those present. As we advance closer and closer toward walking in the fullness of God's glory, not just peace or joy but the fullness of God's love will overtake our services. This end-time outpouring of love will then transform every arena into which we enter.

When we carry the love of God, those people that we come in contact with who are carrying strife, are in bondage to bitterness, or have erected isolating walls, may often be delivered by our presence alone. Love can so permeate the soul realm about us that it drives out demonic forces and allows us to witness to people who couldn't be reached before. We will look at the results this atmospheric force produces in more detail as this chapter proceeds.

When we're under the influence of the anointing of love, the actions of love attributed in First Corinthians 13:4-8 become spontaneous. Have you ever had the experience of trying to get to church and your car was messing up, your computer crashed, you just got into strife with your spouse, or your kids weren't doing what they were supposed to do? Perhaps this has never happened to you or possibly it's all happened on the same day. By the time you arrived at church you were ready to cry. However, you declared: *"I'm just going to worship God by faith! I am going to praise Jesus with everything left in me!"* And as you began praising and worshipping God, supernatural peace manifested around you and all of your cares were swept away.

Suddenly, all of your thoughts were easily centered on God and often you didn't even remember why you were previously frustrated! All of that oppression that you were dealing with left. What happened? Attributes of the love of God bore them away.

It's *easy* to *bear all things* when under the influence of the love of God.

Glory to God! I'm looking forward to flowing full-time in God's love rather than just trudging my way up the mountains. And I believe that God's going to blow some mountains out of our way in these last days.

In Corinthians, Paul declares that he was caught up to the Third Heaven.

> *2 Cor 12:3 – "I knew a man in Christ above fourteen years ago, (whether in the body, I cannot tell; or whether out of the body, I cannot tell: God knoweth;) such an one caught up to the third heaven."*

The Third Heaven refers to the Spirit Realm - the location where the Throne of God resides. That there is a third heaven lets us know that there are two other heavens as well. In our examination of love as the atmosphere of heaven, it will aid us to know what each of these realms consist of.

The First Heaven is comprised of The Earth, the sky, and the remainder of the universe in which we dwell. Whereas our spirit man is situated in the Spirit Realm - the Third Heaven, our physical body is positioned and interacts with the First Heaven. In fact, each aspect of our triune nature corresponds to and is positioned within one of each of the three heavens.

The Second Heaven is the realm of the soul. It is a realm where thought and emotion have voice. When we speak of creating an *atmosphere of love*, we are not referring to the First Heaven atmosphere around The Earth. The *atmosphere* that we need charged with the love of God is the soul realm. The soul realm is an actual heaven or dimension positioned between the First and Third Heavens in which our own soul resides. All information and instructions passed to us from our spirit man must pass through the reasoning processes of our soul before our bodies may comply in obedience. However, in this realm thoughts and emotions have tangibility.

When satan was cast out of the Third Heaven, he took up residence in the Second. Now he acts as the master of thought and emotional manipulation. Paul referred to satan as the *"prince of the power of the air"*:

> *Eph 2:2 –"Wherein time past ye walked according to the course of this world, according to the prince of the power of the air, the spirit than now worketh in the children of disobedience;"*

The devil is a master at controlling people by negatively bombarding their thoughts and emotions. As the seeming master of the Second Heaven domain, he endeavors to rule the world through filling this *atmosphere* with demonic activity. Even though God has given Christians all authority, it is through much soul-oriented warfare that we reject satan's efforts to manipulate us and we possess the arena of our own minds.

When a demonic entity enters an area, it endeavors to impart its own personality to the soul atmosphere of that space. Strife, hate, rage, lust, and grief are often the results of satanic forces dominating an area. Once saved, we are now charged of God to displace this demonic activity.

God never intended for us to make decisions based on our emotions; to always react in agreement with how we *feel*. Our emotions are given to us as sensors in the realm of the soul to inform us of what is going on around us. Just like our natural bodies have senses to tell us what's going on in the physical realm, emotions are our senses that alert us to what is going on in the soul realm. Have you ever walked into a room where two people have been arguing? You didn't hear a word of the argument, yet as you walked into the room you *felt* the thickness of the anger present! We may have walked into a funeral home and felt like crying when we didn't even know the person. Grief had charged the soul realm atmosphere with sorrow.

Did you know that animals are able to sense fear or even eminent threats? This is because animals have learned to use their emotions to detect danger for their own survival. And God means for us to do the very same thing.

Have you ever been in a church service when the presence of God moved in and you went from feeling discouraged to feeling wonderful? Our emotions are designed to pick up either the presence of God or of the demonic in a room. As such, they become the primary detectors of what's spiritually going on around us. And God never meant for us to react negatively to what we feel. If there are spirits of frustration or bitterness in operation, we're not meant to respond in agreement with them. God intends for us to be alert and sensitive everywhere that we go to use our emotions to detect what is going on in the air around. And if it is not of God, take actions to change it.

Scripture declares that God will draw near to us if we draw near to Him:

> *Jas 4:8 – "Draw nigh to God, and he will draw nigh to you ..."*

As we praise and worship God from our First Heaven position, He draws near to us from His Third Heaven Dwelling place. Our meeting place is the realm of the soul - the Second Heaven. As we take steps to seek God, His presence will fill the dimension of the soul and we will *feel* Him with our emotions. As we do this, demonic forces are displaced along with their emanations of strife, hate, and grief. In this fashion, God intends for His end-time church to eradicate darkness and likewise manifest His glory.

As we take radical steps to pursue the love of God in these last-days, we are endeavoring to draw the atmosphere of the Third Heaven into the Second.

THE EVANGELISTIC ANOINTING

The first time that God ever placed the anointing of love on me in public was an evening when I had volunteered to go out and perform some street witnessing. I had done this many times in the past, usually with very limited results. But this night, He coated me with His supernatural love and in 45 minutes I led five people to the Lord. The force of love was so powerful that it literally transformed the atmosphere about me. As I approached people on the street, this impartation of love in the air produced a clarity of mind in nearly everyone that I approached. As I would speak the truths of The Word to them, there was little to resist their ability to receive what I was saying.

I, without question, believe that God is going to harvest the earth through this anointing. The effects of genuine love permeating the atmosphere around us will produce unparalleled results. Love becomes God's *harvest magnet*.

When all is said and done, I believe that God's going to have more people in Heaven than the devil has in Hell because He's going to harvest the earth. And the way that God is going to bring in His harvest in the last days is by a manifestation of His love that is going to draw people from every direction. Up until now, as *fishers of men*, we have been trying to snag new converts with a hook and line and not very good bait. To lure in prospective converts, we have been using stink bait - condemnation preaching. Rather than draw people in with an atmosphere of love, we have attempted to scare people into church.

Isn't that an exciting way to get people to want to serve God - by scaring them into church? Condemnation ministers decry: *"You're going to hell if you don't get saved."* Oh yippee! **God's genuine evangelism plan is to draw in His sons and daughters through the goodness of His love.**

> *Rom 2:4 – "Or despises thou the riches of his goodness and forbearance and longsuffering, not knowing that the goodness of God leadeth thee to repentance?"*

The Bible infers that God is going to *harvest His catch with nets.* We see that when Jesus started His ministry, He told Peter and John to launch out into the deep and let down their nets for a draw. They brought in so many fish that the boats nearly sank. In this, we have a representation of the harvest that God wants to bring in during the last days! When he arose from the dead a similar event took place. They had fished all night and had caught nothing, yet in the morning He again instructed His disciples to let down the nets. But this time they were instructed to fish on the other side of the boat. They caught 153 fish of every type; also representative of the last day harvest. God wants to bring in His harvest through nets comprised of the power of His love.

God's *finishing work* involving His church is going to be a revival marked by an outpouring of His love. And this revival will never cease until the return of Jesus. There have been none like it before, nor will there be any like it thereafter. I'm excited about this, how about you?

As we walk in the true supernatural love of God, it will have an effect on the atmosphere of the soul realm – and not just the atmosphere three feet around us – it will affect entire rooms. And as we get into agreement with *two or more*, it will affect city blocks and beyond. **Think of it, as churches begin to corporately walk in the power of this love regions will be affected!** And God's going to use this as a magnetic force to draw His harvest to the church in the last days. Think of it as fishing with nets instead of with hooks, lines, and sinkers.

THE ANOINTING THAT ERADICATES STRIFE AND REMOVES OFFENSE

The anointing has been framed from Isaiah 10:27 to be the *power of God that removes burdens and destroys yokes*. The love of God may take the form not only as God's divine nature, the fruit of the Spirit, and as an atmosphere, but also as an anointing. And this most powerful of all anointings is the power of God that eradicates strife and removes offense. **Under love's influence, we become Teflon to all feelings of rejection and inferiority.**

As people experience the anointing of love, they may be instantly set free from decades of emotional abuse. No matter what the form of past disappointment, love contains the power to deliver. Rejection, isolation, bitterness, and mental bondage must bow to the anointing of the love of God. Paul refers to this in the book of Philippians:

> *Phil 1:9-11 –"And this I pray, that your love may abound yet more and more in knowledge and in all judgement; That ye may approve things that are excellent; that ye may be sincere and without offence till the day of Christ; Being filled with the fruits of righteousness, which are by Jesus Christ, unto the glory and praise of God."*

As the anointing of love develops in our lives, we will not only be set free of all offense ourselves but we will be able to liberate others as well. As an atmosphere of love is established in a location, deliverance from every form of oppression will often automatically take place. It is as tangible as any other anointing of God such as those available to deliver from sickness or lack. God is raising up a church *without spot or wrinkle*. The anointing of God's love is the key cleansing agent that eradicates such blemishes to our garments.

AN ANOINTING THAT CAUSES THE DEMONIC TO MANIFEST AND FLEE

The love of God is a supernatural force that can literally wipe the atmosphere clear of demonic presence and oppression. As the *evangelistic anointing*, the genuine love of God when manifested allows the unsaved to suddenly see clearly to receive the revelation of the reality of Jesus as Savior. This is possible because the power of love drives forth mind-blinding spirits from deceiving the souls of men. It is this capacity of the love of God to drive out darkness that will bring in His abundant harvest.

As an anointing that drives out strife and removes offense, love displaces demonic spirits that keep people bound through the inability to forgive. By driving out the spirits that are continually dominating men's thoughts and emotions, true peace may be realized. Under the influence of supernatural love, the atmosphere of strife is eradicated.

We will later discover that the *Glory of God* is the tangible manifestation of His love. One of the key aspects of God's glory is that oppression cannot penetrate the shielding sphere of love's influence which it produces. **The force of glorious love creates such a shielding effect against oppression that we will never experience another down day in our lives.**

Wherever Jesus traveled, demons were forced to manifest. Jesus as the ultimate man of love, broke up demonic gatherings. Love set multitudes free wherever Jesus was received.

AN ANOINTING THAT DELIVERS FROM FEAR AND FEAR OF DEATH

An obvious witness to the power of love to displace demonic activity is found in First John:

> *1John 4:18 – "There is no fear in love; but perfect love casteth out all fear: because fear hath torment. He that feareth is not made perfect in love."*

Supernatural love, as it approaches the perfection of the glory will deliver us from all fear. Because *"fear hath torment"*, it becomes imperative that we overcome fear's effects. Fear as the opposing force to faith, would attempt to hinder all that we desire God to accomplish in our lives. While fear may be rooted in both demonic and psychological causes, love is well able to eradicate the result of each.

Where faith declares that *"no weapon formed against us shall prosper"*, fear opens doors for satan to move against us. Fear of rejection attempts to keep us from voicing truth in vital situations. Fear of lack would hinder us from tithing and sowing. Fear of man transforms *called* men and women of God into *people pleasers*.

But perfect love overcomes all fear. Under the influence of God's love we become totally aware of the Father's great desire to bless us. **Why would we fear when we gain comprehension that we have been made one with the Creator of the Universe?** Not even the threat of death holds any power over one who knows that for him to be absent from the body is to be united with the God of love. When we become saturated with the fullness of God's love, to some extent, the declaration from Corinthians is fulfilled - *"O death, where is thy sting? O grave, where is thy victory?"*

Added to the buffering effect against fear provided through merely knowing that God loves us is the power of deliverance love possesses to drive out spirits of fear. Whenever demonic powers are confronted with the intention of casting them out, the initial counterattack against the exorcising minister will be an assault of fear. Fear is the first wall of defense that demons use to shield themselves against being driven out.

At times, when addressing the demonic you can physically feel as if fear punched you in the chest. Feelings of fear will try to grip your soul. To proceed any further in driving out the spirits of evil, this fear must be addressed. You must override the fear with your own faith to complete your task.

But perfect love casts out all fear. Once the full blown love of God manifests upon our lives, such levied attacks of fear will become merely an amusement. With great boldness, we will cast out legions of demons and set the captives free. No longer will rejection, disappointment, fear of failure, or any other type of fear be able to render us ineffective. The devil's number one wall of defense will be obliterated by love.

AN ANOINTING THAT DISPERSES DARKNESS AND BRINGS LIGHT

Gross darkness veils men's ability to perceive truth. A small light may disperse darkness produced through the absence of light, but it is of little effect to pierce through the demonic smoke screen produced via *"gross darkness"*. Only the glory of God has the power to do that. Isaiah prophesied of the coming glory that would disperse all darkness!

> *Isa 60:1-4 –"Arise, shine; for thy light is come, and the glory of the LORD is risen upon thee. For, behold, the darkness shall cover the earth, and gross darkness the people; but the LORD shall arise upon thee, and his glory shall be seen upon thee. And the gentiles shall come to thy light, and kings to the brightness of thy rising. Lift up thine eyes round about, and see: all they gather themselves together, they come to thee: thy sons shall come from far, and thy daughters shall be nursed at thy side."*

Verse two refers to both *"darkness"* and *"gross darkness"*. In this verse, the Hebrew word for *"darkness"* refers to the *absence of light."* Where there is merely an absence of light, the proclamation of the truths of the Gospel alone may be adequate to illuminate men's souls to receive salvation. However, the Hebrew word for *"gross darkness"* means a *thick cloud.*

Where gross darkness has rolled in, no little candle belonging to the baby Christian will penetrate the demonically induced haze. As multitudes flounder in the deception that gross darkness produces, those revivalists who have held tight to The Word will manifest God's tangible love that is able to penetrate mass delusion. As we see in Isaiah 60, as the glory of God arises upon the end-time church the multitudes will come from far and wide to make up His harvest. Praise God for the power of perfect love in the form of His glory!

In some cases of scripture, this same word translated as *"gross darkness"* is alternately referred to as God's *"glory"*. God has designed His thick cloud of Glory to eradicate the enemy's thick cloud of darkness.

AN ANOINTING THAT CHARGES, MOTIVATES, AND DIRECTS OUR FAITH

This book will reveal that supernatural love cannot be manifested without faith. In like fashion, faith cannot effectively work unless it is empowered by love. Love becomes both the motivation for the proper release of our faith as well as the fuel that energizes it.

Recall that one of the fruits of the spirit listed in Galatians is faith.

> *Gal 5:22-23 – "But the fruit of the Spirit is love, joy, peace, longsuffering, gentleness, goodness, faith, meekness, temperance: against such there is no law."*

Some Bible versions translate the Greek word used here as *"faithfulness"* rather than *"faith"*. However, the word being translated is *pistis* which always represents *faith* rather than *pistos* meaning *faithful*. The faith that allows us to remove mountains is a fruit of being rooted in love. The same Word of God that builds our faith is the same Word that we must abide within to dwell in His love.

All that the believer endeavors to accomplish by faith must be motivated by love. God's Word makes it clear that He will not answer prayers initiated from the flesh.

> *Jas 4:2-3 – "Ye lust, and have not: ye kill, and desire to have, and cannot obtain: ye fight and war, yet ye have not, because ye ask not. Ye ask, and receive not, because ye ask amiss, that ye may consume it upon your lusts."*

The only proper and effective motivation for the release of our faith should be love. God implanted the nature of love within us when we were born again. Now He wants us to develop and use our faith to manifest the fruit of that love outwardly. But faith is also fueled by the anointing of love upon us. As Paul wrote in Galatians:

> *Gal 5:6 – "For in Jesus Christ neither circumcision availeth anything, not uncircumcision; but faith which worketh by love."*

The Greek word used for *"worketh"* is *energoumene* inferring to be *energized by*. Love becomes the raw fuel that energizes our faith to produce. It is not by accident that when our time with God is stretched thin and as our love reserves become depleted, our faith grows weak as well. **Faith and love are intended by God to operate fully dependent upon one another.** As we experience more and more of the love of God, our faith level soars. Conversely, as our faith capacity rises, we are able to experience an ever increasing overflow of the love of God.

During the two week period of my life when I was caught up in the glory of God, faith became automatic. I was so energized by love that I knew that everyone that I prayed for would be healed. The intense love that I experienced clearly related to me God's desire to bless. My only responsibility became to lay hands on the people to provide God an avenue for His anointing to flow.

AN ANOINTING THAT IS TO BE DEVELOPED AND POURED OUT UNTO THE GLORY

An entire segment of this book is dedicated to this topic in the chapter *The Glory of Love*. There it will be pointed out in more detail that the glory of God is actually concentrated, outpoured love. As this love flows from the Third Heaven to the Second, it will reach a point that it overflows into the First. Here, all Hell will break loose attempting to find a place to escape. No time in all of prior human history will approximate this culmination of God's purpose for the church. His bride will have completed 2000 years of preparation and be enveloped in His glorious love.

God is raising up an end-time *Glorious Bride* saturated in His love. The Bible is packed with last-days prophecies decreeing and celebrating this event. In this final, ultimate revival which will usher in the rapture, God is going to unleash His church with nearly unlimited power. **The results produced through this end-time unveiling of His body include:**

- **Miracles, signs, and wonders as never before witnessed in all of history;**
- **The inversion of the wealth of the wicked into the hands of the righteous;**
- **God's end-time harvest coming forth;**
- **The restoration of all things that the enemy has kept back from the church since their inception;**
- **Peace and joy producing fulfillment as we have never thought possible;**

And much more!

AND SO -

Through the remainder of this book we will be examining specific steps the on-fire Christian will need to take to manifest this love and glory. Only a sold out attitude toward The Kingdom may produce the desired results. These first two chapters of this book have been designed to provide a peek as to what is available to us. **The chapters that follow provide us with the 'how-to' steps.**

CHAPTER 3

GOD'S RECIPE FOR LOVE

EMBRACING NEW REVELATION

Now we're going to step forth a little deeper in our teaching and look at *how* we can manifest the love of God. That's the thing that confounded me for years. I knew I was supposed to walk in love but I didn't know how to do it. After many years of study and seeking God on this subject, I believe that He has revealed to me some of the primary keys.

As you may have already experienced in the first two chapters, there are some things that you are going to read in this book that you may not have read or heard of in the past. So I will ask starting out to not *freak out* and throw this book across the room shouting: *"I've never heard this before!"* I will endeavor to make plain what I relate by the Word of God.

This chapter really might challenge some peoples' theologies but please hear what the Word of God has to say on these things because not all of our traditional doctrines that we have been taught have been correct. If I bring forth a teaching that you do not agree with or perhaps understand just proceed to the next section. It may make better sense to you later.

In order to get into some of the deeper revelation of how to walk in supernatural love, it is necessary to discuss some basic teachings regarding righteousness and faith. For some this will be a review of what they already know, but for others it will be brand new revelation.

Jesus said that we would do *greater works* because He was going to the Father. And I challenge you to find in this world where the greater works really are in manifestation. It's certainly not in every church on every street corner. And God says in Hosea:

> *Hos 4:6 - "My people are destroyed for lack of knowledge and because you've rejected knowledge, I will also reject you."*

So we discover a primary reason that churches aren't manifesting the power of God is because they lack knowledge. Right now, we're in a season where God is bringing forth revelation and understanding of the Word of God at a level previously unknown. This is to allow us to step out of our old limited ways of thinking and into the fullness of what God wants us to do and become today.

The Word declares in The Gospel of John:

> *John 8:32 - "You shall know the truth and the truth will make you free."*

Right now, most of the church is in bondage. They're bound up, they're weighed down, and they're not even enjoying their Christianity. If I took a poll and you were truly honest with yourself, a lot of you reading would say: *"You know, I'm really not enjoying my walk as a Christian much of the time."* And we've still got a situation where to many, the things of the world look more enjoyable than the things of the church. It was never intended to be that way. **God is bringing forth revelation of the Word regarding how we may truly step into being fulfilled as Christians. However, we've got to be willing to change our mindsets to line up with what He is revealing in these end-times.**

TARGETING GENUINE LOVE

In Chapters 1 & 2 of this book, we taught why Christians need to walk in and manifest the love of God. We found that it fulfills God's commandments for our lives. Love demonstrates that we're His disciples. It brings in the harvest, and much more.

You may already know that First Corinthians 13 is referred to by many as the *Love Chapter*. We examined the first three verses of this powerful chapter in the initial chapter of this book. Doing so, we discovered that without love, it doesn't matter if we speak with the tongues of angels, move mountains, give all of our goods to the poor, or give our bodies to be burned - it will profit us nothing. We are hollow and empty without love! Let's now continue reading again from First Corinthians, starting with verse 4:

> *1Cor 13:4-8 – "Charity [agape love] suffereth long, and is kind; charity envieth not; charity vaunteth not itself, is not puffed up, Doth not behave itself unseemly, seeketh not her own, is not easily provoked, thinketh no evil; rejoiceth not in iniquity, but rejoiceth in the truth; beareth all things, believeth all things, hopeth all things, endureth all things. Charity never faileth: but whether there be prophecies, they shall fail; whether there be tongues, they shall cease; whether there be knowledge, it shall vanish away."*

Years ago, I decided to target walking in love after God convicted me to come out of my Mr. Spock mentality, where I had targeted living totally without emotion. Discovering that God had commanded us to love, I tried everything I could to accomplish this. I wasn't going to become angry with my wife or children anymore. I wasn't going to express impatience, lack of kindness, or any other actions that violated God's standards of love.

As I mentioned earlier, I'd review verses 4-8 and say: *"Today, I'm not going to mess up a single one of these directives."* And by mid-morning I'd blown half of them. So then what happened? I'd get mad and condemn myself: *"You thought you were a Christian. You said that you loved God.. You thought you were going to be such a powerful man of God, and you can't even walk in love for 15 minutes!"* And of course, the devil would remind me of which ones I had blown.

But, the revelation then came that I was trying to reinstitute law in my life. As we discovered in Chapter 1, we'll never manifest the love of God in our lives through law. Legalistic living will never be qualified to manifest the love of God.

So, I started seeking and asking: *"God, how can I walk in this love?"*

Let's review and throw in some additional aspects of the five verses we just read that will start to give us a little more appreciation of just what is contained in the love of God. First of all, in the Greek every aspect mentioned in these five verses is an action; each one is a verb. Also, they are all present tense. It's not good enough to have loved in the past. We must stay in love; we must walk in love full-time.

Everything mentioned here is an attribute of God, so these verses give us a glimpse of who God really is. God is love. He's not a mean-spirited entity, dangling us like some spider on a thread over a fiery pit. **He's not looking to throw us into hell at the first opportunity.** He **"*beareth all things,*" "*endureth all things,*"** and He **"*never faileth.*"**

We find out as well that every one of these attributes of love is a key for maintaining integrity in our lives. We'll never accomplish anything for God without integrity. The loss of integrity has been the number one smear against ministry in the past several decades. Men and women of God who lose their integrity end up introducing hypocrisy into the church.

And so it tells us in Luke:

> *Luke 8:15 - "But that on the good ground are they, **which in an honest and good heart**, having heard the word, keep it, and bring forth fruit with patience."*

Understand that if we're going to walk in love, it's going to require us to guard our integrity. Love is all important and demands that we become people who guard the truth with all diligence. Know, however, that once love arises in our lives, walking in integrity becomes much easier.

The fruit of the Spirit are all attributes of our reborn nature. We are born again with the nature of the love of God. As well, all of these items mentioned are interlinked. For instance, we can't believe all things unless we can also bear all things. We can't be kind unless we can equally endure. In other words, to walk in the fullness of the love of God, nine out of ten won't do. And, as we begin to endeavor to manifest the true supernatural power of the love of God, God is going to deal with us in areas that apply to every one of these. Any area in which we are negligent will become the weak link in our chain that will limit how much we can really carry the anointing of love.

Remember, the love of God is beyond just bringing somebody a Jell-O salad when they feel low. God is love, and when His love manifests on this earth, it does so in a supernatural fashion. To truly walk in the love of God provides a power supply to our lives; an anointing that's going to enable us to do what we could not do of ourselves.

The love of God is God's highest level of empowerment. Many of you reading this may have done just what I did. You may have tried to walk in love and you only made it so far before you fizzled out. You exhausted yourself in your efforts to be a nice enough person or do enough good deeds. You couldn't bear this load by yourself for more than a few days.

I like what I once heard Joyce Meyer minister regarding her early days of Christianity. She had young children, and at times she had to get away from the kids for a few minutes to regain her sanity. She'd go lock herself in the bedroom to get some time alone with God to recharge. The children would then come knocking on the door saying: *"Mommy, mommy, mommy! We need you! Can you come out? Mommy, mommy, mommy!"*

And she'd answer back: *"You don't want mommy to come out right now!"* What happened? She walked in love to the level or extent that she was capable of on her own but there came a time when she needed God to take her beyond her own personal ability.

Jesus said that we're supposed to abide in Him. When we step beyond - into the supernatural realm where we are truly abiding in Jesus, we'll walk in love full-time. I'm convinced that before Jesus comes back for His church, we will be doing just that. Understand, if we do what we've always done because we believe what we've always believed, we'll get what we've always gotten. ***So we've got to change what we believe - to alter what we do - to get something new.***

The love of God and these attributes defining the love of God, all describe the walk of a perfect man or woman as far as God is concerned. We found out in Chapter 1 that even a man is supposed to walk in the love of God and it does not challenge his masculinity to do so. And each of the verbs in these five verses are all in the continuous tense. So it's not enough to manifest only part-time love, we are instructed to walk in continual love.

God understood these verb tenses when He spoke this and led Paul to write it down. For God to list all of these descriptors that love accomplishes, and for Him to decree love as His will for us in the eternal scriptures lets us know that it is available for us today. The Word of God is full of verses about walking in love. And again, God didn't mean merely performing a set of good deeds. He was talking about a supernatural, present tense, continuous divine empowerment in which we're supposed to live and dwell.

If it's in His book, then I know that it should be available for us today. All we've got to do is discover *how* to do it.

This will be discussed in more depth later on, but God showed me how to manifest the love of God somewhat by accident. Having tasted of this supernatural love, I then found in the Word of God why it manifested as it did.

Here is the key verse that came alive to me:

> *1Tim 1:5 – "Now the end of the commandment is charity out of a pure heart, and of a good conscience, and of faith unfeigned."*

Here we see what I call God's *Recipe for Agape* – a three-part recipe of how to manifest the love of God. There are three primary components to this: "***A pure heart,***" "***a good conscience,***" and "**genuine faith.**" (The word *"unfeigned"* means *genuine*.)

Notice that it says that *"the end of the commandment"* is *agape*. In other words, the end of everything that God's directing us to do is fulfilled when we walk in love. Every instruction that God ever gives us has one end goal – to get us to walk and live in His love. Everything that He tells us to give; every verse that He tells us to read; every person that He tells us to speak to; and every church service that He tells us to attend has one end goal in mind.

That goal is to get us doing something to manifest the love of God in our lives. Even learning how to be miraculously healed is a component of manifesting the love of God. After all, it's hard to walk in love if we're sick; or at least we can't take it to very many people. That the end of the commandment is love means that everything the Word has to declare to us and everything God instructs us to do is targeted to get us to walk in this love.

So now we want to examine these components that bring us into His supernatural love - one at a time.

A PURE HEART

Our first ingredient is a *"pure heart"*.

What does it mean to have a pure heart? Let's look at First Peter 1:22 to find out:

> *1Pet 1:22 -"Seeing ye have purified your souls in obeying the truth through the Spirit unto unfeigned love of the brethren, see that ye love one another with a pure heart fervently."*

It says that we are to *"love one another with a pure heart fervently."* **Understand that it is impossible to love one another with a defiled heart.** If we are going to manifest the love of God, we must have this contamination-free nature. Let's read on:

> *1Pet 1:23 –"Being born again, not of corruptible seed, but of incorruptible, by the word of God, which liveth and abideth for ever."*

To walk in the love of God we must be born-again of the *"incorruptible"* seed. However, it will aid us to understand what actually takes place when we are saved.

Do you understand that we as human beings are really triune beings? We're made up of three parts. The part of our three-part being that we are most acquainted with is the body. But that body is not who we really are - it's just the tabernacle that enables us to walk in the natural world.

God placed five senses in our bodies so that we can detect what's actually going on in the natural world where we live.

Without these five senses, we wouldn't know what was going on about us. And so, we live in a physical body.

Our true eternal being is a spirit. Our spirit-man is the part of our triune being that becomes born-again upon salvation. When we were saved, we were born again by incorruptible seed. Someone came to us and related to us the Gospel message and we believed and received it. Supernaturally, our inner man was purged of sin and recreated righteous. Through this transformation, our spirit becomes the part of us that has continual communion with the Holy Spirit within. Our spirit-man in actuality is who we really are. And when we die, our spirit goes to heaven leaving this body behind.

As well, we possess a soul – the soul is the component of our triune being made up of our mind, our will, and our emotions. The soul is the portion of who we are where we process the majority of our conscious thoughts. Not being purged by the blood upon salvation, our souls still retain the memories of sin, the hurts of the past, and are programmed with many of the improper reactions we experience. **Our souls become that part of our triune being that must be transformed by the Word of God.** And so contrary to much Christian teaching, our soul is not the same as our spirit although they are closely linked.

Now some might have just gotten saved only to obtain fire insurance - i.e. to escape hell. However the truth is, when we did give our lives to God a supernatural manifestation took place on the inside of us. The Bible says that God came inside of us and took out our heart of stone and replaced it with a heart of flesh. We actually became new creations in Christ.

> *2Cor 5:17 –"Therefore if any man be in Christ, he is a new creature: old things are passed away; behold, all things are become new."*

When we were born-again, we became a new species of being. We became a new person made in the image of God on the inside. God came into us and took out our sin nature and put in its place the nature of love. He put in us once again the image of Himself.

Did you know that Adam carried the image of God originally? We'll look at this in Romans shortly, but when we became born again, God *restored* our God image on the inside. God, being love, put into us His love nature and now we are a new species of being. Hallelujah! Once saved, Jesus took our sin and the Bible declares that we are now the righteousness of God in Christ Jesus!

Now here is a statement that may rattle some chains: Once we are born again we are no longer a sinner! Now understand that I didn't say that we would never sin again. I didn't say that we wouldn't make another mistake. However, when we became saved, God did a miracle on the inside of us. He took out our old nature of sin and totally eradicated it from our lives.

The problem is, when we were born again He didn't do anything to change our souls. We still have the same mind that we possessed before. We still have the same memories that we held before. We still have the same memories of *enjoying* sin in the past that we did before.

And so, because the Word of God has not yet renewed our minds, we still know how to sin and there's still the potential that we can be tempted by sin. But inwardly we already detest iniquity. We just read in First Corinthians 13 that love *"rejoiceth not in iniquity"*. Well, this love is now on the inside of us. We hate sin. That's why a person who becomes born again may have been a fun-loving sinner before but now he despises his old ways.

You may have witnessed many people who have been born again but later became backslidden. However, a backslider can never enjoy a life of sin again. They enjoyed life as sinners before because the actions of sin they performed were in agreement with the fallen image that they had imprinted on the inside of them. However once they became saved, they received the love of God imprinted within instead - a nature that despises sin. And now when the born-again individual sins, it grieves him. A saved person can never return to sin again and enjoy it because it is in contrast to and grieves their new inner man.

To really enjoy life, we must commit acts or experience activities that fulfill who we are on the inside. And so from that standpoint, if we really want to be fulfilled in life then we will have to walk in love. Only the love walk can align our lives with who we are on the inside. Understand that we are now reborn the righteousness of God in Christ Jesus. When we were saved, incorruptible seed transformed us. That seed, when we received it, germinated, produced growth, and now the DNA code of that incorruptible seed has been released into our lives. And the DNA code of that seed represents the very nature of God Himself.

Do you understand that Jesus became the Bible in human form? He is the Word made flesh. So when we receive the seed of the Word, we receive the entire DNA program of incorruptible seed on the inside of us. **Now, through that DNA code, we are a new species of being that never existed before the cross.** We are a born-again saint. Glory to God!

One of the most important things that we have to learn is to realize who we are on the inside. This is because a defiled vessel cannot manifest the love of God to any high level. Know that there was a great exchange made on the cross - as it was there that Jesus took our sin upon Himself while imparting to us His love nature. Most Christians understand that Jesus, through His blood paid the price to wash away our sins. But actually, it's really a step deeper than what many have perceived in the past. Let's look again at this important verse of scripture:

> *2Cor 5:21 -"For he hath made him to be sin for us, who knew no sin; that we might be made the righteousness of God in him."*

Notice here that it doesn't say that Jesus only paid the redemption price for our sins committed. The Word declares that He took sin upon Himself. It says that He was made sin. He was actually made a sinner upon the cross because only by doing so could He go to hell and pay the full price of redemption for us. Not only that, but Jesus on the cross cried: *"My Father, my Father, why have you forsaken Me?"* Why did He say that? He voiced this because that was the point at which He was made sin. For the first and only time in all of eternity past, present, and forever, Father God and Jesus were separated. And this division was the result of Jesus being *"made"* sin.

Jesus took upon Himself through the cross not just sins, but He took upon Himself the very fallen nature of Adam himself. The Bible declares:

> *Gal 3:13 - "Christ hath redeemed us from the curse of the law, being made a curse for us: For it is written, Cursed is everyone that hangeth on a tree."*

By being hung on a tree according to Deuteronomy 21:23, Jesus became accursed. He was made sin. And to be freed of this sin impartation, Jesus also had to be born again from the dead. He had to be born again just like you and me. He arose via the prophetic declarations that He had spoken over himself as the redeemer. Jesus was raised by the power of His own blood.

So we being a born-again Christian are more than someone who has been washed by the blood. We are a new species of being with a new nature that's been made in the image of God. We are a species that didn't exist pre-cross. And once we realize who we are as a born-again saint, it will allow us to walk in more power than we have ever thought possible. The devil's number one tool to disable Christians from walking in the power of God is to make them think they're not worthy of that power. And the number one tool the enemy uses to disable people from walking in the love of God is to make them think that they're not worthy of possessing His divine nature.

When we were saved and received the nature of love, our assignment in life became to take that love image that's on the inside of us and get it to the outside. God wants us to be fulfilled. He wants us to enjoy life. And God wants us to learn how to get what's on the inside of us and bring it to the outside to experience that fulfillment.

Let's look further at this righteous nature. Paul writes in Romans:

> *Rom 5:12 – "Wherefore, as by one man sin entered into the world, and death by sin; and so death passed upon all men, for that all have sinned...For if by one man's offence death reigned by one; much more they which receive abundance*

> *of grace and of the gift of righteousness shall reign in life by one, Jesus Christ."*

Here it says that death entered and reigned through Adam's transgression. However, those who receive through Jesus the righteous impartation of God - His love nature, become qualified to access grace to reign in life. In other words, once we begin walking in the love of God which is the manifestation of our righteous nature, we'll then walk in a God-given authority that will far transcend any weaponry the enemy has been able to use to oppose us. Paul goes onto say this:

> *Rom 5:19: - "For as by one man's disobedience many were made sinners, so by the obedience of one shall many be made righteous."*

Here Paul confirms that Christians have been born-again righteous. Did you know that if we weren't made the righteousness of God then we couldn't get to heaven? After all, sinners aren't going to heaven - only those born-again. **And the truth is, we being born-again Christians, internally are just as righteous as Jesus.**

Did he just write that?

That's what is written in the Bible. Because we've been born-again and received His new nature, we are just as righteous as Jesus. And if we weren't, we couldn't go to heaven. The Bible says in Matthew:

> *Mat 11:11 – "Verily I say unto you, among them that are born of women there hath not risen a greater than John the Baptist: Notwithstanding he that is least in the kingdom of heaven is greater than he."*

Those who are in the kingdom of heaven include not just those who have died and received their heavenly reward, but also all of those currently living who have been born-again. We don't wait to die to become citizens of heaven. We are kingdom citizens now. Why are born-again Christians greater than John the Baptist? Is it because of what we've done? *No* - but it is because of who we have become on the inside. The new heart of love makes us greater than anyone who has not received this God-given nature.

I'm telling you, God's bringing a revival in these last days that will be renowned as an outpouring of His love. On the leading edge of this revival will be an overflowing revelation of believers discovering who they are in Christ. We cannot operate in the authority of the Word of God beyond our level of knowing who we are in Him. Yet through love, miracle power will overflow the end-time church. We as saints have been born into a royal family.

There have been many royal families where, when the king died, his child was crowned monarch at a young age. (In fact, there are instances of that in the Bible.) And a young child who has been made king, no matter how powerful that nation, is not going to walk in any meaningful authority until he discovers who he is. However, once he discovers his identity, he will begin to wield power to the utmost levels of his dominion.

In the same fashion, when we find out that we are made in the image of King Jesus, we will then begin to walk in the full authority and power that God has intended for us to carry. It will allow us to step into a realm of anointing beyond anything we have thought possible. I am convinced that God is even now bringing about a revival among His people who really know who we are in Christ Jesus. This then enables us to access His power to do the greater works – including walking in the love of God.

Remember that Ingredient #1 is a pure heart. Therefore a person with a nature of sin cannot walk in love - primarily because, he has no access to the third heaven in which love originates. Ephesians tells us that we are seated in *"heavenly places"* in Christ Jesus.

> *Eph 2:6 – "And hath raised us up together, and made us sit together in heavenly places in Christ Jesus:"*

Do you know why we are seated there? It is because we've already been made in God's image; we've already been made *"sons of God"* according to First John.

> *1John 3:2 – "Beloved, now are we the sons of God, ..."*

We've already been given all authority. We're already seated in heavenly places. As far as God's concerned, we now have access to every promise contained in the Word and to every form of anointing.

So out of our heavenly position, we now have access to the raw material of love. Through this connection, we can bring this supernatural force to the earth. A non-Christian does not possess this heavenly access, so there's no way that they can manifest the God-kind of love. (Not to mention the fact that a non-Christian has limited motivation to do so - the main focus of a non-Christian is *me*.) Let's look again at First John:

> *1John 4:7 "Beloved, let us love one another: for love is of God; and every one that loveth is born of God, and knoweth God."*

Here John declares that everyone who loves is *"born of God."* So conversely, we can state that everyone who isn't born of God cannot manifest *agape* love. If it says that everyone who *"loveth is born of God"*, then we must of necessity be born-again to manifest that love. The Word as well declares that we have to also know God (we'll get to that later).

First John 4 goes on to say this:

> *1John 4:8 - "He that loveth not knoweth not God; for God is love."*

Here it says that if we don't display love, then we don't *"know"* God. To walk in *agape*, it is not enough just to be born-again but we must also come to know Him. I might throw in that if we don't flow in love, we most likely are not abiding in the Word. After all, the Word is the revelation of who God is. As we spend extensive amounts of time in the Word, the Word will get in us. It will allow us to step into more and more of the love of God through knowing Him.

So that's Ingredient #1 – a pure heart. So now let's go to Ingredient #2.

A GOOD CONSCIENCE

Let's look again at our recipe for love:

> *1Tim 1:5 –"Now the end of the commandment is charity out of a pure heart, and of a good conscience, and of faith unfeigned."*

Ingredient #2 is a **"good conscience."** To walk with a good conscience implies that we walk free of condemnation. Condemnation becomes a logjam to the flow of love in our lives. If we're going to walk in the love of God, then we've got to realize that we are worthy to carry it. And condemnation targets our *worthiness mentality.*

After all, the enemy is going to come to us and say: *"Who do you think you are? Do you really think that you are holy enough to see God answer your prayers? Who do you think you are that you can carry a supernatural force to transform the lives of the people around you?"*

The devil is going to bring up every mistake we've made for the past ten years – especially those this morning. He'll say: *"Remember when you got frustrated this morning? Remember when you were going to read the Scriptures this morning and instead you watched the news for 15 minutes? Remember how you were going to fast for 40 days and you only made it for three?"*

Satan will come to us and say that we're unworthy to carry this power. That is where we've got to *know that we know* that we are the righteousness of God in Christ Jesus. We've got to in return boldly declare: *"No, I cast that down, I'm a carrier of the love of God! I'm made in God's image! Get thee behind me, Satan!"* As we do so, we stand to eradicate condemnation from our minds. Thus it clears the blockages hindering the love of God from freely flowing through us.

But there's another aspect in our thinking where having a good conscience becomes necessary. When we're going to pray for someone else, the enemy will also be sure to remind us that they are not worthy of having our prayers for them answered.

Just as the devil will assault our faith in our right standing with God, he will also remind us of the shortcomings of everyone around us. He will say: *"You know that they are not spiritual enough to have their prayers answered. Do you remember that time you heard them gossiping? They once even sat in the church pew position where you normally sit."*

To truly pray and believe that we can access and release the love of God, we've got to both believe that we are worthy to release it and that those we are praying for are worthy to receive it. Because, if the devil's an expert at launching condemnation arrows into our minds, he's even more adept at trying to get us to entertain judgmental thoughts regarding the faults of other people.

Let's look in the book of Romans to gain some additional insight regarding this topic of condemnation:

> *Rom 5:18 – "Therefore as by the offence of one judgment came upon all men to condemnation; even so by the righteousness of one the free gift came upon all men unto justification of life."*

Through the offense of Adam, condemnation, guilt, and shame entered the world. When guilt and shame arise, it becomes difficult for anyone to receive from God because the subsequent condemnation neutralizes the operation of faith. For our faith to work, God had to address this condemnation issue. Praise God for verse 19:

> *Rom 5:19 – "For as by one man's disobedience many were made sinners, so by the obedience of one shall many be made righteous."*

Here we see that God's free gift of righteousness not only imparts within us His divine nature, but it also carries the power to deliver us from all condemnation. Again, condemnation is reversed by finding out just who we are in Jesus.

Another note regarding condemnation - it attacks people regardless of their level of fire for God. In fact, I have discovered that it is usually the believers with the greatest heart for Him that often battle the most condemnation. The more that they are after God, the more the enemy points out their lack of perfection. People with little desire for God have often seared their hearts to the point that the Holy Spirit can no longer convict them. And at the same time, the devil sees little need to condemn them.

So we must access a good conscience. The way that we develop a good conscience is by renewing our minds to the Word; renewing our minds to the fact that we are the righteousness of God in Christ Jesus. Even though we have a pure heart, if we don't realize it we still won't effectively walk in the love of God.

We're going to find out that if we're going to walk in supernatural love, these three ingredients all apply to a different aspect of our triune being. A pure heart applies to our spirit man. A good conscience applies to our soul – involving the renewing our mind. And genuine faith refers to actions that we're going to need to enact through our flesh to release the love of God through our lives.

To walk in love, we must renew our minds to realize the full potential of our pure hearts. Within our soul resides not just our mind, but also our will. We usually describe the soul as being made up of our mind, will and emotions. Even though our real man on the inside is made in the image of God, our will embedded within our soul still becomes the decision gateway for our lives. Every decision that we make, spiritual or not, has to be enacted by our will.

When we became saved, our spirit man wanted to go to church right away. The Holy Ghost was down on the inside of us saying: *"Go to church!"* However if you're like me, your head was arguing: *"Why do I want to go to church? There's a bunch of hypocrites in the church!"* But when we got in the Word of God, we discovered that it says that we are *"not to forsake the assembling of yourselves together."* Our soul, enlightened to the truth of the Word of God was then able to make a willful decision that agreed with our spirit-man. And we reversed our decision to skip services. The same held true for tithing and many other spiritual principles to which we had to reeducate ourselves.

So God has to get us to renew our minds to the Word of God in order for us to make spiritual decisions. Once our mind is renewed, we become 'spiritually minded' and can make decisions that agree both with the Word and also with our reborn spirit-man. You see, the most powerful two that can come into agreement for our lives are our spirit and our soul. As we get our minds renewed by the Word to what already took place in our hearts when we were saved, we will then be able to walk in the fullness of our God-given authority. Once we find out that we are made in God's image, we have taken a giant step toward being qualified to manifest His supernatural love.

Once saved, we should target the rest of our Christian life to discover the fullness of what took place at that moment. **You see, when we became saved, there was such a miracle that took place - such an impartation released - and such an inheritance made available to us - that we'll now spend the rest of our lives in the Word finding out just what happened in that moment.** And the more that we can find out what happened at that moment, the more we'll walk in the power of God that was then made available. So it is imperative that we renew our mind to our new righteous nature.

Romans chapter one lets us know without question that God wants us to personally build our faith in comprehension of our righteous nature.

> *Rom 1:16-17* – *"For I am not ashamed of the gospel of Christ: for it is the power of God unto salvation to every one that believeth; to the Jew first, and also to the Greek. For therein is the righteousness of God revealed from faith to faith: as it is written, The just shall live by faith."*

Our revelation of our new righteousness nature is revealed from *"faith to faith."* In other words, we must continually develop our faith regarding our new identity. Faith however does not come by accident. It is best developed when it is targeted intentionally. Romans chapter 10 lets us know:

Rom 10:17 – "So then faith cometh by hearing, and hearing by the Word of God."

I like to state this verse in this fashion: *"Faith cometh by **hearing and hearing** the Word of God."*

Faith is developed by meditating the Word of God! We can intentionally develop our faith by meditating scriptures that target specific promises of God in which we desire to walk. In the case of ingredient #1, we want to meditate scriptures that refer to our righteous nature once born-again. **Once we develop faith in our new nature, ingredient #2 - a good conscience will take place automatically.**

To walk in the supernatural power of the love of God we must make the effort to build our faith in who He has now made us. We are not who we used to be. It is important that we develop a list of scriptures upon which we would like to meditate regarding this new nature. It is valuable to write them down and speak them out several times a day. We must let them roll over and over again in our minds. As we do so, an amazing process will take place - we will begin to believe what we have been meditating because faith is being developed. We will begin to realize that love *is* on the inside of us.

Chapter 4 is where we're going to find out that it's going to require *radical faith* to access this love. And not just faith in who we are, but aggressive actions of faith representing that we believe this power is available to us. We may be required to bless people that have just ripped our heart out, sliced it in pieces, and stomped it on the floor. And God's going to say: *"If you want this anointing, you need to go and bless them."*

Let's go on to ingredient #3.

CHAPTER 4

THE SEED OF LOVE

GENUINE FAITH

Now we are ready to look at Ingredient #3 in the 'Recipe for Love'.

> 1Tim 1:5 – *"Now the end of the commandment is charity (agape love) out of a pure heart, a good conscience, and of faith unfeigned."*

Ingredient #3 is *"unfeigned faith"* and that really becomes the most challenging of the three.

When we think about it, it doesn't really take a lot of effort for someone to get born again. They confess: *"Jesus, I believe your words, save me! I receive you as my Lord and Savior!"* That wasn't too hard, was it?

And actually, it's not too hard to renew our minds to the Word of God. It mainly takes time in the Book. It demands the re-prioritizing of our days to spend adequate time in study to fully discover who God says that we are. Renewing our minds and developing a cleansed conscience is really just an educational process.

However, ingredient #3 is really where the rubber hits the road. Ingredient #3 is where it's going to take some effort and it's going to stretch us significantly. It's going to require us to grit our teeth and bite our tongues to activate the faith necessary to manifest the love of God. The phrase *"unfeigned faith"* means *genuine faith*. As such, we need to discuss faith for a bit. If we don't really comprehend what faith is then we won't be able to effectively utilize it.

We understand that God has placed us in this natural world - this first heaven realm where we experience many frequent challenges. Through the Word, we should also understand that God has promised us power to overcome these challenges - not just when we die and go to heaven, but now in this world as well. Through the spiritual principle of faith, God has given us a tool whereby we can bring forth His power and resources out of the third heaven. As we bring His provision from the Third Heaven into the First, we are able to change our circumstances and live victoriously. Glory to God!

In fact, faith is the *only* avenue to supernatural power that God has given us which will give us victory over all of the challenges of life. Without faith, we cannot access the supply of the Kingdom of God. That's why according to Hebrews 11:6, *it's impossible to please Him without faith.*

We will need to have faith to access anything that God has promised us, including the supernatural power of love. I'm referring to the power of God that will take us beyond ourselves - that will take us beyond our own willpower and strength. I'm referring to an anointing that will literally destroy devils out of our presence, deliver us from strife, and rid us of offense. The power of love will heal our hearts of every past scar and allow us to enjoy a fulfilled life such as we have never dreamed possible. Love is a supernatural force, and it's only available through faith.

Let's now take the time to look at this biblical principle a bit further to see what is required to walk by faith. If you've been under any faith teaching for very long then these Scriptures will be familiar to you, but we need to cover them to lay the right foundation for where we want to go.

A common statement that we use regarding the teaching of faith is that *everything we experience in this first heaven realm is temporary and subject to change.* Everything in this universe operates by certain established rules or principles that we refer to as the *'laws of physics'*. These laws are so reliable and well defined that through applying them, we can send men to the moon and bring them back safely. Everything built or designed by man takes these laws into account. I am thankful that these laws are reliable; otherwise how would we know if it were safe to cross a bridge or whether the brakes on our car would stop us.

In the same way, the Kingdom of God operates by spiritual principles. And if the laws of this natural realm are repeatable and well defined then we can also know that the laws of the spirit (the third heaven realm) are equally reliable. This first heaven universe was created out of the realm of the spirit; God spoke and the entirety of this universe came into existence. Therefore we know that the principles and the power upon which the spirit realm operates have authority and precedence over this natural world and its physical laws.

Do you remember when Jesus walked on the water? He defied the law of gravity. He knew how to apply faith to access a level of spiritual power that would give Him priority or precedence over the established laws of this natural realm.

And that's the way that faith operates. **If we understand faith, we then understand that everything we experience in this natural life can be changed if we will access the power and provision available to us through God's Word.** For example, sickness is a fairly universal natural event. Nearly everyone experiences sickness and disease at various times. However, the Bible declares that *through the stripes of Jesus we were healed.*

> *1Pet 2:24 – "Who his own self bare our sins in his own body on the tree, that we, being dead to sins, should live unto righteousness: by whose stripes you were healed."*

By utilizing our faith, we can access healing power provided through the kingdom of God and bring it into our lives. We can be healed from any disease or injury that would afflict us. How does this take place? Through faith, we bring in a higher truth with greater power from God's Word - and that higher truth changes the facts of our natural experience.

Jesus made this statement regarding faith in Mark 11:22-24:

> *Mark 11:22-24 –"Have faith in God. For verily I say unto you, That whosoever shall say unto this mountain, Be thou removed, and be thou cast into the sea; and shall not doubt*

> *in his heart, but shall believe that those things which he saith shall come to pass; he shall have whatsoever he saith. Therefore I say unto you, What things soever ye desire, when ye pray, believe that ye receive them, and ye shall have them."*

So we have the ability to command natural circumstances to change. And if we believe and act on what the Word of God promises us, then we can see our circumstances change to match what He has declared in His Word. If we experience financial lack in our lives, the Word of God promises that we may prosper. And if we will use our faith to apply God's spiritual principles of seedtime and harvest, then we can see our finances totally turn around.

A pivotal truth of this book is that we can see our relationships turn around by faith in the Word as well – through the anointing and empowerment of supernatural love.

Let's look at another testimony of faith related to us in the Word. Romans chapter 4 speaks of Abraham - the father of faith:

> *Rom 4:16 - "Therefore it is of faith, that it might be by grace; to the end the promise might be sure to all the seed; not to that only which is of the law, but to that also which is of the faith of Abraham; who is the father of us all, (As it is written, I have made thee a father of many nations,) before him whom he believed, even God, who quickeneth the dead, and calleth those things which be not as though they were."*

Abraham, when he was still named Abram was told that he was going to be a father of nations. In an effort to keep Abram continually mindful of His promise, God told him: *"When you gaze at the stars, that's how numerous your seed is going to be."* And also: *"When you look at the sand, it indicates the number of descendants that will come from you."* God needed Abram to meditate the promise that He had given him to build up his faith within.

Then when Abram was ninety-nine years old after years of carrying this promise, God came to him and directed him to take a more radical step of faith. He commanded him to change his name to *Abraham* – meaning *Father of Many*. At the same time, God changed his wife's name to *Sarah – Mother of Nations*. To get Abram's faith activated, God decreed that he must begin to declare the promise over himself and his bride. It was vital that they speak the promise. At this time, the reproductive capabilities of both of their bodies were dead. Yet because they began *calling those things that were not as though they were*, Isaac was birthed into what had been a dead situation.

In this book we're going to learn how to resurrect relationships from the dead. I don't know about you but I've had relationships that were dead in the water. Accessing the power of love has enabled me to see many such relationships restored. It also has aided me in taking the right steps of faith to maintain relationships that the enemy has targeted.

Without doubt, I would not be married today if not for what God has taught me regarding how to access His supernatural love. And I believe that if you will apply the teachings of this book, it will turn the relationships in your life around as well.

Faith can raise dead situations - but we have to be willing to call things that appear not as though they are. That's where it begins to get tough.

FIVE STEPS OF FAITH

When I teach faith, I like to break it down into five basic steps. No matter what we are believing God for, operating by faith will require us to follow this same foundational progression:

1. **REVELATION,**
2. **MEDITATION,**
3. **APPLICATION,**
4. **MANIFESTATION, and**
5. **RESTORATION**

We have discussed several of these previously but we are now going to cover a brief summarization of each.

Before we can believe God for any of His promises, we must first get a **REVELATION** that the promise exists and that it is available to us. In the case of love, we must gain the knowledge that it is a supernatural force that we can access and carry.

Once we realize that a specific promise is available to us, in order to develop our faith for that promise we must spend time in **MEDITATION** of what the Word declares. Regarding love, we must focus on meditating scriptures that declare our righteousness and that speak of us being able to manifest this power.

Once developed, we must then take steps toward **APPLICATION** of our newly produced faith. Application of faith involves three steps of its own:

    A. SPEAKING,
    B. ACTING, and
    C. STANDING

SPEAKING is the initial step that we take to *release our faith*. As Jesus taught in Mark 11:23, we must *speak to the mountain!* Until faith-filled words are spoken, no authority for change is released. Proverbs lets us know:

> *Prov 18:20-21* – *"A man's belly shall be satisfied with the fruit of his mouth; and with the increase of his lips shall he be filled. Death and life are in the power of the tongue: and they that love it shall eat the fruit thereof."*

Our words have the power to decree both death and life into our situations. Those who walk by faith use this capacity to release the power of God for good. As we speak the promise of God that we desire, we forcefully take hold of it to bring it into our life.

ACTING refers to the actions that we will take once we truly believe that the promise of God is ours. If we genuinely believe what the Word declares for us, then we will act like it. I am not referring to acting as in an actor in a play - as if one were merely pretending to fill a role. I use the term *acting* for those *actions* that we will take when we really believe that we can step out on the water by faith. In the case of love, we are referring to actions that we will take to bless others where we desire love to flow. In many cases, we may be required to bless those who have risen up against us.

The term **STANDING** applies to the time period between when we have spoken and acted upon the promise *up to the point that* we see the promise actually manifested.

During this time frame, it is vital that we maintain our confessions of faith and continue to act as if the promise were ours. Otherwise, contrary words and actions will most likely neutralize our ability to receive what we are believing for. Opposing words and actions reflect that we really are not fully convinced that the promise of God is ours and demonstrate wavering in our faith stand. James lets us know that we cannot expect to receive anything from God in those instances:

> *Jas 1:5-7 – "If any of you lack wisdom, let him ask of God, that giveth to all men liberally, and upbraideth not; and it shall be given him. But let him ask in faith, nothing wavering. For he that wavereth is like a wave of the sea driven with the wind and tossed. For let not that man think that he shall receive any thing of the Lord."*

MANIFESTATION is what we are looking for. *Manifestation* represents that we have now received the *end of our faith* - the promise of God being fulfilled in our lives. Regarding love, our manifestation will often be a damaged relationship supernaturally repaired.

RESTORATION implies that everything that the enemy has stolen from us or has damaged has been replaced or repaired. Often *restoration* produces conditions superior to the original. It is not unusual that those who experience divine healing discover that the area touched by the power of God is stronger than ever. Regarding love, our relationships will end up more gratifying than we ever thought possible.

At a higher level of living by faith, restoration implies that *all* of the promises of God have been manifested in our lives - including us walking in the love of God. Full restoration of our lives manifests as *zoe* life where we experience nothing missing or broken. As well, as we partake of this end-time outpouring of love, we will find that manifestation of all of the promises of God is much easier.

Understand that there are innumerable books that can teach us, in detail, to walk by faith. In this book, we will only touch on some of the highlights.

SPEAKING LOVE

Since we are targeting the release of love in our lives by faith, what we speak becomes a major factor in this process. **Therefore, it is vital that we develop a regimen of confessing scriptures that declare that God's love operates through us.** There are numerous passages that declare this but my personal preferred passage is from Ephesians chapter 3:

> *Eph 3:17-21 – "That Christ may dwell in your hearts by faith; that ye, being rooted and grounded in love, May be able to comprehend with all saints what is the breadth, and length, and depth, and height; And to know the love of Christ, which passeth knowledge, that ye might be filled with all the fulness of God. Now unto him that is able to do exceeding abundantly above all that we ask or think, according to the power that worketh in us, Unto him be glory in the church by Christ Jesus throughout all ages, world without end. Amen."*

As we confess this passage of scripture over our lives, we are declaring that Christ (the anointed one and His anointing) is resident and active within us. As well, we are stating that we have a full comprehension or understanding of His love - and that through this love, our potential to serve God is unlimited.

Let's look at some other passages that will be of value for us to speak over our lives:

> *John 17:25-26 – "O righteous Father, the world hath not known thee: but I have known thee, and these have known that thou hast sent me. And I have declared unto them thy*

name, and will declare it: that the love wherewith thou hast loved me may be in them, and I in them."

Imagine that, here Jesus lets us know that the same love that the Father has for Jesus may be within us. If our minds can ever really get a hold of this fact then nothing will ever stop us.

1John 2:5 –"But whoso keepeth his word, in him verily is the love of God perfected: hereby know we that we are in him."

God wants to *perfect* His love in our lives. Perfect love infers that we are walking in all of the attributes of love that are discussed in chapter one. We will never be oppressed, fearful, or offended again. A harvest of souls will come freely to learn from us the secrets to our joy.

2Tim 1:7 –"For God hath not given us the spirit of fear; but of power, and of love, and of a sound mind."

As we confess this verse, we are declaring that we have been given a spirit (nature) of love. That love is within us now. Our confessions are working to bring this love into full operation in our lives - manifesting as the fruit of the spirit. As we speak these verses over ourselves, not only are we releasing our authority for love to rise to its fullness within us but we also are building our faith to walk in this love as we continue hearing ourselves profess these promises. Again, faith comes through hearing and hearing. The more that we speak that we walk in the love of God, the more our faith will increase enabling us to do so.

ACTING IN LOVE

As mentioned, the second step one takes in application of their faith is to *act* on their desired promise from the Word.
We see this part of the faith process declared by James:

Jas 2:17 "Even so faith, if it hath not works, is dead, being alone."

The release of our faith requires not only our declaring of the promise, but also our acting upon that which we believe we have received.

If you have been exposed to teachings on faith in the past, then you have learned how this must be applied to access the power of God for divine healing. If we are fighting symptoms of sickness in our bodies and want to access the supernatural healing power of God then we must take aggressive steps which oppose those symptoms. Let's say for example that we wake up one morning and we have a headache, a little nausea, and some cold chills. If we want to access the supernatural healing power of God, we won't be able to by saying: *"Honey, please bring me some chicken soup."; "Call my boss and tell him I'm sick" or "I'm staying in bed."* Even though we know of God's promises for healing, if we don't step out with actions that agree with those promises then we'll stay sick.

So to receive the power of God to be healed, we've got to say: *"No, the Word of God says that I'm healed and I now receive that healing."* And we've got to make an effort to put into action that which we believe. Just as Joshua had been promised that God had given them the Promised Land, it wasn't until they marched on Jericho that its walls fell flat. Joshua had to put action to his faith. And faith works in the same fashion if we are sick. We've got to put action to our faith. We've got to kick off the covers, jump out of bed, get in the shower, and declare over and over again that we are healed. We must refuse to focus on and speak of any of the symptoms that have attacked us. As we hold to our faith, *we thus walk straight into the healing power of God that is subsequently released into our lives.* Usually before an anointing manifests in our life, we'll have to step into it forcefully.

I remember the first time that the flu hit me after I'd learned this. I fought the flu for five days - and for all five days *I was very sick.* However, I fought it. I spoke forth that I was healed - getting up and doing what I could. Then after about five days my healing manifested. You might say, but that's probably all the longer that flu normally would last. Well the next time I got the flu, it lasted for about a day. Then after that, it could remain only for about an hour. It's now been over twenty-five years since I've been down with the flu. Why? Because I learned how to access God's healing anointing by stepping into the promise of God by faith. And with anything that we're believing God for, we'll have to *act in faith* to step into it. And, when the Word informs us that we can access supernatural love, then we're going to have to *forcefully step into* this love despite significant demonic and emotional opposition.

Let me tell you about the first time I learned to act in faith to release the love of God. It took place even before God illuminated to me His *Recipe for Agape*. He showed it to me by example.

There was one night many years ago that my wife and I got into a knockdown drag-out battle. I don't remember what the disagreement was about but we were in a huge argument. In my mind, I felt that I hadn't done anything wrong and that I was being attacked without merit. Without doubt I'm sure that she felt innocent as well. However, we were in possibly the biggest battle our marriage had ever experienced. We had strife devils everywhere holding up big flashing signs over our house announcing: *"DIVORCE! DIVORCE!"* And all of this was over just one fight!

We retired that night to our queen-sized bed. That was the first step of faith we took. Neither one of us left the house and neither one went to sleep on the couch. And, you have to picture the scene although I am exaggerating a bit. She was leaning over the edge at her side of the bed and had one foot on the floor so she wouldn't roll over and touch me. As well. I had a handful of carpet on my side so I wouldn't roll over and touch her. We didn't want anything to do with each other. If you had put a bucket of water between us, you wouldn't have been able to pour it out because it would have frozen solid in seconds. I mean, it was cold in that bedroom that night. Without doubt, she hated me at that moment in time.

Understand that neither of us had really done anything horribly wrong - we both loved and served God and we were faithful to one another. It was just a disagreement, however, it resulted in major strife filling the air. She had the attitude of *"I'm-going-to-move-out."* And, I had the attitude of *"I-don't-really-care-if-you-do."*

So as I was laying there, I began silently speaking to God: *"God, I don't care about this marriage right now but I know that you put us together."; "I know that we're not supposed to divorce."; "I know that we're not supposed to be angry, but, I don't know what to do!"*

And God spoke to me and said: *"I want you to rub her back."* Now understand, my wife would rather have me rub her back more than anything in the world other than perhaps buy her a Dairy Queen Blizzard. She loves back rubs. Normally when I rub her back, she backs into it and, via her soft moans, lets me know that she's enjoying it.

And I said: *"God, I don't want to rub her back, You rub her back."*

And God replied: *"I'm going to rub her back but I need your hands."*

Swallowing my pride I began rubbing her back and her neck, though I must admit that my hands wanted to reach around her neck and squeeze a little bit. (I know you've never been there!) I wasn't happy about being requested of God to do this, but I was using my faith whether I realized it or not. I had said: *"God you've got to do something."* So he was leading me in what to do to bring His power upon the scene.

Anyway, I might as well have been massaging a block of granite because she was in no way even acknowledging my action. So I said under my breath: *"God what do I do now?"*

And, He said: *"All right, now apologize."*
What?

I responded: *"God, I didn't do anything wrong!"* (At least I felt like I was innocent.)

I persisted: *"God, I didn't do anything to apologize for."*

His response was: *"What does that have to do with anything?"*

The truth is, in our relationships, God's not concerned as much with who is right in a squabble as he is in eradicating the strife - because strife opens doors to increased demonic operation. He's more concerned about what type of atmosphere that we are inviting in and entertaining. And God needed the atmosphere in our home adjusted in order to repair our marriage. And ... HE INSTRUCTED ME TO APOLOGIZE!

So I'm sure my first apology was something to the effect of: *"Babe, I'm sorry that you are mad at me."* (Which probably didn't fly very far either.) However before I was finished speaking I said: *"Babe, I just want to apologize."*; *"If I've done anything wrong to offend you; if I've said anything that hurt you; I'm sorry."*

And she responded - *Not a word!*

As I looked over at the bucket of water it was still frozen solid. She still had one leg on the floor. It was colder than ever in that place! And I said: *"God, I don't know what to do."*; *"I've given it my two best shots."*; *"What do I do now?"*

Then He really upped the ante and said: *"Tell her that you love her."* And under the influence of the emotion-altering strife, I thought - *"I'm not sure that I do at this moment."*

Understand the environment. We'd just come through a knockdown drag-out battle. Words have been spoken that were not edifying one to another. Now men often don't carry the same expertise in verbal jousting as ladies, but a woman when properly set off knows how to reach inside of a man and pull out his heart while it's still beating. She then may proceed to slice it and dice it comparable to the best sushi chef in the world and then throw it on the floor and stomp on it.

Now I know that you ladies have never done that and you guys have possibly never had that done to you, but at that moment I felt that way. And when we've taken a hit to our heart by someone close to us as with a covenant partner, there is major pain of rejection attached to that experience. There's not just strife spirits attacking your relationship, they are being reinforced by spirits of rejection. After all, I was as many who have been through some rough relationships in the past. Before I met my wife, I had put up a wall against women that you couldn't chisel through with a jackhammer! And all of a sudden, here arose that same wall that I had spent significant effort bringing down in the past.

So then what happened? God continued dealing with me on, not what I wanted to do, but on what He wanted accomplished. At that time, I was not operating out of how I felt, but instead was operating 100% out of obedience to Him. At times like these, it is imperative that we let the Spirit of God take over our decision making processes. And in this case, it took *all of the faith that I had to do so.*

See, when First Timothy 1:5 is speaking of genuine faith, this is what it's referring to. It's speaking to us about going through the scars, going through the hurt, and going through the opposition to become *peacemaker*s in these situations. Remember Jesus said: *"Blessed are the peacemakers."* And there is no greater blessing that we can ever encounter than to be enveloped in the love of God.

We will often need to act as the peacemaker *even if, at times, we are innocent!*

And He said: *"Tell her that you love her."*

So I choked down every bit of pride that I had remaining - while refusing to look at my heart which was still scattered in pieces all over the place - and said: *"Babe, I just want you to know that you're my princess and that I love you with all of my heart."*

And suddenly something happened in the atmosphere!

Literally, *instantly,* something happened that was so tangible that we could identify it immediately! Love filled the air.

All of a sudden I heard soft sniffles coming from her side of the bed and she said gently: *"I love you, too!"*

And in an instant, that bucket of ice that was between us began boiling! Amazingly as it seems, we couldn't even remember what the fight was about! God came into that situation with the miracle anointing of love and fused our marriage together stronger than ever before. However, it came forth via someone stepping forth in faith and acting as a peacemaker. (Follow me on this because I'm not trying to exalt myself on this - I'm merely giving an example of how it worked so powerfully in my own life.) God needed someone who would demonstrate spiritual maturity and go beyond their thoughts that were being viciously bombarded. Someone had to go beyond their fickle emotions that had rapidly moved out of bounds and do what God said to do. And by doing this in faith, *we accessed a supernatural empowerment - an anointing that literally eradicated strife out of our house.*

And there was no residual effect from that fight. Often when couples have a fight, one may receive the *three-day silent treatment* - where they just kind of cohabit until things finally cool down. In our case, there was total restoration in the relationship. And miraculously, the relationship was taken to an even higher level.

That's one of the phenomenal things that takes place when we access the power of love. Normally (in the case where the supernatural power of love is not accessed) as people experience battles, scarring develops on the heart. The cumulative effect of these disagreements and this scarring causes them to grow further and further apart. Over time, they may come to the conclusion that they have lost their love for their partner and separation takes place. They may have survived individual battles, but because there was no supernatural manifestation of the love of God then no power was released to remove the scars.

Built up scarring to the heart over time produces built up resentment toward those who have hurt us. The good news is - when God heals our relationships through love, He takes even the scars away. And in this case, God came in and *removed* the offense, *changed* the atmosphere, and actually *healed* our hearts of past damage. He took our marriage to a much higher level.

THE FIGHT OF FAITH

I believe that manifesting the supernatural love of God works in the same fashion as when we manifest divine healing by faith. At times, you have to forcefully oppose the symptoms. For me, an example of this came years ago when I was suffering with migraine headaches. I had never experienced migraines until I became saved. Afterwards, the devil started hitting me with one of these nuclear headaches every week or two where the pain was excruciating. I battled them for several years but the only resolution seemed to be to take pain pills, go to bed, and try to fall asleep in hopes that the pain would be gone when I awoke - usually the next day.

I remember when I finally obtained victory over them. Now this testimony is going to seem preposterous to some, but in 1992 I became determined to lock horns with these headaches with my faith. I was at a party (alcohol free) when there arose a major migraine. Normally I would have excused myself and gone home but on this occasion, I decided to have a showdown with this tormenting affliction. I left my wife inside and told her I was going to our van to battle this attack. I climbed into the passenger side of the vehicle and declared: *"I don't fear you anymore migraines."; "You will not hinder my life nor alter it any longer."*

Now here's the part that may seem a bit unusual but I was determined to fight this assault to the finish then and there. Our van was a 1987 Chevrolet which had a steel dashboard with no padding. The only covering over the dash was a sheet of vinyl. Normally with a migraine, every movement of your head sets off nuclear explosions of pain within.

However in this case, I declared: *"I don't fear this pain any longer."; "I refuse to bow down to this pain."* Then I slammed my forehead down on the dashboard with as much force as I could. When I did, as I sat up the pain level went off the meter. Quickly recognizing that the migraine was still in full blown manifestation, I again said: *"Migraine, you don't belong to me"* and slammed my head on the dash again. In fact, I continued to speak to the headache and slam my head on the dash even to the point that I proclaimed: *"Either I am coming out of this van delivered from this or I am going to split my head wide open."; "I am not living like this any longer."* I kept this up for quite a while but on around the twentieth head slam, I sat up totally healed without even a mark on my head. And I've never suffered with migraines since then. On top of this, I stepped into an increased anointing to pray against migraines in others. I have seen numerous people delivered from migraine headaches as I spoke to the pain or laid hands on them. The victory brought me to a new level of releasing the power of God

The point of this is that, as we manifest the love of God by faith, not only will it deliver us from any strife in operation during that moment but it will take all of our future personal interactions to higher and higher levels. As we mentioned in chapter two, those who learn to step into the power of love on a daily basis and take it to elevated levels will be able to control the soul realm atmosphere every place that they go.

So then faith regarding the manifestation of love is activated by our ability to go beyond what we're feeling. It operates the same as when we receive healing by faith. Healing manifests as we press through physical symptoms and continue to speak God's promise. In the same fashion with regard to love, we must press beyond the pain of personal attacks and emotional rejection while holding to our confession. We must become the one determined to bring the love of God into our situations. The devil is our adversary - not other people.

Many times the situation or relationship that we want to see turned around is one that appears dead. It may even be dead. Our marriage, our interaction with a co-worker, and often involvement with a relative may all be relationships that seem dead in the water. And the truth is, we may not feel as if we want these repaired but God will often instruct us to restore them. He wants to save our entire household, our fellow workers, and our extended families. And we're the ones assigned to bring contrary walls down in order to get them saved. We may think: *"But it looks so dead."; "What's the point?" or "Why even bother?"*

Understand that when we begin releasing actions of love toward others, there will be an investment of our time and effort into their lives that many times will make us question whether we are letting ourselves be taken advantage of. After all, there I was rubbing my wife's back somewhat feeling like a sucker. I had to progress beyond thoughts that cried out: *"Here I am trying to bless her and she's not even acknowledging it; she's throwing it back in my face."* and *"I'm the one apologizing when she knows she was the one who was wrong."* These are the types of thoughts that will go through our minds in such cases. Despite these, we've got to be willing to take aggressive steps of service and blessing unto the manifestation of His love.

I have fought many spiritual battles in the process of manifesting the numerous supernatural healings I have experienced. As well, I have continually watched God bring finances into my life as I would confront *lack* to sow seed with regard to His promises to prosper me. However, to step out in faith for God to release love into our relationships requires a whole other level of battling through demonic and emotional opposition.

Because the devil knows that the love of God is the highest level of anointing attainable - that love fulfills all of the intention of the Word, he will try to hinder us at all costs. The devil doesn't like it that we access healing through the Word of God but it doesn't ruin his day. He likes it even less when we begin to prosper, but again, as long as he can keep prosperity localized he knows that he will survive. **However, satan understands that if we begin manifesting the love of God then his kingdom is finished.** The devil knows that the love of God is the power to evangelize the planet.

A revival of love is exactly what God is going to bring in these last days because it's the anointing that He's going to use to harvest the earth. Through manifesting His glory - the concentrated love of God, the Father is going to bring in His end-time harvest of souls. Amen!

LIVING AS A BLESSING

So then, what other steps can we take to accelerate our stepping into this marvelous anointing of love? Well, let's take a look at First Peter again:

> *1Pet 1:22 - "Seeing ye have purified your souls in obeying the truth through the Spirit unto unfeigned love* [phileo] *of the brethren, see that ye love* [agape] *one another with a pure heart fervently."*

As you will recall, there is more than one word in the Greek translated *"love"* in the King James Bible. The word *phileo* represents a conditional, reciprocal type of love. *Phileo* is the highest level of love that a man may operate in who is not born-again. *Phileo* at its highest level may represent the love of that one has for their spouse and even the love that a mother has for her child. It falls short, however, of the type of love that proceeds forth from God - His *agape*. **Agape is God's own unconditional love, the love that prevails when all other types of love give up. This *agape* is the love that stays in operation even towards those who have turned against us.** It is the love that both Jesus and Stephen accessed when they prayed that the Father would not hold sin against those who were having them executed.

From this verse, we can gather that the Holy Spirit will direct us into acts of *phileo* - actions of friendship and kindness. And this *phileo* is a step we will take toward moving into the fervent *agape* of God. To step into the supernatural *agape* of God by faith will require us to first release actions of *phileo* to those around us. Those whom we target for blessing will especially be those within the church since we are commanded in the above verse to *love the brethren*.

We've touched on this already but let's look at it again from the perspective of this verse. If we want to manifest the supernatural anointing of healing, then we will have to produce appropriate actions to oppose any physical symptoms. Again, *"Faith without works is dead."* In the same way, if we want to manifest the supernatural love of God then we will have to step out in *phileo*. We may not feel loving, we may not feel as though we want to demonstrate kindness, but we will have to act as a friend and as a blessing stepping forth as if the relationship were strong. We must show kindness to those whom the enemy is attempting to separate from us. The actions that we produce through *phileo* will become the steps of faith that we must take to access the anointing of love. We see this again in Second Peter in the passage I refer to as God's *Stairway to Agape*:

> 2Pet 1:5-7 –*"And besides this, giving all diligence, add to your faith virtue; and to virtue, knowledge; and to knowledge, temperance; and to temperance, patience; and to patience, godliness; and to godliness, brotherly kindness; and to brotherly kindness, charity."*

Here we have a progression that God will take us through in the process of developing within us the highest level of anointing that exists - the *agape* of God. The Spirit of God will guide us through steps intended to fully develop us spiritually. He will challenge us to exercise *faith*, walk in *virtue*, develop *knowledge*, and so on - all of the way through this list. The last attribute being mentioned is of course the *agape* love of God. Because of the repeated use of the phrase *"and to"*, it is clear from this passage that this entire list of attributes indicates a progression. Before we can step into the development of one spiritual element, we must first experience growth in the prior element. And here we see that the step just prior to manifesting the love of God is brotherly kindness - *philadelphia*. And, the root word to *philidelphia* is *phileo*. To step into agape, we must first target a lifestyle of walking in human kindness; *phileo - friendship love*.

Here's a key point: **If we want to become a person who walks in the love of God, we've got to become full-time servants to men.** We will have to seek opportunities to bless others, especially others within our church. We will have to show ourselves friendly, even and most importantly at times when we don't want to. Others will rise up against us and we will have to reject attitudes of offense and vindictiveness. These actions, combined with our confession of love along with our cooperating with God to develop within us all of the attributes of Second Peter 1:5-7, move us into position to manifest *agape*. Each of these progressive steps are designed of God to bring us to the fullness of this supernatural empowerment.

The in-born, sin nature of man is self-focused and self-serving. Fleshly mindsets reflect an attitude of: *"It's about me"* and *"What can I get out of each situation?"* The first word that a baby learns other than *"mama"* or *"dada"* is usually *"No," "me,"* or *"Mine!"* All of these responses reflect man's fallen nature. The sin nature decries: *"What can I get out of this relationship?"; "What can I get from this person?"* and *"What do I have to do for them to get them to do something for me?"*

The nature of God is the opposite of the sin nature. The nature of God is one of giving. John 3:16 declares to us that *"God so loved the world"* that He *"gave"* His best on our behalf. He sacrificed His own son on behalf of a world that rejected Him. A part of the process toward walking in the love of God requires that we revise the ways that we think and act. We must dispose of critical attitudes. We must put down judgmental mindsets and refuse to make statements that condemn those around us. We've got to change the way that we react to every encounter in life to manifest a love that the world cannot produce.

When there's an opportunity, we must ask God: *"How might I bless this person?"* We should petition God for divine appointments in which we may be a blessing to others rather than go through our lives wondering: *"What can I get or even take from those around me?"* **Again, it will be very difficult for anyone with any form of an entitlement mentality to ever carry the supernatural power of love.**

And as we change the way that we think and the way that we operate, it's going to allow us to step by faith into the supernatural power of love. Again, this is where it becomes difficult as we must press through the thought bombardments of the enemy proclaiming that we are suckers. It will seem at times as if we are always doing good deeds for others often with minimal appreciation. I'm telling you right now, we're not going to be appreciated every time that we bless someone. Some people are going to laugh at us. Some are going to use our niceness against us. But you know what? *The anointing is worth it!* Furthermore, the effect that the anointing has to restore our relationships is worth it! However, it will require a totally different way of thinking from us and a subsequent altered lifestyle.

Many of you reading this have already been doing exactly what I've described. You already know that we are *blessed to be a blessing*. However, you may not have known that we can access an anointing through these seeds of kindness.

So we see here that we have to act as a friend to access this anointing - this supernatural, spiritual empowerment. In Luke, Jesus speaks the following:

> *Luke 6:27-32 - "But I say unto you which hear, Love your enemies, do good to them which hate you, bless them that curse you, and pray for them which despitefully use you. And unto him that smiteth thee on the one cheek offer also*

the other; and him that taketh away thy cloak forbid not to take thy coat also. Give to every man that asketh of thee; and of him that taketh away thy goods ask them not again. And as ye would that men should do to you, do ye also to them likewise. For if ye love them which love you, what thank have ye? for sinners also love those that love them."

Jesus is stating here that when people attack us *we should then bless them* - we should not curse them but bless them in some fashion. He also declares: *"If we give to those who give to us, what profit or reward do we have from that?"* See, if all we do is bless people who are kind to us then we have only replicated what the world does.

Let's keep reading:

Luke 6:33-36 "And if ye do good to them which do good to you, what thank have ye? for sinners also do even the same. And if ye lend to them of whom ye hope to receive, what thank have ye? for sinners also lend to sinners, to receive as much again. But love ye your enemies, and do good, and lend, hoping for nothing again; and your reward shall be great, and ye shall be the children of the Highest: for he is kind unto the unthankful and to the evil. Be ye therefore merciful, as your Father also is merciful."

Jesus tells us to: *"Bless those who curse us."* and to *"Be kind to those who do evil to us."* Now when I first came across this, I thought that the reason He was telling us to bless our enemies was so that they would feel bad regarding their behavior toward us. However I came to realize, that such mindsets represent an effort to manipulate others by producing guilt in them. Now in my studies of the Word, I can't find the term *guilt* anywhere listed as one of the fruit of the Spirit. Manipulation is a form of psychological witchcraft and God informs us in His Word that He hates witchcraft. Therefore we can know that He would never instruct us to utilize manipulation to alter anyone's viewpoint toward us.

So what was Jesus speaking about when He told us to bless our enemies? He was stating that even though they may not pay us back, God will reward us. And one of the ways that God is going to reward us is through the release of His love into our lives. **The good news is - if we will develop the anointing of love in our lives, within the atmosphere that we then carry resides the potential to win our enemies to God's kingdom.** Jesus wanted us to bless our enemies; not to manipulate them but rather through the power of love to convert them!

Let's read further in Romans:

> *Rom 12:18-21 –"If it be possible, as much as lieth in you, live peaceably with all men. Dearly beloved, avenge not yourselves, but rather give place unto wrath: for it is written, Vengeance is mine; I will repay, saith the Lord. Therefore if thine enemy hunger, feed him; if he thirst, give him drink: for in so doing thou shalt heap coals of fire on his head. Be not overcome of evil, but overcome evil with good."*

Again, from this passage I originally assumed that for us to heap coals of fire on the head of someone inferred that they would experience guilt for being nasty to us. Now follow me on this. When God is going to deliver someone from darkness, He's going to do it through an anointing not via a manipulative act. Jesus declares that we are to overcome evil with good - which goodness is inherent in the anointing of love. Once when Jesus was called *"good"*, He responded with the statement; *"There is none good but God."* He was indirectly letting them know that He was God and that everything He did originated from the throne of God. And God is *agape*!

Recall that goodness is one of the nine fruits of the Spirit mentioned in Galatians 5. Goodness is therefore an attribute of the supernatural anointing of love. We have previously discussed some of the mechanics of strife and of the devils' strife parties. If our enemy attacks us and we retaliate in the same manner, then we're inviting increased demonic activity to come between us. And Jesus commanded us not to give way to such evil; we must not give way to a strife-filled environment. When we begin to operate in a lifestyle of blessing rather than retribution, we will begin to carry an anointing by which evil will be overcome.

Let us also keep in mind that in Paul's day, women placed clay jars of coals upon their heads to transfer fire from place to place. We can compare this with the modern process of getting out jumper cables to start our neighbors' vehicles, providing them with power where they previously had none. The coals of fire were not designed to burn their neighbors' heads, but rather to ignite and warm their homes with fresh power.

Recognize that we will never cast out a devil merely with a good deed and that the evil that people experience is most often the result of demonic activity. Hate, anger, strife, bitterness – whatever it might be – is usually the result of a demonic presence. Therefore, the source of conflict we are experiencing will not be limited to the person that is coming against us. That person is possibly being goaded by forces of darkness to which he has opened himself.

Again understand, we'll never cast out a devil with a good deed. When Jesus came down from the Mount of Transfiguration and the disciples had been trying to cast out a devil. Do you remember what Jesus did? He brought the lad a Jell-O salad and said: *"Here's 20 bucks."* Of course that's not what took place! Jesus commanded the spirit to leave and the anointing that He carried forced the demon to comply. Again, good deeds won't displace a demonic spirit but the anointing will. And I believe that Jesus and Paul were both letting us know that our good deeds are a step that we are to take in accessing the power that will produce deliverance. The anointing of love that we manifest and carry will become our number one weapon to displace demonic forces - thus delivering the captives from darkness.

GREATER LOVE

As we explore using our faith to access *agape* love, we find that John chapter 15 holds vital teachings that are key to our pursuit of this vital force. This passage lets us know that the more we abide in God, the more we will abide in love. This will be covered in detail later but right now we want to focus on one specific passage:

> *John 15:12-13 – "This is my commandment, That ye love one another, as I have loved you. Greater love hath no man than this, that a man lay down his life for his friends."*

That's an amazing statement! This appears to inform us that if we desire to carry the fullness of love then we've got to be willing to die for a friend. I assumed for some time that apparently the willingness to die for a friend was *the definition* of the highest level of love attainable. After all, this appears to be what these verses state. However, in our studies of the Word we discover another passage:

> *Rom 5:7-8 – "For scarcely for a righteous man will one die: yet peradventure for a good man some would even dare to die. But God commendeth His love toward us, in that, while we were yet sinners, Christ died for us."*

The Bible informs us that many might be willing to die for a good man. There is no doubt that many mothers would give up their lives on behalf of their children. Yet as we have already discussed, *agape* represents a supernatural love that extends far above the natural love of a mother for her child. These verses let us know that Jesus, while we were yet His enemies died for the ungodly.

See, I previously thought that John 15:13 was a *definition* for the highest level of love attainable - that in which you would be willing to die for a friend. However, this cannot be true. Surely it would represent a higher level of love to die for an enemy. And Jesus did just that - and there can be no question that Jesus walked in the fullness of the love of God.

So I don't believe in any way that dying for a friend can represent the definition of the highest level of love accessible. I believe instead that **John 15:13 is the PATHWAY to the highest levels of love attainable**. John 15:12 lets us know that we're supposed to love one another with the same love in which Jesus walked. So following with verse 13, slightly rewritten to indicate a pathway versus a definition, we get: *"And greater levels of love accesses no man than in this fashion; that he lays down his life for his friends."*

And, if we look at that word *life* from this verse in the Greek, it's not the word *bios*, from where we get our word biology - it's the word *psuche*, the word normally translated *soul*. *Greater love accesses no man than this - that he lays down his* **soul** *for his friends*. What does this mean? When I was telling you about the battle over my marriage, I related how I had to go through rejection, strife, and all of the other thoughts and emotional onslaughts that were trying to rise against me. This setting aside of our natural desire to strike back versus bless represents the *'laying down of our souls'*. I had to lay down what my soul was feeling. I had to lay down what my soul wanted to say and wanted to do. I had to go *past my soul* and complete what God instructed me to do to see supernatural love released.

In the Garden of Gethsemane anticipating the upcoming agonies of the cross, Jesus laid down his soul. It was a battle that deprived him of so much strength that he pleaded with the other disciples to pray for Him. The soul battle that He engaged in required an angel to appear and strengthen Him. **Before Jesus laid down his life at the cross, He first laid down his soul in the garden.** Jesus cried: *"Father, if there is any other way that I might fulfill what You've called me to do, let this cup pass from before me. Nevertheless, not My will but Yours be done."* What did He do? He laid down His soul and accessed so much love that it enabled Him to follow through with the most difficult assignment in human history. Remember that on the cross, He didn't only experience the most excruciating form of punishment ever devised by man but He also willingly took upon Himself the sin of the world. That's the definition of the greatest level and form of love that has ever been manifested.

If we want to access the greatest levels of love that God possesses, then we will have to lay down our souls as well. We will be required to bless those whom we do not want to bless. We may be instructed to apologize to others who have misused us. And I assure you, The Holy Spirit will lead us to enter into a lifestyle of continuous giving, at times being required to sow major seeds. We will have to develop the mindset to be a blessing to everyone with whom we come in contact. And it's going to require *all of the faith that we have.*

I am convinced that God is raising up a triumphant church in these last days. In Joel, this church is prophesied to be an army which *will not break rank nor run each other through* (attack one another). Many people are going to move from the city where they currently reside to attend the church to which God assigns them. And once they get there, He's going to raise them up in an accelerated form of training. Such Holy Spirit training will stretch us to the highest limits but because we have lain down our souls, we will refuse to cut and run.

I don't know about you, but there have been times when I've wanted to run. And God has said: *"Where are you going to go?"* That's what Peter said - *"To whom else would we go? You alone have the words of eternal life."*

God's going to say to us: *"I sent you there."; "There's no other place that you can go."; "That is the place where I'm going to raise you up."* and *"Don't even think about leaving."* We won't be able to rely on how we feel. We will have to lay down our souls, including those fickle emotions.

As we obey these directives, we are thus laying down our souls on behalf of a covenant assignment. And it's going to bring us into an empowerment that will allow us, not just to stay where God has sent us but to flourish in that place. God intends to radically change our lives via His love. If we cannot lay down our souls to any great level, then we will not manifest His love to any great level either.

When we commit to God to walk in *agape*, He will begin dealing with us about our relationships - from the worst to the best. You see, we always want to love those people close to us. We prefer to love our best friends, our children, and hopefully our spouses (when they've treated us right for that week). However, God wants us to bless our spouses when they've treated us less that perfectly. He will guide us to speak a kind word to that person who has risen up against us. That's when we'll start accessing increased anointing - anointing that will take us beyond ourselves. And here, I would like to insert a word about *strife parties.* Did you know that devils like to feed upon their own presence? Let me clarify that statement. Demons like to congregate in the atmospheres that they create. Here's the way that they will attack a relationship and particularly a marriage.

One demon will come to the husband and say: *"Your wife doesn't love you anymore."* and *"She's not giving you the respect that you deserve."* And with these critical thoughts, the demon will bring forth contrary emotional reactions as well - most likely involving feelings of rejection. So during that day, instead of responding in love toward his bride, he's going to respond instead in a critical fashion. The words that he speaks toward her will have a sharp edge to them. And since that demon is trying to create his own little party, he'll come to the wife and say: *"You know, your husband doesn't love you."*; *"He wants to get rid of you."* and *"He wishes you were dead."*

The next thing you know, rather than exhorting one another they begin attacking each other instead. They start tearing each other down. They say little picky things to each other like: *"Are you going to wear that?"* or *"Can't you do something with your hair?"*; *"You always ... ."*

Subsequently, one becomes outwardly offended. And as such, wicked spirits begin to call to one another declaring: *"There's a party over here right now."* So then demons start coming in from every direction. Some will continue speaking to the husband and some to the wife. Their goal is to get a demonic party activated where the atmosphere becomes so charged with strife that the couple feel they have no choice but to separate and go in opposite directions. And the truth is, that's how most divorces take place.

What God desires in those situations is for us to recognize the trap that's being laid for us and to respond in a fashion that will shut it down. He wants us to detect what's going on in the *atmosphere* around us and say: *"Wait a minute, this is not the presence of God I'm feeling right now."*; *"I'm not sensing my home charged with the anointing of love."* The Lord then wants us to take active steps toward blessing our spouse to reverse the adverse atmosphere.

This is where stepping into the love of God becomes demanding. Blessing someone when our thoughts and emotions are being overwhelmed by the enemy is a challenging task. Again, at times it will take all of the faith that we possess. However the rewards are well worth the effort. Paul relates to us:

> *2Cor 4:17-18 -"For our light affliction, which is but for a moment, worketh for us a far more exceeding and eternal weight of glory. While we look not at the things which are seen, but at the things which are not seen: for the things which are seen are temporal; but the things which are not seen are eternal."*

Before we can step into the glory of God we will at times have to battle through severe pressure. Our role in the battles will require us to counter every effort of the enemy to bring strife or division into our lives. If we will respond to the pressure of these attacks in the right fashion, then according to the Word of God it's going to produce the glory of God in our lives - concentrated tangible love.

GIVING LOVE

From John 3:16, we understand that God by love offered on our behalf His very best in Jesus. The very nature of love is a giving nature. By contrast, the nature of sin is a taking nature. **So if we want to manifest the nature of God which is the nature of love, then we must become givers -** ***radical*** **givers.**

In fact, a stingy Christian will never be able to manifest the love of God. He cannot because his lifestyle is in contrast to God's divine nature. The love of God is going to be poured out through radical givers who trust God in every area of their lives - including their finances.

Let's look at what the Word lets us know in First John:

> *1John 3:16-17 – "Hereby perceive we the love of God, because He laid down His life* (His soul) *for us: and we*

> *ought to lay down our lives* (our souls) *for the brethren. But whoso hath this world's good, and seeth his brother have need, and shutteth up his bowels of compassion from him, how dwelleth the love of God in him?"*

The person who can repeatedly ignore the obvious needs of others when it is in their power to aid them is obviously living out of a stingy mindset. According to this verse, there is no love of God in operation in their life. He goes on to say in verse 18:

> *1John 3:18 –"My little children, let us not love in word, neither in tongue; but in deed and in truth."*

Here again, we see that the love of God produces tangible actions or deeds. The individual who carries this love will, of necessity, be a giver.

Let's look at another passage that further brings to light the tie between a person's giving and their personal manifestation of love:

> *2Cor 9:6-7 –"But this I say, He which soweth sparingly shall reap also sparingly; and he which soweth bountifully shall reap also bountifully. Every man according as he purposeth in his heart, so let him give; not grudgingly, or of necessity: for God loveth a cheerful giver."*

This verse seems to indicate that if we will become a cheerful giver then God will love us. However, there is a problem with this interpretation. The Bible makes it clear that God loves everyone. He even loves the sinner! God does not love at different levels. Since He is love, He loves the sinner and the saint alike.

So we have a quandary. If God loves everyone alike, then how can He love us more when we become cheerful givers? If we look closely however, we find the answer. The Greek word translated *loveth* in Second Corinthians 9:7 is actually *agapao*, the verb form of *agape*. We understand that verbs are action words, so we can know that the love referred to in this verse is *love which is put in motion*. What I believe this passage actually tells us is that: **God's love is put in action on behalf of, through, and toward a cheerful giver.** The person who *lives to give* activates the love of

God in their lives. Because God is a radical giver, cheerful givers have best positioned themselves to reflect His full manifested nature - love.

A person who has made the transition to give, not just out of necessity because he feels pressured to do so, or grudgingly just because the bucket is being passed, is demonstrating the very heart of God. And one of the greatest reasons to give cheerfully is because we understand that we are taking an aggressive step of faith to manifest the supernatural power of *agape*.

In fact, a person who is giving cheerfully may do so because he is activating multiple spiritual principles. He gives cheerfully because he knows that God is going to bring the harvest on his seed back to him in multiplied fashion. And, he gives cheerfully because he knows that the anointing of love is going to be released into his life.

For years, many have been giving not knowing that they could access either of these blessings. Others may have been sowing extensively believing God for financial increase. However, we also have a right to release our faith for the supernatural anointing of love via our giving. People who are exuberant, radical givers position themselves to manifest maximum levels of love.

Knowing that the anointing of love will be released in the life of a cheerful giver is something to become excited about. And God is looking for people who get excited about what He's doing in their lives.

Let me throw out another reason why we should be excited about giving. There are a lot of frustrated non-cheerful Christians out there. We have found out that our inner nature is that of love. In Chapter 1, we discussed how the person who wants to be fulfilled in life must allow their inner nature to have outward expression. We've got to walk in love. To not walk in the manifested love of God outwardly is to live in a fashion that is in disagreement with who we have become inwardly once we are born-again. We must endeavor to live in that anointing. We've got to let our inner nature have full outward expression to enjoy life. And now, we have found that our new inner nature is one of giving.

So giving fulfills the characteristics of our inner person, and that's why we become cheerful! Do you know why some people are not cheerful givers? It's because they've not yet renewed their minds beyond stinginess - beyond the mentality of lack (i.e., *"If I give, I'm not going to have anything."*). They don't really have any faith in the financial principles of the Kingdom of God. This then causes them to bottle up their giving and subsequently limit the amount of love which they can experience. This thus prevents them from living a fulfilled life.

The next verse of this passage in Second Corinthians goes on to say this:

> *2Cor 9:8 -"And God is able to make all grace abound toward you; that ye, always having all sufficiency in all things, may abound to every good work."*

The grace of God is more than His unmerited favor. It is His supernatural ability and provision granted us to fulfill the call of God on our lives. Grace represents the gifts, the finances, and the anointing our callings demand. In our case, His grace package includes not just the anointing of love but also the financial seed that we will need to remain in the flow of our assigned giving lifestyles. And here the Word says that we will *"abound"* in this grace thus permitting us to sow into *"every good work"*.

When God relates to us that we can abound to every good work, He is saying that as we give, He's going to bring more back to us so that we can give even more. In fact, once we comprehend that giving releases the love of God into our lives, we can realize that God has established for us a vital spiritual cycle. I call it the **Love-Giving Cycle** - where as we give, the anointing of love is released into our lives and we then want to give even more.

So what does God do? Because He wants to get His glory manifested in our lives in the form of greater and greater levels of love, He is going to multiply the seed that we sow to enable us to sow in extreme levels. And as we give at even greater levels, there will be even *more* love released into our lives. So we see a cycle established alternating between God manifesting both financial increase and supernatural love to us. As we continue in this cycle, it will exponentially increase our love anointing resulting in the overflowing glory of God.

We see the love-giving cycle confirmed in the Word as we read further in Second Corinthians:

> *2Cor 9:9-10 – "As it is written, He hath dispersed abroad; he hath given to the poor: his righteousness remaineth forever. Now he that giveth seed to the sower both minister bread for your food, and multiply your seed sown, and increase the fruits of your righteousness."*

In verse nine, as we have stated previously we find that our actions of blessing reflect our reborn righteous nature. This verse even infers that this lifestyle of giving works to keep us in right standing with God. Not that we are earning salvation but our actions demonstrate that we are remaining steadfast in His kingdom.

Verse ten relates to us the results of entering into the lifestyle of a giver. We see **four areas of blessing that come back into the life of a sower**:

First, God brings seed to the sower. He will bring us specific funds and other blessings meant to be sown forth, not consumed by the receiver. It is vital that we actually develop the ability to be Spirit-led to discern what God has brought to us to be consumed personally versus what He has delivered to us to be used as seed. If we consume the seed, we will be unable to reap our necessary harvest.

Second, God assures us that **there will be food for our households**. In that we are meeting the needs of others, He will meet our needs as well. The consistent sower never needs to fear missing a meal.

Third, God will multiply the seed that we sow back into our lives. Jesus spoke in the parable of the sower that it will come back to us in measures of up to 100-fold. God wants to bless us, not just spiritually but financially as well. In fact, God desires that His professional sowers become wealthy thus enabling them to radically impact their surroundings.

And **Fourth**, God says that **He will increase the** *"fruits of our righteousness."* We have discovered that *"righteousness"* is embedded within our new born-again nature. The fruit of that righteous nature is the fruit of the spirit - the love of God. Here scripture lets us know that when we take up the lifestyle of a sower, not only will God bless us financially but the anointing of love will manifest in our lives as well! Again, this demonstrates to us the *Love-Giving cycle*.

Do you recall from scripture when the glory of God manifested in the Old Testament? When they built the first tabernacle, the glory of God came in such that Moses could not enter. And when Solomon built the temple, the glory of God appeared with such intensity that the priests could not even stand to minister. We find in both cases that they gave radically just prior to both of those manifestations of God's glory.

Further, if we study the prophetic passages in scripture regarding the last days and the outpouring of God's glory, we will discover that repeatedly the glory is tied to not just a harvest of souls but of finances as well. Scripturally, the outpouring of God's glory cannot be separated from *the inversion of the wealth of the wicked coming to the hands of the righteous*. Why does this take place? It will all involve the *Love-Giving cycle*. God is going to release to His glorious bride both finances and the anointing of love in a simultaneous, interactive fashion.

I recognize that this may seem preposterous to many. However right now, an outpouring of revelation regarding biblical prosperity stands at the forefront of what God is releasing to His leading edge church. At the same time, much of the Body of Christ is learning to walk by faith and also discovering who they are in Christ Jesus - the righteousness of God in Him. These all act together as the primary spiritual anchor points to usher in the radical love of God and subsequent glory. This topic will be discussed in more detail in our chapter on *The Glory of Love*.

Understand fully, what I've said in this chapter involves much more than merely memorizing a few verses. It becomes a whole revised way of living and it's going to take all of the faith that we've got and more.

This brings us to an assignment that I'd like to challenge you to do. Find somebody to bless who you wouldn't normally bless. Whether it be through doing a good deed, whether it be through sowing a seed, or buying them lunch. Set goals to do this on a daily basis. These are actions that will continue to cause this book to become alive in your hands as you experience the living power of God.

In doing this, see if you can become addicted to it - addicted to being a blessing to other people. You will discover that your life will become so fulfilled that you will never want to depart from this newly learned lifestyle. Watch and see if God doesn't bring blessings back into your life. He'll begin to restore relationships and bring you to a higher level of walking in His presence than you have ever thought possible.

CHAPTER 5

ROOTED IN LOVE

THE KEY TO SUCCESS

I believe that there is so much restorative power in the love of God that in one moment, regardless of our past, love can repair our lives. Regardless of past abuses that we may have suffered whether physical, sexual, or mental, the power of love will deliver us from any limiting emotional strongholds that have been established. Love, once accessed will redeem us from all distrust, rejection, and any other disappointments where we have been unable to forgive those who have wronged us. Love will take down the emotional barriers in our lives such that we can view people and life from an entirely new perspective. And through faith, we can access this love!

In this chapter, we're going to take an extended look at how faith and love function together. Let's lay some groundwork for this by looking at the first Psalm:

> *Psa 1:1-3 -"Blessed is the man that walketh not in the counsel of the ungodly, nor standeth in the way of sinners, nor sitteth in the seat of the scornful. But his delight is in the law of the LORD* [the Word of God]; *and in his law doth he meditate day and night. And he* [the meditator] *shall be like a tree planted by the rivers of water, that bringeth forth his fruit in his season; his leaf also shall not wither; and whatsoever he doeth shall prosper."*

Here it says that a person who meditates on the Word of God becomes like a tree that brings forth *"fruit"* in the proper season. The Bible informs us in Galatians 5 that *"the fruit of the Spirit is love."* The fruit of our reborn spirit with its righteous nature is the love of God. And, the one who meditates in the Word day and night is going to become like a tree that brings forth the fruit of love as they access it by faith.

"His leaf also shall not wither" - declares that the person who meditates scripture will continue to produce fruit and *will thus never dry up*. From Second Peter 1:10, we have ascertained that the individual who walks in the love of God *will never fall*. In John 15:6, we discovered that those who abide in Jesus and His Word *won't burn out*. Obviously, the love of God carries within it the full potential to reverse *spiritual burnout*.

Psalm 1 also lets us know that if we are full of the Word and manifest the love of God then whatever we set our hands to accomplish is going to prosper. And God wants us to prosper in every area of our lives - especially within our relationships.

You see, love becomes the key ingredient to our prosperity - whether financial, spiritual, or physical. Love becomes the fertilizer for the seed that we sow. Without operating in the love of God, we will not see the manifestation of our harvest. Without love, our faith is neutralized.

> *Gal 5:6 –"For in Christ Jesus neither circumcision availeth any thing, nor uncircumcision; but faith which worketh by love."*

Love becomes the catalyst which empowers our faith to produce. And meditation of the Word is a critical step to see the fruit of love developed in our lives.

THE ROOTED REMNANT

Looking further into the Word regarding the topic of trees, we find in Isaiah:

> *Isa 27:6 –"He [God] shall cause them that come of Jacob to take root: Israel shall blossom and bud, and fill the face of the world with fruit."*

Here is a prophecy declaring God's plans for His last-day church. Although He is speaking to Jacob, this verse really gives reference to what God has in mind for His bride. We, as The Church, are the prophetic Israel of God in this passage. We are the seed of Abraham. We are the wild olive branch that was grafted into the original tree because the first olive tree did not produce the desired fruit.

So we see from Isaiah, God is going to cause us to take root like a tree and bear fruit. **This blossoming fruit-bearing event will subsequently cause the entire world to be filled with love.** Before you are finished reading this chapter, you're going to see more fully that the love of God is going to be God's harvest tool. And this harvest magnet is going to bring in the multitudes that he's been after since creation. Let's take a look at another verse in Isaiah:

> *Isa 37:31 - "And the remnant that is escaped of the house of Judah shall again take root downward, and bear fruit upward."*

Again we see that as a tree, in order for God's people to produce fruit - roots must be put down. But here we discover that the *"remnant"* is to bring forth this fruit. But who is this remnant to which God is here referring? I believe it is His end-time revivalist church composed of radical believers from diverse backgrounds.

God is raising up a remnant body in these last days. In fact, the church that I pastor in Georgetown, Kentucky is a *remnant church*. Our membership is composed of people from many different denominations and backgrounds. Some of them were raised totally outside of church as I was, and some were Baptist, Lutheran, Catholic, and many other denominations. God is even now extracting numbers of people out of different church systems who are hungry for a move of God. God is seeking out disciples who believe that there's more to God than just going to church. He's assembling a remnant church composed of Christians who refuse to stay locked in organizations that will not progress with Him.

Remember the remnant quilts of the past? They were comprised of various and diverse cloth scraps sewn together into a quilt. Well I believe that's what God is doing with the Church in these last days. He's bringing forth those who will fully go after the things of God. He's pulling them together and using them to produce an anointed church *covering* for His end-time purposes. And it says that this remnant church is going *to "root downward and bear fruit upward."*

From the Word, we can see that God repeatedly compares us to trees. Let's look at this further in Isaiah 61. This is the passage that Jesus quoted in Luke chapter 4 referring to Himself - but which to some level, really applies to all of us.

> *Isa 61:1-3 -"The Spirit of the Lord GOD is upon me; because the LORD hath anointed me to preach good tidings unto the meek; he hath sent me to bind up the brokenhearted, to proclaim liberty to the captives, and the opening of the prison to them that are bound; To proclaim the acceptable year of the LORD, and the day of vengeance of our God; to comfort all that mourn; To appoint unto them that mourn in Zion, to give unto them beauty for ashes, the oil of joy for mourning, the garment of praise for the spirit of heaviness; that they might be called* **trees of righteousness**, *the planting of the LORD, that he might be glorified."*

This verse refers to the anointing that Jesus and His followers would carry. As well, it refers to his disciples as **"trees of righteousness."** We have already discussed the fact that as born-again believers, we have been made the righteousness of God. There are oak trees and apple trees and pear trees, however we are *righteous* trees. That is the spiritual DNA program inherent on the inside of us. God declares us to be trees that are programmed for righteousness. We are the planting of the Lord! In other words, God sowed the incorruptible seed of the Word to rebirth us. And here God says that this was done so that He might be glorified. Again, we're going to see before we're done that this love we're going to walk in is going to manifest as the glory of God and bring in His last-day harvest.

Let's keep going because I want you to see the context of these verses:

> *Isa 61:4-7 – "And they shall build the old wastes, they shall raise up the former desolations, and they shall repair the waste cities, the desolations of many generations. And strangers shall stand and feed your flocks, and the sons of the alien shall be your plowmen and your vinedressers. But ye shall be named the Priests of the LORD: men shall call you the Ministers of our God: ye shall eat the riches of the Gentiles, and in their glory shall ye boast yourselves. For your shame ye shall have double; and for confusion they shall rejoice in their portion: therefore in their land they shall possess the double: everlasting joy shall be unto them."*

Here God is speaking of an inversion of wealth - a last day move where unbelievers are going to serve the people of God. And this move is going to take place through the efforts of trees of righteousness. Up until now, most trees of righteousness have been producing the wrong fruit. Instead of manifesting the love of God, they have been displaying the sorrow produced through condemnation. Because they have allowed a sin mentality to be grafted to their righteous nature, Christians have walked with a heaviness instead of the fruit of peace.

Now let's take a deeper look at this in Luke:

> *Luke 6:43-44 - "For a good tree bringeth not forth corrupt fruit; neither doth a corrupt tree bring forth good fruit. For every tree is known by his own fruit. For of thorns men do not gather figs, nor of a bramble bush gather they grapes."*

It says here that men won't gather figs out of a thorn bush nor grapes from a bramble. Whenever we read about thorns, brambles, and thistles in the Word of God, all are representative of the curse. Remember when Adam fell? God said that the ground would consequently produce thorns and thistles such that Adam would now have to work the land. So thorns and brambles represent aspects of the curse. By applying this understanding to this passage, we can ascertain that proper fruit will not be gathered out of curse oriented situations.

Let's apply that to the church. **We will not see God's anointings manifested at their highest levels in a church that continually proclaims the curse.** We will never see the fruit of the love of God manifested through people who are repeatedly told that they are sinners. The message they continually hear is that *they're falling short of the glory.* All they ever hear about is *"sin, sin, sin"; "This is a sin, and that's a sin";* and *"Have you sinned today?"* It is a proclamation which focuses primarily upon the curse - thorns, thistles and brambles. Understand that sin is real and there is no doubt that God demands holiness from His church. However, sin is never overcome by informing Christians that they are failures. Sin is defeated in the lives of a people who genuinely discover who they are and step boldly into their new identity.

God wants to elevate us far above sin mentality and sin-focused ministry and bring us into the realm of acting as trees of righteousness. Only then will we be able to produce the fullness of the fruit of the Spirit. This last day move of God is going to be highlighted by a people who are finding out who they are in Christ Jesus. To operate in the love of God, we must discover from the Word that we *really* do have a *pure heart*. We must develop the *good conscience* to which we have referred and purge ourselves of any condemnation mentality.

We must become very selective of who we can listen to on the radio or watch on television. Too much of Christian programming is primarily proclaiming the curse. The other half of Christian programming is declaring that once we are saved, God can't witness any of the actions of sin that we do commit. This doctrine is even much more damaging than sin focused ministry. In fact, this message of hyper-grace stands to lead multitudes to hell. Let's continue further in this passage:

> *Luke 6:45 -"A good man out of the good treasure of his heart bringeth forth that which is good; and an evil man out of the evil treasure of his heart bringeth forth that which is evil: for of the abundance of the heart his mouth speaketh."*

This passage doesn't say that we **should desire** to bring forth the treasure that lies within us! It says that we **will** bring forth that which is within us. Even though God has rebirthed us righteous, if we continue to fill ourselves with sin-centered teaching we will be unable to bring forth good fruit. However if we fill our lives with teachings focused on our new divinely created spirits, we will bring forth the fruit of love. Understand that we as trees of righteousness should be speaking forth words that align with our divine nature. We should be bringing forth fruit that agrees with whom God has now made us.

Let's view a passage in Ephesians that we covered earlier. My desire is that you now see this verse in a new light.

> *Eph 3:14-19 - "For this cause I bow my knees unto the Father of our Lord Jesus Christ, Of whom the whole family in heaven and earth is named, That he would grant you, according to the riches of his glory, to be strengthened with might by his Spirit in the inner man; That Christ may dwell in your hearts by faith; that ye, being rooted and grounded in love, May be able to comprehend with all saints what is the breadth, and length, and depth, and height; and to know the love of Christ, which passeth knowledge, that ye might be filled with all the fullness of God."*

Here again, we are compared to trees. It recommends that we be *"rooted and grounded in love."* **If we as trees want to produce God's end-time fruit, then we will need to be rooted into the right soil.** Knowing that the roots of the tree bring in minerals and moisture which cause that tree to grow, if we are rooted into poor soil then it's going to enable limited growth in our lives. Therefore as trees, we must be absorbing the proper nutrients to produce savory fruit. The roots of a tree - the unseen portion, are actually more important than the above ground growth. If a tree is cut off at its base, the seen portion of the tree becomes dead. However, the root section of the tree may again put forth branches and eventually bear new fruit.

Now let's examine a bit of the structure and operation of trees. If we were to look outside our window and see a tree, how much of that tree would we actually see? We would be able to view only the part of the tree which is above ground. Half of that tree actually exists underground - the roots. The roots of the tree actually parallel to some level the size and shape of the portion of the tree that exists above ground. So when we look at a tree, we only see half of it.

That applies to us as well. As a tree of righteousness, people only see of us that which is *above ground*. They only see that portion of us that is apparent in the natural realm - our flesh bodies. As with the tree, the most important part of us is unseen to the natural eye.

Paralleling the tree, our real person - our spirit man, dwells in an unseen realm - the realm of the spirit. And we as born-again representatives of God *must be rooted into the kingdom of heaven*. When people view us and our daily actions, the results of what they witness will arise from what we are producing out of our root system. And here in Ephesians 3, it says that we are to be *rooted and grounded in love*. Since God is love, if we are rooted and grounded in love, then we are automatically rooted and grounded in God. This of course infers that we have an active relationship with God, and this then demands that we know His voice. We of necessity must know how to hear the Spirit of God and flow with what God is attempting to accomplish in our lives.

As we previously discussed, the Word of God is Jesus in print form. Jesus was the Word made flesh - so the Word represents the very DNA code of God Himself. Thus our Bible becomes the very essence of God in print form. To be rooted and grounded in love implies that we're rooted and grounded in God, and equally that we're rooted and grounded in the Word. All three are synonymous.

CONVERTING LOVE TO FRUIT

Once we've become rooted and grounded in the Word and have established an active relationship with God, our roots penetrate deep into His love. We have then made a supernatural connection to heaven's supply. We now have the ability to bring into our lives the very sustenance of love itself. We can draw it into our lives through the roots that we have developed in the realm of the spirit.

Now, the righteous nature within us has the phenomenal ability to transform that pure raw material of love that we have absorbed into precious manifestations of the fruit of the Spirit.

Galatians 5 states:

> *Gal 5:22-23 - "But the fruit of the Spirit is love, joy, peace, longsuffering, gentleness, goodness, faith, meekness, temperance ... ."*

Each of these represent outward manifestations of the pure love of God that our roots have tapped into by faith. As we continue to abide in Christ and utilize our faith to access this anointing, a miraculous process takes place from within us. The raw material of the anointing of love is converted to the fruit of the spirit in our lives. Thus we can enter the funeral home at a time of great loss and when everyone else believes that we should be falling to pieces, we display forth the supernatural fruit of peace. The raw material of love enables us to access and demonstrate all of the fruit of the spirit.

We may have everything collapsing around us yet access the raw material of love, process it through our righteous nature and manifest the joy of the Lord. Circumstances may arise that would normally drive us to have a *fit of carnality*, but temperance arises from within that quenches any inclination to throw a tantrum.

The raw material of love if accessed, will take the form that we need to provide the power necessary to give us timely victories in every situation. God gave us His divine nature which is able to take the raw material of love and transform it to display publically these manifestations of fruit in our lives.

ROOTS OF FAITH

One particular verse that we just read in Ephesians states:

> *Eph 3:17 - "That Christ may dwell in your hearts by faith; that ye, being rooted and grounded in love,"*

Remember that we said that there is a tie between faith and love? The Bible declares that we are rooted and grounded in this love *by "faith."* Here we have another aspect of the tree that carries spiritual connotation. **When we read about *roots* in Scripture, it's referring to *faith*.**

Let's examine a verse from Colossians chapter 2:

> *Col 2:6-7 - "As ye have therefore received Christ Jesus the Lord, so walk ye in him:* **Rooted and built up in him, and stablished in the faith**, *as ye have been taught, abounding therein with thanksgiving."*

Here the Word tells us to *"walk"* in Christ *in the same fashion in which we were saved*. And Scripture makes it clear that we are saved - *by faith*. We know that we are to *walk* in the outward manifestation of *love*, and here we see again that we are rooted by *faith*. Let's envision ourselves as trees again. Our physical, natural body is the above ground section of the tree that everyone can see. And as a natural tree produces fruit that all may see, others should witness us manifesting the supernatural force of love in the form of the fruit of the spirit. They should see love in our lives; they should see joy; and they should see peace, far beyond that which we can produce of ourselves. As spiritual beings, part of our total man operates in the seen realm but another part of us exists in the unseen. The internal part of us functions from within the realm of the spirit.

We find in First Corinthians 2 that we have spirit to Spirit communion with the Holy Ghost - that the Spirit searches within us the deep things of God. And we're rooted in that realm of the spirit *by faith*. Understand that the visible portion of a regular tree does not normally grow beyond the length of its roots. In the same way, we will not develop spiritually beyond the level of our faith. Faith acts as our root system that connects us to the realm of the spirit – The Kingdom of God. As we are rooted into God's kingdom, it allows us to draw the sustenance of love into our hearts and manifest it outwardly in whatever form of the fruit of the spirit which we need.

Notice this as well. For some time, having a science oriented background, there was a part of this verse that confounded me. I would go to the section of the verse that states: "[You] *May be able to comprehend with all saints what is the* **breadth**, *and* **length**, *and **depth,** and **height;** and to know the love of Christ, which passeth knowledge."* What confused me was that this verse lists four dimensions; *"breadth," "length," "depth,"* and *"height."* However, I understand that our natural realm contains only three physical dimensions. How can it be referring to four dimensions when there's only three?

I had been teaching on love from this verse for years, when suddenly I saw the answer. The tree has three dimensions in the visible realm but it has a fourth dimension in the unseen - *"depth."* So we're not just three-dimensional beings, we're *four-dimensional* beings. The roots represent our extension by faith into the realm of the spirit and *depth* indicates our true spiritual stature.

The level that we're rooted down into the Word of God is also the level that we're rooted deeply via our relationship with God. Subsequently, this is also the depth that we're rooted into the love of God. And this rooted depth determines our spiritual capacity to produce fruit.

BALANCED ROOTS

Let's take a step further in our examination of tree roots. Did you know that the Word of God is a promise book? It is God's last will and testament to us. And in the Bible, there are all types of promises that God says that we can have if we will develop faith for them. And as trees of righteousness, we get to determine the promises toward which we're going to develop our personal roots. The first thing that we had to root to was salvation. That's our taproot. If we cut the taproot of a tree, that tree will die. The same thing is true with us. If our taproot of salvation is cut off - we're doomed.

However once we as trees begin to grow through understanding faith, we can choose which promises toward which we desire to extend and develop roots. Initially, we may want to target growing our faith for divine health. And so, what do we do? We get into the Word of God and we begin stretching a root intentionally into Scriptures that promise healing. Since faith comes by hearing and hearing, the root of faith that we are intentionally sending forth extends more and more into God's provision of healing. Perhaps then we may want to start believing for our family's salvation, for finances, for divine protection, and of course for the love of God. As we begin developing our roots toward these primary promises of God, we then develop a balanced root system thus stabilizing our lives as trees of righteousness.

Our previous passage from Colossians chapter 2 also declares that we are to be *"established in the faith."* A balanced root system of faith makes us immovable to the storms of the enemy. We see the promise of divine shielding expressed in Ephesians chapter 6.

> *Eph 6:16 – "Above all, taking the shield of faith, wherewith ye shall be able to quench all the fiery darts of the wicked."*

This shield of faith is designed to provide us with supernatural protection for our lives. With a properly raised shield there is nothing that the enemy can do to harm us.

However, for this defense system to work, more is required than just proclaiming: *"I take unto myself the shield of faith"*. The true shield of faith is a result of developing roots of faith to all of God's promises of provision and protection. For us to ignore developing our faith to any of the major promises of God is to supply the enemy with an opening in our shield through which he WILL attack us.

The devil is an expert at locating holes in our shields and accurately hurling poisoned darts through those openings. Anywhere that we have an opening in our shields becomes the point where the enemy is going to target our lives. If we develop faith for finances but not for healing, then he will attack our health. If we develop faith for finances as well as healing, then he's going to attack our marriages. He's going to hit us in any area where we have an opening in our shields. The reason that I'm bringing this out is to let you know that we can't just choose to develop a root to one area of promise. We're going to have to develop our faith toward every major promise of God. Hebrews chapter 4 declares that we should *fear to leave a promise of God unclaimed*. To do so hinders us from *entering into His rest*.

Anywhere that we don't develop faith becomes a potential hole in our shield and will permit unrest in our lives. God's plan is that we develop a balanced root system into all of His promises. By faith, we must receive all of His provision for protection such that when the storms come, we can't be uprooted by an attack in any one area. A tree that has roots that have somehow been damaged on one side is likely to be uprooted. And if we are unbalanced in our development of faith, then we stand a chance of being uprooted as well.

So what does this have to do with our teaching on love? Keep in mind that the purpose of the tree is to produce fruit. In our case, that fruit is the love of God. Without developing faith for all of the promises of God, it is unlikely that we will stand long enough to manifest any measure of fruit. As trees, we will have unbalanced root systems.

And the truth is, when **the enemy brings storms** into our lives, they have two major purposes:

1) **To strip us of our fruit**
2) **To uproot our faith.**

He wants to strip us of our fruit before it can ever be developed to maturity. He brings hurricane level storms to get us frustrated and oppressed such that we no longer walk in love. Or, he wants to uproot our faith such that we won't believe God for His blessings any longer. When we're undergoing potentially horrendous attacks, understand that the enemy is attempting to uproot us. However, if we'll develop a full root system representing faith in all of the major promises of God, it will make us impossible to overturn.

Remember that Jesus said in John 14:30 (paraphrased): *"The devil comes, but he has nothing in me."* What was He saying? He was declaring that there were no holes in His shield of faith through which the enemy could attack. And we're supposed to do the same thing. So as we develop faith in all of God's promises including of His love, it allows us to manifest the full fruit of the spirit that people will then see.

Let me introduce a few other things with regard to this. The tree in Scripture many times represents both us individually and also the body of Christ. When we read about trees, sometimes it's referring to individuals and at other times to the church - and sometimes both.

Understand, a tree cannot effectively grow beyond the size of its roots. Know as well, that a tree's roots cannot extend far beyond the length of its branches. Roots and branches have to grow simultaneously. In fact, the leaves of the tree form what is called a *drip-line*. As water rains upon the tree, the leaves shed that water to the outskirts of the tree where the roots ends truncate. This allows the roots to absorb the maximum amount of moisture possible thus optimizing potential growth. If the roots try to grow far beyond the drip-line - the upper leaf covering of the tree, those roots will dry out and be forced to pull back.

In the same fashion, if we try to grow our faith in an effort to access the promises of God but we don't commence producing above-ground visible growth, we will dry out as well. To demonstrate no seen change in our lives indicates that we have become *"a hearer of the Word but not a doer."* As we build our faith, God will then lead us to activate that faith. Otherwise, *it is dead, not being mixed with works.*

Also, the branches of a tree cannot extend beyond the root system. Without an equivalent root system, a tree that is attempting to produce abundant fruit will not be able to absorb sufficient nutrients to sustain that fruit. As well, any strong winds that hit that tree will threaten to uproot it since the wind load it receives on the branches will tend to be greater than the root system can endure.

This applies to us as trees as well. Should we attempt to produce fruit beyond our faith level, we will run short of sufficient supernatural supply. This is the state of many ministers who have attempted to accomplish a work for God without learning to use the principles of faith. The end result is that they go about trying to complete a work for the kingdom without God's supernatural provision and end up in spiritual burnout. Burnout is the end result of trying to produce for God without accessing His divine power and supply.

Delving deeper, the branches of a tree represent divine order within the church. The nutrients that produce growth in the tree are initially brought into the trunk. From there, the sap flows out through the branch system of the tree. This is synonymous to the anointing originating from the head of the church - Jesus, and spreading out to the furthermost members of the body through God's divinely assigned government structure. And if you'll notice, the fruit on a tree is always produced in the outer branches. That's our job - to display to the world the fruit of the spirit. We're to be raised up in the power of the Kingdom to be fruit producers. However, to be an individual who possesses the anointing, we must be under someone who carries the anointing. Now as never before, God is raising up anointed pastors and leaders in the church to channel the anointings to the body.

ATTRACTING THE HARVEST

Now we're going to bring forth a key point from Genesis chapter 1:

> *Gen 1:26-29 -"And God said, Let us make man in our image, after our likeness: and let them have dominion... So God created man in his own image, in the image of God created he him; male and female created he them. And God blessed them, and God said unto them, Be fruitful, and multiply, and replenish the earth, and subdue it: and have dominion over the fish of the sea, and over the fowl of the air, and over every living thing that moveth upon the earth And God said, Behold, I have given you every herb bearing seed, which is upon the face of all the earth, and every tree, in the which is the fruit of a tree yielding seed; to you it shall be for meat."*

Here we see that God made man in His own image and gave him an assignment. Adam was placed in the Garden of Eden and told to multiply and fill the earth. Originally, Eden did not fill the entire world. It was a garden plot from which man was to take seed into all the earth. Through the power of seed, God's plan was for Adam to transform the entire world into a paradise.

It is theorized that prior to the flood, the earth was about 98% land and 2% water versus its composition being 2/3 water as it is today. The flood was primarily the result of the release of underground waters – *the fountains of the deep* that produced the oceans that we have today.

Originally, God's assignment to Adam was to take multiple types of seed into all of the earth, which at this time was comprised almost totally of dry land. Adam was to take forth the seed of the garden, the seed of the trees, the seed of the animals, and the seed of man to transform the entire earth into the Garden of Eden. God's primary goal was to fill the earth with people made in His image. The fall of man did not change God's plan - it only revised the process by which it would take place. God still has in mind to fill the earth with men who carry His divine image.

Through the fall, Adam lost the image of God. Through the cross, Jesus made available the restoration of this God image. And now our commandment is: *"Go ye into all of the earth and make disciples of all men."* The assignment of man has never changed. However, now we take forth the seed of the Word of God and sow it into the hearts of men. Those that receive this divine seed become born-again and are once again transformed internally into the image of God. God's not out to save only a remnant of the planet. He's looking to save everyone that he possibly can. And I believe that by the time that the church has completed their assignment, there will be more people in Heaven than there are in hell. There will be far more. And we're the harvesters!

Whenever God *calls* someone to a position or assignment, He always sets aside everything that they will require to fulfill that assignment. We have previously defined this as God's *grace* package - God's provision for us to complete our vision. When God commanded Adam to fill the earth, He provided him with the grace to do so. To complete this challenge, this grace came in the form of five tools - all described in Gen 1:26-30. Each of the tools that Adam was given in the garden has a New Testament counterpart available for us today. Jesus recovered for us, not just the opportunity to fulfill God's original assignment to Adam but also the same tools that man was given in the beginning.

The first tool that God gave Adam was **image**. And now through Jesus, we have again been given His image via our righteous nature. It is of paramount importance that we come to understand that we carry the image of love on the inside of us. Knowing who we are in Christ becomes the foundational truth by which all of the other tools function.

The second tool that He gave Adam was **dominion**. And our dominion today is equal to if not greater than Adam's. Dominion indicates our jurisdictional rights over the earth. It is this dominion that allows us to operate in authority upon the earth. Through this authority we have been given the power of **binding and loosing**.

The third tool that God gave Adam was a wife - **a covenant partner.** In the New Testament, we have been made members of God's *covenant body*. Through our covenant relationships, we can operate in the **principle of agreement** producing amplified release of power. Jesus declared in Matthew 18:19: *"if two of you shall agree ... it shall be done."* As well, since we are the *Bride of Christ* - we have our covenant husband, Jesus, standing with us.

The fourth and fifth tools that Adam was given were **seed and fruit**. The fruit was to eat and the seed was to sow. Our fruit is the love of God - the outward manifestation of our inner righteous nature. We are going to see in a moment that it is our fruit that will draw the harvest to God. The seed is the Word of God that we are to sow. Whosoever receives the incorruptible seed of the Word will be engrafted into the kingdom.

The FRUIT OF THE SPIRIT combined with our IMAGE, COVENANT, DOMINION, and the WORD OF GOD are all that we as the church need to accomplish God's original goal.

Again considering the tree, I want to relate an example of how I believe that much of this will take place. When I was growing up, I lived on a farm in Tennessee where we had a very small orchard. We had about five trees and they were all pear trees - but the pears that they produced were enormous. When those pears became ripe we took advantage of our harvest. We had pear butter, pear preserves, canned pears, and every other food made from pears that you can imagine.

We would watch these pears grow during the summer until they looked like oblong softballs. And most of the year, as these pears were growing there was little activity in the orchard. They were green, and if you tried to eat one your lips would pucker. They didn't taste good and no animals bothered them.

However, a shift took place around late September when the pears began to ripen. Even though all of the local critters had left those pears alone all summer, all of a sudden we had opossums, skunks, raccoons, and every varmint you could think of trying to get to those pears. We had red wasps and yellow jackets. We were equally visited by every other type of insect in the vicinity. They were all coming for those pears, especially when they started falling off the trees. Even the horses wanted over the fence to get to the ripened pears.

As those animals would come for the pears, they would consume it - **seed and all**. Remember from Genesis chapter 1 that God said that *the seed was in the fruit*. These animals would eat the fruit and as well consume the seed. But guess what? They were doing the tree a favor. They were taking forth that seed of the tree and depositing it elsewhere - pre-fertilized. Through this process, other pear trees were potentially being birthed.

But how does this apply to us? We are trees of righteousness. And many have been trying to bring in God's harvest for years through evangelistic efforts consisting primarily of passing out gospel tracts with little flames drawn on them. All too often, Christians are trying to scare people into the kingdom! And it's been scaring people – they've been running away from the churches as fast as their legs will carry them. They will see Christians coming with their handful of tracts and they'll cross the street to avoid them.

But there's a better way to bring in God's harvest. If we will commence walking in the love of God, it will put forth an aroma - a fruitful perfume that will draw the harvest to us. Just like the animals came for those ripened pears, as we begin manifesting the fruit of the Spirit people will flock to us. They will come to us and say: *"What is so different about you?"; "Why do I feel so drawn to you?"; "Why do you always seem so happy?"* And then, *"How can I have what you seem to have?"*

What happened? They've responded to the aroma that we're giving off. They've come for the fruit, and we now can sow into them the incorruptible seed of the Word of God. Once they come under the influence of our atmosphere of love (remember, a love atmosphere will drive devils out of the area!), their hearts will become wide open for us to impart to them God's seed. When this takes place, we will tell them a bible story - how *"Mary had a little lamb and His name was Jesus"*. Once their heart has been softened by love, we won't need to spend hours and hours convincing them of the truths of the Gospel. Through the influence of love, their hearts will become fertile soil for the Word!

That's how God's going to bring forth the harvest of the last days! He's not going to do it through scaring people into the kingdom. Christians are going to begin manifesting this love anointing and thus draw in the lost. God desires to get the whole body operating in the supernatural force of love. Once entire churches begin operating in this anointing, it will affect entire regions! People will flock to the churches! The church gatherings will become so charged with love that people driving near will be drawn to stop and investigate. They will want to find out what is different about this city! They will cry out: *"I feel so drawn to stop here... what can you tell me?"*

Multitudes will come in! In Luke, we see Jesus giving instructions to the disciples *to let down their nets into the deep for a draught*. In these last days, God's going to bring in His harvest with nets - and that net that He is going to use is the anointing of His love! Oh, praise the Lord! We get to be the carriers of this transformational end-time force!

In my early days of ministry I performed quite a bit of witnessing on the streets. Like many others, I pounded the streets trying to get people saved with minimal results and it was somewhat frustrating. I might have handed out a hundred tracts only to return from the direction I came to find them strewn everywhere. Few wanted to hear what I had to say! They seemed to avoid me more than be drawn to me. I would have to keep exhorting myself, *"Maybe the next one will be open to listen to me."* I was usually mistaken.

It was tiring. However one Friday night years ago, God let me experience a supernatural event. As I went out to witness in downtown Lexington, Kentucky, the anointing of love came upon me. Suddenly I supernaturally loved everyone that I saw. It was one of the most amazing experiences of my life. I actually loved everyone with the *agape* love of God. I was able to approach people without apprehension. I was able to speak to them without any expectation of rejection. **God descended upon me with the supernatural atmosphere of Heaven.** I could walk up to anyone and strike up a conversation and, the amazing thing was, they wanted to hear me. The anointing stayed on me for around 45 minutes, and in that time I was able to lead five people to Jesus in three different groups. I had never encountered such witnessing success. God later let me know that He was giving me a taste of how He intends to bring in His last day harvest - with nets comprised of the anointing of love!

I want to throw in here an interesting potential tie between the level of faith we develop and the fruit capacity that we can produce. Recall that once we target manifesting any promise of God, especially love, the devil is going to attempt to stop us. He will tell us: *"That 'faith stuff' won't work"*; *"It just isn't worth the effort,"* and *"It costs too much"; "It's too challenging"; and "It's too stressful."* There may even be seasons where we are tempted to feel that our faith is not fully producing for us.

However, at the same time that the devil is attempting to lure us away from faith, God will be countering these assaults with an invite to spend more time in His Word and in prayer. Where the enemy is trying to get us to give up on our faith, God is attempting to stretch it.

When a tree is faced with a season of drought, that tree will take one of two courses in response. Either that tree will drop its fruit and try to survive the dry season or it will extend its roots more deeply into the soil in search of increased moisture. **The devil will try to get us to drop our fruit but God will draw upon**

us to extend our roots. These become *make or break times* when we must either quit or go on forward. And God will always challenge us to stretch our faith. He will call us to go on forward and believe for something greater.

With my mathematical background, I began wondering what effect it would have if we were to double our faith level - if we stretched the length of our roots to double their current level. Geometrically, the fruit bearing capacity of a tree will be proportional to the volume of its branches. Since the branches of a tree will somewhat parallel the size of the root system, if we double the length of the roots, the branches should double in size likewise. Mathematically, the volume of a tree will be a cubic function of the length of its branches. Therefore, if we double the length of the branches by doubling the length of the roots then the tree's fruit-bearing capacity should increase eight-fold.

Therefore, rather than drop our fruit and have a pity party, if we will instead double up on our faith building efforts, our anointing stands to increase eight times based on this example. I understand that this model is not an exact replica of how things actually develop in the spirit and that this example just 'lost' some of you. However, the point I'm making is - whatever stretch we will make into the things of God will increase His love and blessings that we step into several times over.

We must realize that the rewards of pressing into the Kingdom of God far outweigh the challenges that we face! God is raising up majestic oaks of righteousness to overshadow any schemes that the enemy may have in mind in these last days. God is going to shine forth His glory upon and through us as these immovable trees!

CHAPTER 6

THE GLORY OF LOVE

"Now the end of the commandment is charity [agape love] out of a pure heart, and of a good conscience, and of faith unfeigned."

-- 1 Timothy 1:5

This verse in many ways is the launching point for everything that we've been discussing. We've discovered that God has an anointing of love into which we can purposefully step. We have examined this *Recipe for Agape* that requires that we mix together three mandatory ingredients:

Initially, we must become born again and discover the depth of blessing inherent in our new righteous nature.

Second, we must renew our minds to the reality of the supernatural love of God.

Third, we must forcefully step out in genuine actions of faith to see this power released into our lives. The resultant love anointing will destroy strife from our midst; it will take from us all offense; and it will make us immovable from the assignment that God has placed upon us.

To combat the advancement of God's anointed church, satan works overtime to get people to abandon the churches where God has placed them. The primary reasons people move from their assigned church bodies are offense, strife, or some form of disappointment. And God's raising up a group of revivalists in these last days that are becoming immovable. When God sets them in a church or in a position, they won't move from that position until God directs them to do so. Too often, Christians allow their emotions to run wild forcing them to make changes that God never ordained.

That's why there exist so many *church hoppers*. Because members refuse to confront discomfort, they've never been able to access the power of God to stay in their assigned positions. Since they have not taken the appropriate steps via the anointing to overcome the pressure of demonic attacks, they have no choice but to be moved. Offense then, has become the enemy's predominant weapon against revival. He stirs up strife, initiates feelings of rejection, and creates distrust to produce church fractures. Even in the revivalist churches where people should know better, he's got members arguing with one another and even dividing into little cliques. In the church of the last-days these things ought not to be. We're going to find out in this chapter that God is going to use the power of love to put a stop to unwarranted church splits.

At this point, we're going to begin pulling together some of the pieces of what we have already discussed and start examining further how God's going to progress in this end-time revival. We've already mentioned that God intends to bring forth His harvest from the earth. He is going to use His fire-baptized revivalists as His harvesting instruments as they manifest the full fruit of the spirit. We are going to sow the incorruptible seed of the Word of God into lives that are drawn by genuine love and witness the number of people saved multiply exponentially. Instead of just fishing with a hook and line, we will really go out there and bring in God's full harvest with nets of the love of God!

A GLORY REVIVAL

A primary passage regarding God's end-time outpouring lies hidden in the obscure book of Habakkuk:

> *Hab 2:1 - "I will stand upon my watch, and set me upon the tower, and will watch to see what he will say unto me, and what I shall answer when I am reproved."*

Here the prophet Habakkuk declares: *"I'm going to go pray."* The term *"watch"* indicates that Habakkuk had an assigned time of prayer in which it was his responsibility to stand spiritual guard.

That he was praying from a tower indicates the importance of praying from a high place to hear God. In that same way, if we want to hear God we must elevate to our high place. And ours is the recognition that we are seated with Him in heavenly places via the righteous impartation that God has given to us through Jesus.

The prophet Habakkuk lets us know that he was going to pray and that he expected to hear God. I am impressed that Habakkuk, though he was an Old Testament figure, expected to hear from God! How much more should we be expecting God to speak into our lives. Yet in the church of today, most who declare themselves to be Christians do not. Reading further:

> *Hab 2:2 – "And the LORD answered me, and said, "Write the vision, and make it plain upon tables, **that he may run that readeth it.**""*

How about that – this verse informs us that the LORD answered him! He will answer us as well if we will seek diligently and listen in expectation.

But the key phrase is at the end of this verse! Through the prophet, The Lord declares that **all that read this vision should run toward its fulfillment.**

We haven't yet gotten to the verse where God relates to us the vision, but let me ask you a question. Do you have a Bible? And if so, does your Bible have the Book of Habakkuk in it? (You can put this book down and check if you like.) Certainly your Bible has Habakkuk in it. However, many if not most Christians are oblivious to the message that Habakkuk related.

Every genuine, spirit-led Christian believes that the Bible is the inspired Word of God. They also understand that God handpicked the books that are included in our canon of scripture. There are no books missing and none that were meant to be excluded. Therefore, it did not catch God by surprise that Habakkuk ended up in our Bible. As well, since this book of Habakkuk is in our Bible we are aware that we are meant to read it. Since God tells us that *whoever reads this vision should run with it*, we can ascertain that all Christianity is intended to run with this vision! In chapter two of the book from this minor prophet, **God reveals the target toward which every Christian is to be pursuing.**

Habakkuk chapter two contains God's end time vision! And He says that everyone that reads it should run towards this vision. God wants every Christian believer to run toward the same vision. Notice that he didn't say to amble towards it or pursue it at our own convenience. He said to run towards it. Running requires focused and dedicated attention and isn't necessarily always pleasurable. Running takes coordinated and concentrated effort! As we continue in this passage we find:

> *Hab 2:3 –"For the vision is yet for an appointed time, **but at the end it shall speak**, and not lie: though it tarry, wait for it, it will not tarry."*

God lets us know that the vision which He gives to Habakkuk is for the end-time. It will seem as though the vision has been delayed, however it will come to pass. We see also that those who are of the end-time will understand the vision. Up until recently, the Church has only minimally comprehended their actual assignment.

The vision that God relates to us through Habakkuk is stated in verse 14. I say to us rather than to Habakkkuk because the vision was not for his day but for ours.

> *Hab 2:14 -"**For the earth shall be filled with the knowledge of the glory of the LORD**, as the waters cover the sea."*

Oh, hallelujah! God wants to bring His glory to this planet! God's not looking for a church that is just hanging on until the rapture takes place. He's not looking for a survival-minded church. He's looking for a glorious and overcoming church - one that is looking forward to bringing the power and the presence of God into their sphere of operation. And, he says that the earth is going to be filled with His glory as the waters cover the sea. Scripturally, *"waters"* represent *the Holy Spirit and the Spirit-initiated revelation of God's Word.* *"Seas"* represent *the multitudes of peoples.*

God proclaims that as He pours out the *revealed Word* in these last days to the multitudes, His glory will be manifested to the same level. Right now, we live in a period of time when technology has exploded to the point that the Word of God may be instantaneously transmitted worldwide. We now possess the ability to take the revealed Word to even the most remote corners of the earth in a concentrated form. We've got CD's, DVD's, satellite TV, VCR's, MP3's and internet streaming. We literally can take the revelation of the Word around the earth in accelerated fashion, even as it is unveiled unto us!

I believe that this technology explosion we've seen over the last 100 years has been birthed of God. In fact, the beginning of the technology release very closely coincided with the revival that began at Azusa Street in the early part of the last century. At the same time that God brought forth an explosion of the baptism of the Holy Spirit, technological advancement took off as well. As believers are prophesying in their prayer languages, God is releasing necessary knowledge to put in place these inventions. These advancements in information technology will be used to spread world-wide the end-time revelations of the Word that God is even now releasing.

God has been bringing forth these advancements in technology for the last 100 years to allow the Word of God to saturate the planet like never before! This will fulfill the portion of the prophecy that declares *"the waters will cover the seas."*

Verse 4 informs us who these people of the glory will be:

*Hab 2:4 – "Behold, his soul which is lifted up is not upright in him: **but the just shall live by his faith**."*

He whose *"soul is lifted up"* refers to those caught up in pride. The exalted soul represents someone who believes that he knows more than God and subsequently more than His Word as well. The person ensnared by pride cannot manifest the glory of God because God cannot break through his religious strongholds. These strongholds prevent him from receiving the revelation needed to produce the required changes for his life.

Those who manifest the glory will be the *just who live by faith*. And that word *"just"* is the same word that means *righteous*. In other words, *he who understands his own righteousness through Christ shall live – BY FAITH*. I've already explained how we access the love of God through faith. And here we see that God is going to bring forth a people who are going to manifest His glory by faith.

Now I want to define quickly what I believe the glory of God to be. There are many different commentaries available that attempt to define the glory, but I want to relate to you what I'm convinced that it is. **THE GLORY OF GOD IS THE CONCENTRATED, TANGIBLE LOVE OF GOD!** It is love in such concentrated fashion that it spills over from the third heaven into the second, and from there into this first heaven, natural realm.

Previous accounts of the manifestation of God's glory relate that people would actually witness it in some visible form. Jesus shined with the glory of God when He came down from the Mount of Transfiguration. Moses came down from Mount Sinai carrying the glory of God where his face radiated. He shined so brightly that he put a veil over his face while he was addressing the people. Literally, the glory of God when manifested so infiltrates this earthly realm that it can be detected with our five natural senses.

We have previously mentioned that the atmosphere of the third heaven is love. Our spirit man always has connection to this supernatural power source. However, we need love to also dominate the other two heavens to produce the fullness of change that God desires. The Word promises that God inhabits the praises of His people. When we set ourselves to seek and worship Him, His presence bleeds over from the third to the second heaven. Once God's love penetrates and dominates the second heaven atmosphere, it now becomes detectable by our second heaven senses - the emotions.

Our emotions allow us to detect the presence of God as it enters our vicinity. As we step into the presence of God, we will feel love, joy, peace, or whatever manifestation of fruit that may occur. The glory represents an occurrence where the manifestation of love spills over from the second heaven into the first. At this time it then becomes tangible to our five earthly senses allowing us to witness the glory through various physical signs and wonders. This will be a major facet in bringing the multitudes to The Cross. Jesus stated that some people won't believe unless they see a sign, *but blessed are those who believe without seeing.* The glory will provide multitudes with the tangible signs that they need to believe.

If we go to the New Testament and look at the Greek word for glory we find the word *doxa*. *Doxa*, represents *the very image, nature, or character of an individual* or *their most exalted state of being*. So, in reference to the very image, nature or character of God, since He is *agape*, then the glory of God must be His love in some fashion. *Agape* is God's image, it's His nature, and it's His character. He is *agape*.

Nowhere in the Bible does it declare that "God is glory". Instead it says that He *manifests* His glory. In doing so, He is manifesting who He is. He is showing forth who He is in a form that people can detect. So when God brings forth His glory such that it covers the earth, multitudes are going to witness undeniable signs and wonders. But of even greater influence, the peoples will overwhelmingly *feel* His supernatural love.

TABERNACLES OF GLORY

In the Old Testament, God gave Moses specific instructions to build a tabernacle for Him to inhabit. These building parameters were to be carried out with exact precision. Once this tabernacle was completed, the glory of God filled it.

But from the New Testament, we find that the Tabernacle was actually a *type* or *representation* of the Christian.

> Heb 8:1-2 – *"Now of the things which we have spoken this is the sum: We have a high priest, who is set on the right hand of the throne of the Majesty in the heavens; A minister of the sanctuary, and of the true tabernacle, which the Lord pitched, and not man."*

Where the tabernacle was composed of three parts, we are as well. The Outer Court, The Holy Place, and The Holy of Holies all correspond to our Flesh, our Soul, and our Spirit. And as the presence of God dwelled in the Holy of Holies, His presence now abides within our spirit.

As we examine the finishing steps to complete the Tabernacle, we should obtain greater understanding of what is required for us to manifest God's love and glory.

Exodus describes the initial erection of the Tabernacle in the wilderness:

> *Exo 40:1-3 – "And the LORD spake unto Moses, saying, On the first day of the first month shalt thou set up the tabernacle of the tent of the congregation. And thou* **shalt put therein the ark of the testimony, and cover the ark with the veil.***"*

The Ark of the Testimony was the specific location where the presence of God dwelt. The Ark represented the place of God's residence and manifested presence in the earth. As we read further:

> *Exo 40:4 – "And thou shalt bring in the table, and* **set in order the things that are to be set in order** *upon it; and thou shalt bring in the candlestick, and light the lamps thereof."*

Before God brings in His glorious presence, He's going to need a church that's set in order. Divine order in the church and submission to that order will be a major factor in manifesting the end-time glory of God. Skipping ahead to verse 33:

> *Exo 40:33 –"And he reared up the court round about the tabernacle and the altar, and set up the hanging of the court gate.* **So Moses finished the work.**"

Here is a key phrase: *"Moses finished the work."* God is today in the process of doing a finishing work on the church and we're now entering the final maturing stages. Once the work of erecting Old Testament Tabernacle was finished, the glory of God manifested upon it.

> *Exo 40:34-35 —"Then a cloud covered the tent of the congregation, and the glory of the Lord filled the tabernacle. And **Moses was not able to enter into the tent of the congregation**, because the cloud abode thereon, **and the glory of the LORD filled the tabernacle.**"*

What was this cloud? It was the visible, tangible, manifestation of the glory of God. When the glory came on the scene, it filled the tabernacle. Keep in mind that **we are the New Testament temples of God** and He intends for His glory to be seen upon us. This glory stayed with the tabernacle for forty years. During the day it would materialize as a cloud and at night as a pillar of fire. The end-time manifestation of God's glory will also be more than a temporal display. It will be a permanent manifestation upon our lives lasting unto the Rapture.

Now this is kind of a ridiculous illustration, but do you suppose that the glory cloud was kind of rubbery such that Moses - even with a running start in an attempt to enter the tabernacle - just keep bouncing off because it was so dense? Of course not! It wasn't that the cloud was so thick that it kept Moses from entering. Instead, it was the effect that the glory of God had upon his emotions - his second heaven sense detectors. Literally, Moses was so overcome by the love of God that it prevented him from entering into the tabernacle. Moses was so overcome by *agape* that awe drained the natural strength from his body.

You see, when the glory of God comes forth it's going to produce more than a series of visible signs as a tangible witness of God's presence. Love is going to dominate the very atmosphere of this first heaven world. People are going to be drawn not only to signs, they're as well going to experience the overwhelming magnetic power of God's love all around them. This love will totally eradicate every form of resistance within them that might prevent them from receiving revelation of the truths of God's Word.

Here Moses is God's top man for the moment, yet he couldn't penetrate past this cloud because of the impact it had upon what he was feeling.

Not only was the Old Testament Tabernacle a *type* of the revivalist Christian, but so was the temple at Jerusalem.

> *1Cor 3:16 – "Know ye not that ye are the temple of God, and that the Spirit of God dwelleth in you?"*

We can also examine the dedication of this temple to discover God's assigned process for us to manifest His glory.

If you will recall, David wanted to build a temple for God but was denied because he was a man of war. He laid up immense wealth for the building of this temple and his son Solomon took that wealth plus additional of his own to complete the project. Let's examine the building of The Temple in Second Chronicles:

> *2Chr 5:1 – "Thus all the work that Solomon made for the house of the LORD was finished: and Solomon brought in all the things that David his father had dedicated; and the silver, and the gold, and all the instruments, put he among the treasures of the house of God."*

Oh, how blasphemous! Solomon must not have known that God didn't want treasures in His house. Of course I'm just kidding, yet many are deceived to believe that the church should be filled with second-hand junk.

> *2Chr 5:2 – "Then Solomon assembled the elders of Israel, and all the heads of the tribes, the chief of the fathers of the children of Israel, unto Jerusalem,* **to bring up the ark of the covenant of the LORD** *out of the city of David, which is Zion."*

Here, we again have the Ark of the Covenant (representing the place of the presence of God) being brought to the Temple. Reading further:

> *2Chr 5:3-4 – "Wherefore* **all the men of Israel assembled themselves unto the king** *in the feast which was in the seventh month. And all the elders of Israel came; and the Levites took up the ark."*

Now the congregation assembled together with the elders and the Levites fulfilling their assigned responsibilities. God needed to put everything in order to accomplish what He was about to do in the Nation of Israel.

> *2Chr 5:5-6 –"And they brought up the ark, and the tabernacle of the congregation, and all the holy vessels that were in the tabernacle, these did the priests and the Levites bring up." Also king Solomon, and all the congregation of Israel that were assembled unto him before the ark, **sacrificed sheep and oxen, which could not be told nor numbered for multitude.*"*

Everything was in place - the temple and all of the people were assembled in order. Solomon then began bringing forth sacrifices unto God at an overwhelming level. We spoke earlier of how *giving* is a necessary step to manifest the love of God. It is a key step in what transpires in this dedication as well. Let's go on down to Verse 11:

> *2Chr 5:11-12 –"And it came to pass, when the priests were come out of the holy place: (for all the priests that were present were sanctified, and did not then wait by course: Also the Levites which were the singers, all of them of Asaph, of Heman, of Jeduthun, with their sons and their brethren, being **arrayed in white linen**, having cymbals and psalteries and harps, stood at the east end of the altar, and with them an hundred and twenty priests sounding with trumpets:)"*

We know from Revelation 19:8 - that white linen represents *the righteousness of the saints*. That the Levites were dressed in white linen lets us know that God is requiring righteousness from those involved in this glorious event. Looking at the next verse:

> *2Chr 5:13a – "It came even to pass, as the trumpeters and singers were **as one**,"*

By the time that God has completed His finishing work on His remnant church, we will be operating *"as one"*. When we get to the place where we operate as a unit, get ready for it's time for the glory of God to come on the scene. He's looking for a united church, a church without spot or wrinkle - a *glorious* bride. At this time, let me say that I do not believe the glory will be initiated through a unification of everyone who call themselves Christians. The glory is going to manifest initially through a leading edge group of revivalists who have progressed to believe the entire Word of God. They will be those who have refused to bow to the pressures of the world. Reading further:

> *2Chr 5:13b – "To make one sound to be heard in praising and thanking the LORD; and when they lifted up their voice with the trumpets and cymbals and instruments of musick, and praised the LORD, saying,* **For he is good;"** *for his mercy endureth for ever:"*

They had a revelation of the goodness of God. He is a good God. God is not looking for an excuse to throw people into hell. He sent Jesus to deliver us from Hell. People send themselves to Hell when they reject the *goodness* of God. Continuing:

> *2Chr 5:13c-14 –"that then the house was filled with a cloud, even the house of the LORD; So that* **the priests could not stand to minister** *by reason of the cloud:* **for the glory of the LORD had filled the house of God.**"

In the culmination of this monumental event, we see that the priests could not even stand to minister. The glory of God produces such an intense awareness of God's holiness and love that human efforts to approach Him lack the required strength. They were in reverence of the goodness of God manifested in His love. The power of God came in so powerfully that they all were slain in the Spirit - knocked down by the Holy Ghost.

NEW TESTAMENT TEMPLES

Recognizing God's pattern of bringing His glory to the temple, look now at Second Corinthians:

> *2Cor 6:16 –"And what agreement hath the temple of God with idols? for **ye are the temple of the living God**; as God hath said, I will dwell in them, and walk in them; and I will be their God, and they shall be my people."*

We are the New Testament Temples of God. Here we can comprehend that the true Ark of the Covenant is situated within us. In the Old Testament, God filled the tabernacle with His glory when it was completed. However, we are the actual, living habitations of God that the tabernacle and temple represented. If He filled the Old Testament - man-made facilities with the glory of God, how much more is He going to fill His last-day church with the fullness of His glory!

Remember that Habakkuk said that the earth would be filled with the glory? It's not because God's going to wave His hand and all of a sudden glory fills the earth. Rather, as we step forward into the love of God and start manifesting it in greater and greater levels, we're going to become the carriers of the glory. And the earth's going to be filled with the glory because we're going to carry it into all of the earth. God has ordained that His power is to be carried through man. Therefore men will be the carriers of the glory worldwide. Looking further at First Corinthians:

> *1Cor 3:17 –"If any man defile the temple of God, him shall God destroy; for the temple of God is holy, which temple ye are."*

If we are temples of God and the temple of God is holy - then we must also be holy. But how do we *"defile"* the temple? Three obvious ways that we as the temple can be defiled are:

First, we refuse God full access to our triune being. We try to serve God out of our own understanding rather than allow Him to truly be Lord over our lives.

Two, we refuse to deal with the obvious sin issues that may attempt to plague us. The revivalist believer must endeavor to live a holy life.

And three, we defile the temple when we declare ourselves to be sinners. Identifying ourselves as sinners causes us to walk with a condemnation mentality believing that we can do no right. The Christian who entertains any of these three, disqualifies himself from being able to manifest the end-time glory of God.

God is raising up temples in these last days who know who they are in Christ. They know that they're holy and they know that they're righteous. They're manifesting the very image, nature and character of God. God was never really concerned with buildings made of stone. He was looking ahead to living temples - buildings carved out by His Word.

EXCEEDING GLORY

God confirms His desire to bring the glory to the church in Ephesians 5:

> *Eph 5:25-27 –"Husbands, love your wives, even as Christ also loved the church, and gave himself for it; That he might sanctify and cleanse it with the washing of water by the word,* ***That he might present it to himself a glorious church****, not having spot, or wrinkle, or any such thing; but that it should be holy and without blemish."*

Here we see the *"water"* of the *"Word"* of God acting as the cleansing agent to purify and perfect the Bride of Christ. Jesus is not coming back for a broken-down, busted-up church. He's returning for a glorious bride. In prior years, the rapture was often believed to be God's rescue action to deliver Christians just before the devil totally destroyed them. Nothing could be further from the truth. The rapture will be God's final promotion for the church that has manifested the fullness of His glory.

The spots and wrinkles described here refer to divisions - creases in the Body of Christ. God's coming back for a church without strife, without offense, and without any type of division within.

What I want to make clear is that **God is bringing forth a REVIVAL OF LOVE to usher forth His supernatural glory!** This revival is not something that God is going to do just to get us excited about attending church and to get a few people saved. This end-time move is the vehicle that God's going to use to bring in

His harvest. As we step into greater and greater levels of manifesting His love, it's going to develop into the very glory of God in our lives.

I can imagine that someone may now be exclaiming: *"Well, that's pretty way out there preacher."*; *"That's sounds way too radical."*

My answer: *The Bible is a radical book!*

I had been raised as an atheist, so I had never been taught that the power of God has passed away as is instructed in many denominations. So after I became saved, I was made aware of an amazing promise in John 14:

> *John 14:12 – "Verily, verily, I say unto you, He that believeth on me, the works that I do shall he do also; and greater works than these shall he do; because I go unto my Father."*

If the Word ever proclaimed an extreme statement this would be it. However, God had so witnessed within me that the Bible is His inspired Word that I became determined to do this. God is even now raising up a group of revivalists who believe that they can do these *"greater works."* If we believe that we can do the works of Jesus, certainly we should be able to believe that we can manifest His love. We serve a radical God!

Let's now look at Second Corinthians:

> *2Cor 3:6 – "Who also hath made us able ministers of the new testament; not of the letter, but of the spirit: for the letter killeth, but the spirit giveth life."*

Here we discover that we are now God's New Testament representatives - assigned to minister His life versus the condemnation of the law. Looking at the next verse:

> *2Cor 3:7 – "But if **the ministration of death, written and engraven in stones, was glorious**, so that the children of Israel could not stedfastly behold the face of Moses for the glory of his countenance; which glory was to be done away:"*

The ministration of death refers to the Law, including The Ten Commandments. In that the Law can only bring the knowledge of sin, and death by sin, we can ascertain that those Old Testament commandments can never bring us into perfection. Even so, when Moses came down from the mountain, he was carrying the glory of God. He even put a veil over his face such that the people could not see this glory which was fading away. So even the ministration of the Old Testament was able to produce a tangible, visible glory. But read on:

> *2Cor 3:8-9 –"How shall not the ministration of the spirit be rather glorious? For if the ministration of condemnation be glory,* **much more doth the ministration of righteousness exceed in glory**.*"*

If the Old Covenant produced visible glory then the New Testament will display even more. We sit on the precipice of the most exciting set of events to ever take place since the Cross.

The *"ministration of righteousness"* is the message that declares to us that we're no longer sinners. We are now saints. We've been made new creations in Christ Jesus. And we now have within us the very image, nature and character of God. But there's more:

> *2Cor 3:10-11 –"For even that which was made glorious had no glory in this respect, by reason of the glory that excelleth. For if that which is done away was glorious,* much **more that which remaineth is glorious**.*"*

Here Paul says that the Old Testament glory that Moses carried won't even compare to the glory of the last day church. As well, the glory that we will carry will never fade away - it *"remaineth!"* I believe that God is about to use us to fulfill the vision that He gave his people through Habakkuk.

We are the generation that's going to do this! God is raising up a group of people even now that are declaring: *"I want all that God has."; "I want to be involved in the extraordinary."; "I want to fulfill my high calling."; "I don't care what people think."* and *"I must answer the call of God on my life no matter what it takes."*

THE MIRROR OF THE WORD

Now let's go down to the end of Second Corinthians 3 and read two very powerful verses:

> *2Cor 3:17-18 -"Now the Lord is that Spirit: and where the Spirit of the Lord is, there is liberty. But we all, with open face **beholding as in a glass the glory of the Lord, are changed into the same image** from glory to glory, even as by the Spirit of the Lord."*

The glass in this verse is a mirror or a looking glass. This mirror referred to is the Word of God. As we peer into the Word, it has the power contained within it to change us into the image that we see. If when studying the Word, all that we see is our sinfulness then we are going to take on the mindset and image of a sinner.

However, Jesus is the Word made flesh. Therefore, the Word of God is the full representation of Jesus in print form. The image that we should be witnessing as we read the Word is that of Jesus. As we do so with an open face (being willing to change), we are changed into the same image supernaturally. **We are transformed into the visage of Jesus as we spend extensive amounts of time meditating God's Word.** This process of allowing the Word to change us day after day takes us to higher and higher levels of walking in God's glory!

Also, because God is love and Jesus is God then as we are transformed into the image of Jesus we are subsequently changed into the image of love. It is this manifestation of love that takes us from *"glory to glory."* As redeemed Christians, when we gaze into the Word we should view ourselves carrying the very nature of God and shining with His glory.

James also teaches us of the looking glass of God:

> *Jas 1:23-25 – "For if any be a hearer of the word, and not a doer, he is like unto a man beholding his natural face in a*

glass: For he beholdeth himself, and goeth his way, and straightway forgetteth what manner of man he was. But whoso looketh into the perfect law of liberty, and continueth [therein], he being not a forgetful hearer, but a doer of the work, this man shall be blessed in his deed."

Here it says that a man who is a hearer of the word and not a doer is as one who views himself in a mirror but later forgets how he appeared. Traditionally the way this passage has been preached is in this manner: *"When a man looks in the Word of God, he is made aware of his sinfulness and repents. Then as he walks away, the conviction fades away and he returns to sin."*

In actuality, the face we view in the mirror should be the face of Jesus. The man that will not keep this image before him will be apt to remain mindful of his former sinful nature. He will be unable to operate out of His God-given new righteous nature. All of the authority and anointing in which we desire to operate is tied to our recognition that we now carry the image of God within.

The man that is a hearer of the Word but not a doer loses sight that he is now been made the righteousness of God in Christ. He reverts back to walking with the image of his *"natural face"* - his prior unredeemed personal image. Time in God's Word viewed through the revelation of righteousness provides us with the ultimate makeover. We will not recognize ourselves as the same person once we grasp the revelation of who God has now made us.

We must witness our God-given righteous image reflected in the Word. It is imperative that we study scriptures that declare our righteousness. We must study the love scriptures and meditate passages that promise us victory. As we do, watch what God does in transforming our lives. The Holy Ghost is in our lives, not to condemn us but to lead us into the glory.

LIVELY STONES

Let's look at First Peter chapter 2:

1Pet 2:1-5 –"Wherefore laying aside all malice, and all guile, and hypocrisies, and envies, and all evil speakings, As newborn babes, desire the sincere milk of the word, that *ye may grow thereby: If so be ye have tasted that the Lord is gracious. To whom coming, as unto a living stone, disallowed indeed of men, but chosen of God, and precious, Ye also, **as lively stones, are built up a spiritual house**, an holy priesthood, to offer up spiritual sacrifices, acceptable to God by Jesus Christ."*

We have already discovered that we are New Testament temples of God. But here we see that we are being built up corporately - also as a temple of God. God is bringing us together as individual lively stones that are being assembled as an end-time temple for God to inhabit. God inhabits us personally to develop us individually to manifest His calling upon our lives. **But He's also uniting all of our individual callings to produce a corporate body which will manifest the fullness of His glory.**

An end-time Christian will never really manifest the glory of God until he is locked into a body that's endeavoring to walk in love. We must allow God to develop us both individually and corporately in these last days. God has ordained that His power is exponentially increased through assemblage and agreement. When two or more agree, the anointing is multiplied. Therefore, without becoming engrafted within God's last day church building process, no glory will be produced. Jesus is preparing His glorious bride - and The Bride is not representative of a myriad of individual Christians but instead of a united body.

In this construction project, Jesus is the Cornerstone! He is the building block to which the rest of us are being required to conform. And of course, that indicates that we must align our lives with love.

In building a house out of rock, unless the stones are cut just perfectly it can only be erected so high if nothing is used to lock the stones together. And the truth is, when we come to church God will start cutting on us. He'll cut this out of our lives and He'll cut that out of our lives. What's He doing? He's trying to get us cut into shape to place us somewhere within the body of Christ where we can fulfill His divine purpose. He's going to require changes in our lives to reshape us to fulfill that position - and God's primary chisel is the Word. We don't need trials to shape our lives if we will submit to the divine shaping program of the Word of God.

God is building up a spiritual house, but the problem is that these are *"lively stones."* Do you know what the problem is with lively stones? They continually change shapes. A master stone mason may cut a stone to produce an exact fit for an opening in a wall. And because rocks do not ordinarily change shapes on their own, it should stay in position. However with God's construction project, He is using lively stones, and lively stones at times get *all bent out of shape.* One day someone may seem like a perfect fit for a church position but overnight experience a mood swing. Circumstances may not have gone their way or hormones may have become out of balance, but suddenly that stone does some shifting. Before they were in a position where they proclaimed: *"This is where God has called me."* and *"I know this is where I am supposed to be!"* The next moment they may express: *"I don't want to do this anymore."* As well, they likely may become critical of everyone else around them.

As people get their feelings hurt or their toes stepped on, they may become difficult to work with or even totally rebellious. As they do so, shifts take place in the wall of the building making everything unstable. Then one stone takes off and a wall begins to crumble. Or a stone on the bottom decides it wants to be on the top, and it changes position. Suddenly there's a hole in the bottom of the wall and too much weight on the top. In such cases, we may literally have a wall cave in producing a church implosion. Often, one block may even decide to birth their own work and a church split results.

I never realized before I became a Pastor how much need there is to tread softly around many people's feelings. You don't want to say the one thing that will step on a person's toes just hard enough to send them over the edge. So what do you do? You get the Word of God in them. You teach covenant, love, and faith to get them strong enough to stand against the assaults of the enemy. Sometimes toes have to be stepped on to accomplish God's accelerated plans to manifest the glory. Proper teaching has the potential to shod the church members with *steel-toed boots.*

Pastors have been highly limited in how fast they can accelerate the implementation of God's plans. People can only be stretched so far before they want to jump ship to a *zero demands* church. And God's trying to assemble a group of believers that He can stretch to the uttermost levels yet they refuse to flee.

Lively stones often appear to be doing great one day but the next may declare: *"Get me out of here."* It's hard to build a building very high if the stones keep changing shape. We might get one or two tiers high and then as we get to the third tier, the lower tiers may begin to shift in shape or evacuate their space. We're going to have problems getting that building to stand. And realizing this, God has provided a substance to lock the morphing stones together.

Usually, when a building is being constructed of rock, a mortar buffer will be placed between the stones. This mortar layer acts to forgive any imperfections in the adjoining stones and actually use these differences to lock the stones together. In most cases, the mortar doesn't actually stick to the stones. Instead, it uses the stones abnormalities to lock two dissimilar units firmly in place. Mortar actually fills in the imperfections of the stones and places a buffer layer between them - thus producing a perfect joint.

God's building project requires a mortar as well if He is going to build very high. His mortar is specifically designed to adhere lively stones together in the last days. He's fusing together His glorious bride such that they won't jump ship, won't entertain division, and won't get into strife. And **the mortar He is using to bond us together as lively stones is *the love of God*.** Love fuses us together despite our differences and idiosyncrasies. Love keeps us in position no matter how much we feel stretched. Love allows us to share our giftings with one another in the body regardless of the best efforts of the enemy to bring us into strife. And love makes all of this totally enjoyable!

We witness this mortar in Colossians 3:

> *Col 3:14-15* –"*And above all these things put on charity* [agape love], *which is the bond of perfectness. And let the*

peace of God rule in your hearts, to the which also ye are called in one body; and be ye thankful."

Here we see that God has a perfect bond - a mortar that will allow us to adhere to one another and firmly lock us into position. And as we see here, that *"bond of perfection"* is love! God says that we are called into one body, and to stay in that one body we must put on the mortar - His love. Love becomes the *superglue* of the Kingdom.

In prior years and even today, much of the church has more closely resembled a political organization or a social club than a covenant body. Many have been jockeying for position or wearing their feelings on their sleeve. If some don't get their way, offense and chaos result. In these last days, instead of all of that mess, God intends to coat his bride with His amazing love. He plans to encapsulate us in an anointing which makes one *unoffendable*.

When we truly start manifesting the fullness of the love of God, it will shield us from offense. As they did with Jesus, people may spit on or mock us but it won't alter our walk. How did Jesus put up with the persecution and rejection that He endured? He was coated in the love of God, as we will be also.

We will get to the point where it doesn't matter what other people think of us. It won't matter what other people do to us. It's not so much that it's irrelevant, but that it will have no impact upon our emotions. This is because our emotions will have become so flooded with the love of God that no anti-anointing can penetrate and defile our souls.

As people begin to get a hold of this anointing and start walking in it, God will be able to raise up a body of lively stones that can link and lock together and not be moved. As we step into the fullness of love, God will be able to build us into a skyscraper sized temple that can house the entirety of His harvest!

UNITED UNTO GLORY

Regarding unity within the body, let's look at a passage from First Corinthians 12:

> *1Cor 12:14-18 –"For the body is not one member but many. If the foot shall say, because I am not the hand, I am not of the body; is it therefore not of the body? If the ear shall say, because I am not the eye, I am not of the body; is it therefore not of the body? If the whole were and eye, where were the hearing, where were the smelling? But now hath God set the members every one of them in the body, as it hath pleased him."*

God has birthed us onto this planet each with a specific calling upon our life. He has set aside all of the anointing and provision that we will need to fulfill these callings. However, a prime aspect of God's assignment for us is to become united with His revivalist, remnant church. There is a specific position for each of us which no one else on this earth can equally fill. We are precious to God and the calling on each life is similarly precious. We must embrace it with all of our heart. Paul goes on to write:

> *1Cor 12:24-25 –"For our comely* [good-looking] *parts have no need: but God hath tempered the body together, having given more abundant honour to that part which lacked. That there should be no schism in the body; but that the members should have the same care one for another."*

God is letting us know that every member of the body is beautiful to Him. No one is without value in His body building project. We also see again that there should be no division in the body and that God has tempered us together. When steel is produced, carbon and other materials are united with iron to produce a new material. To *temper* the steel, a precise amount of heat is applied over time combined with specific cooling rates to develop the exact properties desired in the metal. And God is tempering His end-time church together. He's bringing us all as dissimilar parts, together to produce through us a body with desired properties we cannot produce of ourselves. **The anointing of love enables us to stand the heat without jumping out of the furnace!**

Let's look in John 17 at a portion of Jesus' last dissertation that we have record of before He went to the cross:

> *John 17:21-23 – "That they all may be one; as thou, Father, art in me, and I in thee, that they also may be one in us: that the world may believe that thou hast sent me.* ***And the glory which thou gavest me I have given them; that they may be one, even as we are one:*** *I in them, and thou in me, that they may be made perfect in one; and that the world may know that thou hast sent me, and hast loved them, as thou hast loved me."*

Reworded, Jesus said: *"Father just like I am in you and you are in Me, I want the body to be likewise."* He lets us know that once the body of Christ unites as one, there will occur a supernatural phenomenon which will convince the world of who He really is. The event that will produce this revelation is the release of the glory of God. We see also in this passage that Jesus ties the manifestation of His glory to the attractive power of His supernatural love. **We cannot separate the glory from the love of God!**

We see again as well, an additional effect that the glory has upon the church is to help to unite us! Why? Because the glory is composed of the love of God - the binding agent or mortar of perfection. Reading further down:

> *John 17:26 – "I have declared unto them thy name, and will declare it: that* ***the love wherewith thou hast loved me may be in them****, and I in them."*

Here Jesus proclaims that the love that He carries is supposed to be in us as His church. What a declaration and what an opportunity! Imagine that - God wants the same love that Jesus carried to be in us. We have been given access to infinite levels of love. God is now releasing this expanded understanding of love in the last-days to bring His glory on the scene. And all of the technology that we've seen come along is to carry this message - that God wants the world saturated with His glorious love!

You probably remember looking at Ephesians 3:

> *Eph 3:17-19 – "That Christ may dwell in your hearts by faith; that ye, being rooted and grounded in love, May be able to comprehend **with all saints** what is the breadth, and length, and depth, and height; And to know the love of Christ, which passeth knowledge, that ye **might be filled with all the fullness of God.**"*

Here it says that we are to be rooted in this love that we may be able to comprehend *"with all saints"* all of God's fullness. And of course, God's fullness is the glory! God intends to pour His love over the entire body as we gain comprehension as to what the fullness of this force actually represents. Until we discover that the love of God consists of more than performing a series of good deeds but is instead the most powerful force in the universe, we will continue to attempt to produce revival out of mere human efforts. This love poured out upon the united church will act to bond us together, manifest His glory, and bring in the harvest.

Now look at Ephesians 4:

> *Eph 4:11-12 – "And he gave some, apostles; and some, prophets; and some, evangelists; and some, pastors and teachers; For the perfecting of the saints, for the work of the ministry, for the edifying of the body of Christ: Till we all come in the **unity of the faith**, and of the knowledge of the Son of God, unto a perfect man, unto the measure of the stature of the fullness of Christ:"*

Here it is clear that the five-fold ministry given to the church is assigned to produce perfection among the members. It is also clear from this that perfection in God's eyes goes far beyond merely living a sin-free life. Perfection to Him is evidenced by unity within His body. Sinners cannot genuinely unite so God indeed wants us to experience full deliverance from carnality. However, He as well wants us to step into supernatural love to produce ultimate unity within His bride. Therefore it becomes crucial that the five-fold ministry teach the process of manifesting the anointing of love.

For years, we've had movements launched among Christians attempting to create the unity of the faith through semi-political efforts. Leaders have stood up and encouraged churches to set aside their differences and just get along. They will say *"Let's not discuss the things that we don't agree upon."* or *"Let's agree to disagree, get together, and we'll all fill a stadium."* However, such efforts demand that we set aside the very tools that produce the genuine unifying power of love.

Paul said to *"be not unequally yoked."* We cannot unite with someone who does not believe in the power of God. Will a prophet be able to unite with someone who doesn't believe in prophets? Should he stifle his gift to prevent offending the spiritually stagnated? Assuming that God has filled your life with the Holy Ghost and you pray in a supernatural prayer language, are you going to unite with someone who believes that speaking in tongues is of the devil? Compromise can never produce true church unity. The unity of the body of Christ can only be the result of people walking in the love of God. As we read further:

> *Eph 4:14 –"That we henceforth be no more children, tossed to and fro, and carried about with every wind of doctrine, by the sleight of men, and cunning craftiness, whereby they lie in wait to deceive;"*

Here he says that we shouldn't be tossed around which includes not being removed from our God-assigned position. Love so cements us in proper place that no demon in hell can move us. Continuing in this passage:

> *Eph 4:15 –"But speaking the truth in love, may grow up into him in all things, which is the head, even Christ:"*

"Speaking the truth" is one word in the Greek which means *actually living*. Until we actually begin to walk in the love of God, to some level, we are still babes in Christ. In fact, when the Corinthian church was squabbling over various topics, Paul declared they were not yet ready to receive the meat of the Word -

but milk only. Walking in love will provide evidence that we are growing up in Jesus and also bear witness of His true headship over our lives. On to the next verse:

> *Eph 4:16 –"From whom the whole body **fitly joined together** and compacted by that which every joint supplieth, according to the effectual working in the measure of every part, maketh increase of the body unto **the edifying of itself in love**."*

Let's break that down in case you didn't grasp all of that on the first reading. The *"whole body"* represents the *united* church, who as lively stones are *"fitly joined together"* by the mortar of agape. That they are *"fitly joined together"* means that they are maintaining more than minimal contact with one another. They are operating as a well-trained, spiritually fit, sold out unit.

The phrase *"compacted by that which every joint supplieth"* lets us know that God is going to fuse us together as each of us brings our God-given giftings and anointing to the table. There are gifts, wisdom, and resources that God has uniquely given to each of us in a fashion that He hasn't given to anyone else. And as we release our gifts into the body of Christ, it will literally lock us together more securely.

And the final phrase of this verse: *"Maketh increase of the body unto the edifying of itself in love..."* - declares that as we're walking in love, the body will experience increase. We will see growth in our churches take place; first spiritually and then numerically. Again, we see that love is the key component to bring forth God's last-day harvest plans!

Isaiah 60 contains a prophetic declaration of what I believe God is doing in the last-days:

> *Isa 60:1-3 –"Arise, shine; for thy light is come, and the glory of the LORD is risen upon thee. For, behold, **the darkness shall cover the earth, and gross darkness the people**: but the LORD shall arise upon thee, and **his glory shall be seen upon thee**. And the Gentiles shall come to thy light, and kings to the brightness of thy rising"*

Here Isaiah prophecied of a time when the multitudes are going to witness the glory of God upon us. And as we are even now experiencing, it will be a time of gross darkness upon the earth. This extreme darkness is going to allow us to shine even brighter. In these end-times, a separation is taking place between those aligned with the forces of truth versus those of darkness. The darkness is getting darker and the truth is becoming brighter! Get ready to shine because it's all a part of God's last-day move. And as Isaiah decreed, God is going to use this glory to bring the peoples and nations to the church. Keeping in mind that the glory is composed of tangible love, we see that again love is going to act as His evangelistic anointing. And those of His revivalist body will become the initial catalysts of it. Hallelujah!

Let's look now at Isaiah 62:

> *Isa 62:1-7 "For Zion's sake* [Zion represents the church] *will I not hold my peace, and for Jerusalem's sake I will not rest, until the **righteousness thereof go forth as brightness**, and the salvation thereof as a lamp that burneth. And the **Gentiles shall see thy righteousness**, and **all kings thy glory**: and thou shalt be called by a new name, which the mouth of the LORD shall name. Thou shalt also **be a crown of glory in the hand of the LORD**, and a royal diadem in the hand of thy God. Thou shalt no more be termed Forsaken; neither shall thy land any more be termed Desolate: but thou shalt be called Hephzibah, and thy land Beulah: for the LORD delighteth in thee, and thy land shall be married. For as a young man marrieth a virgin, so shall thy sons marry thee: **and as the bridegroom rejoiceth over the bride, so shall thy God rejoice over thee**. I have set watchmen* [intercessors] *upon thy walls, O Jerusalem, which shall never hold their peace day nor night: ye that make mention of the LORD, keep not silence, And give him no rest, till he establish, and till he make Jerusalem a praise in the earth."*

Without taking time to teach in detail this entire passage, notice a few of the key attributes of this prophecy. These verses tie together **righteousness, the glory, God's bride, and the harvest**. Since *"righteousness"* is *our reborn inner nature of love* and the *"glory"* is *fully manifested love*, we then know that love is going to be the primary attribute of the Bride of Christ and this love will act as His harvest magnet.

Of course, intercession is mentioned as well. Without intercessory prayer blazing the trail we will not step into this end-time love. God is raising up His last-days prayer warriors.

Do you see the opportunity God has placed at our feet? Are we going to let some little demon-ette ruffle our feathers and take us into strife or get us to abandon our God assigned posts? I don't think so!

CHAPTER 7

COVENANT LOVE

THE DIFFICULTY OF ACTING IN LOVE

To access the anointing of love in our lives will involve some level of work. We live in America - a society that expects instantaneous results. Everyone wants everything done right now. We want to press a button and receive exactly what we desire immediately. Walking in full time love will not be developed quite so quickly.

The love of God requires radical alterations in our lives - alterations both in the way that we speak and act. We have found that the love of God is an anointing that is able to eradicate strife and offense from our lives. It's able to adhere relationships together in an unbreakable fashion. It's able to draw the harvest to us. Love manifests as the most powerful of anointings and it is going to usher in the end-time glory of God. To manifest this love is going to require us to walk more and more in obedience to God and more and more in the actions of a giver - as a sower and a servant. And that's often difficult to do.

Remembering from First Timothy 1, God's *Recipe for Agape*:

> *1Tim 1:5 - "Now the end of the commandment is charity [agape love] out of a pure heart, and of a good conscience, and of faith unfeigned."*

We have discussed that if we want to manifest the love of God, we first must be born-again. Second, we have to renew our souls to develop the *mind of Christ*. And third, by faith, we must forcefully display *actions of love*. And again, I have found that it takes more faith to manifest love than any other of the promises of God.

Let's briefly touch again on the subject of *faith actions* necessary to manifest the promises of God. If we're experiencing pain in our body and are going to exercise our faith for healing, we will need to speak to the afflicted area and take some actions in opposition to the pain.

The same applies if we are going to manifest prosperity. Our finances may scream at us that we cannot afford to tithe or to give. However, we will have to push through those critical voices by continuing or even increasing our giving. Through these actions of faith, we access our breakthroughs at times via even radical seed.

When we deal with the challenge of a broken relationship, we will have to deal with that trial in a similar manner. We will have to fight through the pain of rejection and determine to be a blessing to that person regardless.

When we're sick, we want to become healed. When broke, we definitely want to see financial breakthrough. However, at times there are damaged relationships that we may not want to see restored. Often, a strained relationship has involved critical words spoken to one another and we may not feel as if we want it put back together! At least that is how we may feel momentarily. If we're going to be people who walk in love, then we'll be required to become a repairer of breeches whether we feel like it or not. We will have to confront feelings of animosity and take steps of faith to bring love to injured relationships in order to restore what satan has damaged. The devil has targeted the unity of the body of Christ and love is the only power that can reverse his efforts.

At this point, we are going to discuss a key aspect of being able to walk in the love of God on a consistent basis. As end-time revivalists, we need to target walking in love full-time. When the Bible speaks of us walking in perfection, it's referring to us manifesting the fullness of the image of Christ - God's love '24-7'.

When referring to this level of love, we're speaking of walking above oppression, walking above discouragement, walking above temper tantrums and fits of carnality around the clock. Normally, it is not unusual for there to exist certain personalities that clash.

There are likely to be some people that just tend to rub us the wrong way. How is God going to unite together all of these diverse personalities as one in the body of Christ? He's going to do it with the mortar of the love of God. He's going to encapsulate believers in these last-days with so much of this love that literally no personality or personal interaction will be able to set us off. Nobody will be able to get under our skin. Nobody will be able to rent space in our head. We will become *unoffendable*. God is bringing in His anointing of love such that He may unite us unto the manifestation of His glory.

The enemy knows the danger posed by the church in unity. He knows the power of a marriage where the couple truly act as one. So what does he attack above anything else? He tries to attack a Christian's marriage or a revivalist's commitment to the church. He tries to bring division, strife, and offense to erect walls of division so that no true, united prayer can take place. His ultimate goal is to keep love out our marriages, and most importantly out of the church.

DEFINING COVENANT

The enemy is on the attack against the Body of Christ and we have got to know how to resist the devil to cause him to flee. As we are about to see, the number one area of attack brought by the enemy against our lives is in our *covenants*.

A covenant is an agreement between two people or among a group of people that defines how they are going to interact within a committed relationship. It's an agreement to act as a unit; to operate as one. In the marriage covenant, the Word lets us know that *the two become one flesh*. Two separate people unite as one and advance forward in life together versus individually. This covenant of marriage forms potentially the strongest platform for the *prayer of agreement* that is available in the earth.

It is vital that Christians recognize and understand that through receiving Jesus as Lord, we have come into a covenant with Him. The title *New Testament* means *New Covenant*. And although most church goers may have little problem recognizing that they are in a covenant with God, many may balk at the concept of being in covenant with one another. However, that is exactly the truth.

As a simplified definition, I often describe *covenant* as *a contract with regard to relationship.* The scope of this book does not permit that we go into an in-depth teaching on covenant - that is planned for a future book. However, we need to touch on some of the basics of what covenant truly represents in the eyes of God. You see, back in ancient days, they didn't have the legal systems that we have today. They lacked organized law enforcement bodies and civil courts. And if an agreement was made with someone, there was no entity established to uphold that agreement should the other individual choose to not uphold his end. Man needed a method or system whereby they could be assured that agreements would stand - and God gave us *covenants*.

A covenant acts as the strongest form of commitment into which men can enter. It is a blood sworn oath that declares that we pledge our lives to uphold our part of the declared agreement. In Bible days, to break covenant placed one's life on the line - for the offended party was often bound by covenant to take it. Even the most despicable of men recognized that covenant represented an unbreakable pledge. And God, when He wanted to assure His promise to Abram to make Him the *"father of nations,"* did so by covenant. God has so elevated the concept of covenant that in Romans, *covenant-breaking* is placed in the same category with fornication, murder, and hating God.

Recognize that covenant is more than a casual word spoken or even an earnest promise to fulfill a task. Covenant represents the highest form of oath that can be taken. When God made covenant with us, He swore by His own name. Covenants normally required careful preparation and serious evaluation to enter. Many steps were taken to honor the process of *cutting* a covenant. Our best, passed-down example of establishing a covenant is found in our marriage ceremonies.

Aspects of our modern day marriage ceremony have been passed down for thousands of years. And as with a marriage, a covenant is often initiated through a ceremony. If made between a group of people, leaders would stand in representation of both parties. Covenant vows would be deliberately and precisely spoken. Gifts would be exchanged and a meal shared. Usually blood would be shed as a witness to the precious value of the covenant and as a warning to whosoever might consider breaking the agreement. And, some type of permanent sign would be established as an indicator of the covenant. Before our modern age of disposable rings, during marriage ceremonies of the past the joined couple might have had incisions actually cut into their flesh. The involved person would often have a circle cut into their thumb or finger and then have soot or some other type of dye rubbed into the wound. This process created a permanent tattooed ring in the hand to state that they had come into an enduring oath. All of these ceremonial steps pointed to the sacredness of the covenant.

Unlike many other nations that have perpetuated the foundational truths of covenant, America has not. We have replaced covenant agreements with contracts containing *small print* and may often hire attorneys to find ways to break them. As children we learned that our promises were meaningless by invoking statements like: *"I had my fingers crossed"* and *"We didn't shake on it."* To truly grasp the full impact of covenant requires retraining and experience in application. A person does not truly discover whether they are really covenant-minded until hundreds of demons are jumping on their head telling them to sever a committed relationship. As with love, to hold to covenant will require all of the faith that we possess.

THE CHURCH COVENANT

And so, the body of Christ is assigned by God to be bound together through covenant. God's purpose from the beginning has always been to produce a united people - united with Him and with one another. The Old Testament was God's effort to demonstrate to man that he could not be united by law. The New Testament, replacing the Old, allows us through the cross to accomplish His original plan. Through the born-again experience and subsequently learning to walk in love, the people of God can finally fulfill His assignment to become 'one'.

When Jesus was questioned of what was the *greatest commandment*, He responded by quoting from the Ten Commandments:

> *Mat 22:37 – "Jesus said unto him,* **Thou shall love the Lord thy God** *with all thy heart, and with all thy soul, and with all thy mind."*

The Ten Commandments representing the Law, validate without doubt that the number one target of our love and dedication must be God! However, He did not stop there. Without even being requested, Jesus found it necessary to declare to us a *second commandment*.

> *Mat 22:38-40 – "This is the first and great commandment. And the second is like unto it,* **Thou shalt love thy neighbor as thyself.** *On these two commandments hang all the law and the prophets."*

Jesus here lets us know that God's commandments include the directive for us to love one another. However, if we examine the Ten Commandments in the Old Testament we find that there is no such specific commandment listed. Did Jesus just change the Word? Of course He didn't! He merely summed up the remaining commandments of God in one statement - *we are to love one another as we love ourselves.* If we look at the Ten Commandments closely, we find that many of them involve how we treat other people. Thou shalt not steal, kill, covet, or cheat all deal with actions that produce division among peoples. It is clear here that God's commandments were not just designed to produce unity with Him but also with one another.

As spelled out in the New Testament, love fulfills all of the intentions of the Old. The writer of Hebrews brings out further the need to replace the Law with a better covenant:

> *Heb 8:6-10 – "But now hath he obtained a more excellent ministry,* **by how much more also is he the mediator of a better covenant**, *which was established upon better promises. For if that first covenant had been faultless, then*

> *should no place have been sought for the second. For finding fault with them, he saith, Behold, the days come, saith the Lord, when I will make a new covenant with the house of Israel and with the house of Judah: Not according to the covenant that I made with their fathers in the day when I took them by the hand to lead them out of the land of Egypt; because they continued not in my covenant, and I regarded them not, saith the Lord. For this is the covenant that I will make with the house of Israel after those days, saith the Lord;* **I will put my laws into their mind, and write them in their hearts: and I will be to them a God, and they shall be to me a people.***"*

This passage shows us that The Cross has been provided to enable us to enter into a new covenant. And this covenant is designed to permit us to walk in supernatural love, enabling us to truly become the people of God.

When we became saved, we were assigned to become part of the church whether we knew so or not. As Christians, God intends for us to become intertwined in the activities of the church - to become united as active members.

Our highest level of covenant is with God. Our second highest level of covenant is in our marriages. After that, we are bound by covenant as members of the church. And, it is vital that we learn to operate by covenant within His church.

We found out earlier, that unless we're born again we cannot operate in *agape* love. As well, unless we're bonded to an assigned church we will be highly limited in how much love we can actually manifest. Much of the book of Jude warns of those who despise dominion - those who would resist God's covenant operations within the church. God declares:

> *Jude 1:12-13 -"These are spots in your feasts of charity, when they feast with you, feeding themselves without fear: clouds they are without water, carried about of winds;* **trees whose fruit withereth, without fruit,** *twice dead,* **plucked up by the roots***... Raging waves of the sea, foaming out*

their own shame; wandering stars, to whom is reserved the blackness of darkness for ever."

Such people cannot manifest genuine, supernatural love because they are dried up. They are disconnected from the vine, not being branched to the Body of Christ. God has ordained that His people unite in covenant as the church. Membership and involvement have never been meant to be optional for Christians. Through covenant, we are to be fused to the Body of Christ - mortared into it by love. God's glory is going to come through the church via individual people that will allow themselves to be engrafted to its God-given vision.

God is bringing the glory of God to the earth and he is even now assigning church bodies to manifest that glory in their regions. The only way that we will be an active part of this climactic event is to be involved in a church body that is actually pressing into God's last-day move.

We will not be able to walk in the love of God unless we're connected to His revivalist church; unless we discover just what The Church has really been assigned to accomplish. God wants us to recognize that church activities today are not something to be taken casually. It is an agreement - a bond that we enter into when we become born again that literally is to become the focal point of our lives. Our covenant of the New Testament becomes the guidebook for what is acceptable in our lives. And our top commandments are to love both God and one another.

In the marriage covenant, vows are pronounced of the couple's commitment to each other. The promises *"to have and to hold, rich or poor, in sickness or in health, forsaking all others till death do us part"* all become committed responsibilities that each are to uphold for life. Much of the New Testament becomes our instructions of how we are to interrelate in the *church body covenant* for the rest of our lives. We must locate the church God desires for us to attend and then bond to, endeavoring to follow all of the guidelines of the New Testament.

After all, the church is a whole lot more than just a place God wants us to go on Sunday - as if it were our duty to appease Him by putting in an hour of our time. Church is supposed to be an integral part of our lives. I don't want to throw anybody off on this, but a person who really gains understanding of the priority God places upon the church will rearrange his entire life to connect to the right one. For that person, church becomes more important than where they want to live and may even influence the occupation which they may follow. Many people's jobs are actually interfering with what God would have them do in church, taking away time that He would rather have invested in direct service to Him.

The enemy is doing everything that he can to hold back the revelation of covenant from the people of God. He wants to prevent them from discovering what church is actually to be about and literally sever them from their God-assigned coworkers. The devil hates covenant. He was marked as the ultimate covenant-breaker in his fall from heaven. Why do you think that so many Christian marriages end up in divorce? Even revivalist marriages often end up being divided because the enemy is determined to destroy anything that might resemble unity. Satan knows that covenant unity is a key to release the power and the love of God into the lives of believers.

The enemy is aware that if Christians ever gain full understanding of walking in covenant then he's done for. We are to come into a relationship with our churches that he cannot split - one that's going to usher in God's glory and bring forth His harvest.

THE COMMITMENT OF COVENANT

Let's examine a little further how covenant understanding keeps us in position. In previous discussions regarding the soul of man, we have discovered the true purpose of our emotions. They have not been given to us to force us into decisions based on how we feel. **Emotions exist to enable us to detect and flourish in the presence of God.** They have a dual purpose - to alert us to the presence of God and also of demonic activity. Our emotions will pick up feelings of strife, anger, fear, and the presence of any other demonically induced atmospheres. Through practice, we can utilize our system of emotions to 'feel' who is attempting to pay us a visit. The mature Christian then takes aggressive steps to drive those spirits from their midst.

However, the enemy is an expert at tampering with a person's thoughts and emotions. He will tell them that they are not liked in the church and then couple those thoughts with extreme feelings of rejection. If not confronted, those thought and emotional assaults will work to drive them from the church where God has positioned them.

A person who makes decisions based on what they are thinking or feeling at any moment becomes unstable in their commitments. They may feel like being married one day and not the next.

Covenant represents a commitment sworn; not a temporal decision made. Once a covenant is established, it is meant to deliver our souls from the demonically influenced thoughts and feelings designed to uproot us. If we truly comprehend covenant, then how we feel and the thoughts being sent against us become irrelevant regarding our church or even marital commitment. Covenant declares: *"No matter how I feel, no matter what I'm thinking, nothing will change my faithfulness to this relationship."* Once this revelation is established within us, the number one tool the enemy possesses to remove us from our calling has now been neutralized. And the devil discontinues using weaponry against us that does not produce his desired results. Covenant knowledge and commitment once applied, will halt many of the mental assaults that revivalists repeatedly experience.

Let's look at the initial verse from Job 31:

> *Job 31:1 –"I made a covenant with mine eyes; why then should I think upon a maid"*

Job declared that covenant boundaries had been established limiting what was allowable for him to think. Regarding marriage, covenant establishes limits of what we should meditate upon. The covenant that I entered into with my wife makes clear that she's the only one I'm allowed to do certain things with. But covenant also sets limits to what is permissible thought for me. It is outside of my covenant boundaries for me to ponder being with other women.

It is not allowable for me to think about divorce. It is not profitable for me to think that she is not treating me right. Covenant literally rules out a whole realm of thought that our minds might be tempted to delve into based on emotional whim. The reason that placing boundaries on our thoughts becomes so important is because our minds become the *conception areas* for our actions. Meditations outside of our established covenants will in the long run, potentially give way to sin and possible breakdown in those relationships.

In a healthy marriage partnership where both spouses understand covenant, they reject any thinking that might produce division in the relationship. There are days in any marriage that we will be so infatuated with our spouse that we'll think that they are an angel sent from heaven. But, there may be other days when the enemy may stir us to think that our marriage was a huge error. However if we understand covenant, we will treat our spouse the same every day regardless of how we feel. And if we have been married for very long, we discover that the feelings of infatuation always return. **Covenant keeps us in our committed relationships between the dry spells regardless of how we momentarily *feel*.**

Now that we understand that the Church is a covenant body, membership therein also establishes boundaries of thought for our lives. If we often decide not to go to church because we don't *feel* like it, our understanding of the covenant that God has brought us into is limited. Meditating that we believe that the preacher is after our money is outside the boundaries of allowable thought within that covenant. Roasted pastor for Sunday lunch can no longer be an acceptable meal. We literally must put boundaries around what we permit ourselves to think and ignore any fickle feelings that may arise. Any areas of thought that create distrust or allow us to invite rejection or offense become traps that will hinder our ability to walk in love.

And because we refuse to let our thoughts drift out of bounds, and because our feelings can no longer be used to control us, the enemy no longer has any buttons to push in our lives to destroy our relationships.

Regarding stepping into supernatural love, the importance of learning to become a covenant individual cannot be overlooked. The third ingredient to our *Recipe for Love* was *faith* and as discussed, faith requires action. A covenant person will always respond in actions of love regardless of how he feels at the moment. By honoring our covenants including that with the church, we automatically produce the actions necessary to be positioned for love to manifest in our lives.

Understand however, that possessing covenant knowledge is not enough for us to step into genuine love. Manifestation of love requires that we apply all of the steps of faith we learned in chapter four. Many people have gone through life with the understanding that marriage is to be for life. However, they may merely cohabit for decades with no real love for one another. They just know that neither one of them is willing to get a divorce. How sad to have a relationship based merely on a covenant yet without love. Eventually the partnership is going to grow old, dry up, and have no benefit therein.

If we like many try to establish a marriage based on physical attraction alone, that source of bonding may not be adequate over the long term. There will be disagreements that arise and words will be spoken. Our emotions may be hammered incessantly. If we attempt to establish a bond based on the physical versus upon covenant commitment, the marriage could be short-lived.

Even a marriage birthed out of a deep love for one another will possibly fail if both partners don't learn covenant to some level. Marital love levels, both natural and supernatural are subject to fluctuate until God's glory manifests and we are able to carry love continually. Any marriage operating without covenant knowledge is destined to fail when love levels reach a low enough point.

So what has the enemy been able to do? He has been able to find people in the body who don't understand how to maintain covenant. Through launching divisive attacks against their thoughts, satan has been able to isolate people from the body of Christ. This is especially true of churches in revival. The enemy targets churches full of people who are seeking hard after God. There are demonic assaults that we may never experience until we become involved in an on-fire church, for in prior times the devil never viewed us as much of a threat. But now he views stopping us as his number one priority.

So, what is he going to do? He's going to bring attacks against you that he isn't going to bring against the average Christian. However if we learn how to operate in covenant, we will remain in our assigned positions regardless of the opposition that we experience. The man of faith knows that if he won't quit, he will see breakthrough and subsequent spiritual promotion.

Covenant actions become the *stand-in* actions of love that we take until the true love of God manifests. For example, in our marriages we may not always be thrilled with each other's performance. There are days when one spouse may be having a bad day or perhaps we wake up with an *attitude*. Then without really thinking, we say something to our spouse with the wrong tone. Maybe we just didn't get enough sleep or we've been fasting and we inadvertently grumble something with an *edge* to it. Sometimes we may even say the perfect thing and yet it is misinterpreted. Regardless, our spouse may possibly take it the wrong way. Unless someone learns very quickly to disregard how they feel and act as a peacemaker, a fight is about to erupt.

My wife and I have gotten to the point that when we see the other becoming irritated, we take steps to guard our hearts against any offense that would normally try to arise. We recognize that if something is said in a harsh manner, it does not represent the true heart of our mate but is an attack inspired of the enemy. When we see the devil *on the other's head*, we forcibly act to bring love to the situation.

When the love of God is on our lives, we love everybody automatically - even that person that we didn't care for previously. When the love of God comes in, we automatically act in covenant. Through the influence of love, blessing others becomes automatic. However, there are times when that anointing fluctuates because we have not learned to manifest it consistently. We must learn to operate in covenant - as if we felt perfect towards others at all times. By doing so, we take actions necessary to release love back onto the scene. The more that we get a hold of this, the more the love of God can manifest in our relationships and keep strife and offense out. *Covenant understanding* becomes a key revelation that will provide a platform for this anointing to reside upon our lives full-time. The more we uphold our covenants, the more consistent our love level remains.

As the church, we are commanded to be a united people. God never meant for there to be divisions, cliques, or factions. God declares that we should not be involved in gossip, jealousy, hatred, murder, strife or sedition - all of which represent covenant breaking actions. Covenant breaking is listed as one of the major sins within the church! We found out in the previous chapter that we are to become a body without division, a body without schism.

Because we are to become a unified body, it becomes vital that a pastor teaches his congregation on covenant. Paul spoke in Acts chapter 20 of *"grievous wolves"* entering the church who would not spare the flock. The primary way that wolves operate is by attempting to spread rumors that produce doubt, distrust, and dissension. Unchecked, church hopping wolves can wreak havoc within a congregation. Unless a church is very small, it becomes impossible for a pastor to quickly recognize and extinguish all of the fires that the invader may ignite. However, a church that has learned covenant becomes self-monitoring for wolf activity. They will be ever alert to critical words spoken toward anyone in the body (especially the leadership) and shut down such illicit conversations.

In my church, we have a saying that we have learned to use to shut down rumors and criticism. We express to the potential wolf: *"My ears are not a garbage dump and critical words are not permitted here."* Many a potential pretender has departed our church in disappointment, not being able to produce the division that he sought.

Until we realize that as Christians we are called to be engrafted to the Body of Christ through covenant, then the devil will continue to attempt to seduce us into a loose affiliation with the Church. Our church commitment will oscillate dependent upon how much or little the devil is attacking our feelings and thoughts at the time. There are seasons when the enemy may attack our minds with such a flood of negativity and failure that all we can do is to begin praising God to drown it out. However once we learn to stay in covenant, act in covenant, and think in covenant, it deactivates this weaponry. Rather than pull back from church amidst demonic onslaught, we will instead take active steps to become more involved in actions of faith regarding church unity.

As we covered earlier, the importance of remaining united with the Church lies in what Jesus declared in John 17:

> *John 17:21-23 –"**That they all may be one**; as thou, Father, art in me, and I in thee, that they also may be one in us; that the world may believe that thou hast sent me. **And the glory which thou gavest me I have given them; that they may be one, even as we are one**: I in them, and thou in me, that they may be made perfect in one; and that the world may know that thou hast sent me**, and hast loved them, as thou hast loved me.***"

God has intertwined our commitment to be united to His church with our capacity to manifest His glory. And God has given us covenant to enable us to be firmly established within our assigned church, and thus produce more consistency in our love walk.

So, as we operate in covenant it aids to release love, and as we act in love it enhances our covenant bonds. This interaction becomes what I call the ***Covenant-Love Cycle.*** As we act as a covenant person, love will enter in and our covenant commitment will become automatic. The result is that our relationships become even stronger. And because the strength of our relationships rise to new levels, the love and subsequent glory we produce soars as well. This produces a cycle of self-edifying love and covenant unity that takes us from *"glory to glory."*

THE RULES OF COVENANT

I have been ministering for years of *four basic rules of covenant keeping.* If we will apply these four guidelines to our lives, it will go a long way to maintaining unity within our church bodies. And as such, it will aid us in manifesting the love and glory of God. These rules are as follows:

Rule 1 of Covenant Keeping: *A covenant Christian refuses to criticize, critique or condemn anyone else within the body of Christ.* Critical words sow discord among the brethren. Gossip, backbiting, judgmental and hateful words all represent a lack of understanding of covenant. Such display, even if spoken in perceived confidence act as a cancer within the body of Christ. Paul warned of this in Galatians 5:

> *Gal 5:14-15 – "For all the law is fulfilled in one word, even in this; Thou shalt love thy neighbor as thyself.* ***But, if ye bite and devour one another, take heed that ye be not consumed one of another.****"*

As stated in the outset of this book, critical words within the church produce *Christian cannibalism*!

When we recite or repeat criticism to someone else we may think that it is never going to get out - but it will somehow. The devil is going to make sure that those critiqued discover what we've voiced. So when we begin criticizing others, we release potential division into the body of Christ. And even if no one else heard it, God did.

Criticism, gossip, speaking against the pastor, murmuring against church leaders, and judgmental speech toward anyone in the church all act to limit the operation of the love of God. We are to be a covenant body and we are not permitted to demean our brethren. The revivalist must literally separate himself from critical thought and speech.

A person who understands covenant rule #1, will not only refuse to utter criticism but also will not listen to it. They will not entertain it in their thoughts and they will not listen to it from other people. Such speech will be extinguished immediately by the covenant understanding party. Know also, that gossip may subtly take many forms. Someone may come to you and say: *"We need to pray for this sister because I discern she is filled with lust, covetousness, etc."* Don't fall for such traps. If God revealed this to them, they should pray themselves without making it a public issue.

Have you been made clean by the blood of Jesus? The Bible says that when we judge our brother or sister, we are judging His blood as an unholy thing. Through critical attitudes and words, we declare that we believe that the Blood of Christ is able to cleanse us but not selected others. Do you understand the seriousness of this? Critical words potentially impact the protective covering over a Christian's life.

For a true revivalist church, God establishes a prayer canopy of protection over the members' lives. This umbrella of protection delivers the congregation from many of the temptations and trials that the enemy would bring against them. Again, covenant plays a major role in the functioning of this covering.

In a marriage where God views the couple as one, the primary person that God will assign the husband or wife to pray for will be their spouse. Regarding the church, wherever a covenant body has been established God also views them to some level as one. Because God recognizes and honors covenant, the Holy Spirit will lead intercessors to pray for those in their church bodies in times of challenge. Because He views individual church bodies as one entity, He will assure that people within that church group pray for one another. These intertwined intercessory prayers form a *canopy of covering* over the church. Those who truly come into covenant with that church activate this prayer shield over their lives and families.

And criticism cuts a rift in this canopy giving access to demonic infiltration. Did you know that when we criticize someone it acts as a curse? When we speak negatively against someone, we are cursing - we are decreeing condemnation into that person's life. The authority that we have been given for good is potentially being used to authorize demonic interference instead. A person in covenant will refuse even to see the flaws of those in his church.

We all automatically make judgments about the people that we encounter. Are they rich or poor? Are they clean or dirty? And God wants all of our judgments to be good! He wants us to begin viewing people as righteous. And even when we see people doing something wrong, in most cases unless it's serious we should just let it go and let Him deal with it. Too many believe that they have been made *watchmen* of the church when in fact they are usually critical-minded and potentially full of venom. If we could just cease all of the criticism and gossip in the church, it would literally shut down a great portion of the demonic activity taking place in the body of Christ.

Rule 2 of Covenant Keeping: *A covenant Christian refuses to be offended.* A covenant Christian literally shuts down his or her ability to be offended. They develop in spiritual maturity to the point that literally nothing can upset them. We see this in the Psalms:

> *Psa 119:165 – "Great peace have they which love thy law: and nothing shall offend them."*

Christians full of the Word become unoffendable! If we separate the word *offended* into its component words, it becomes *off-ended*. To be offended doesn't only indicate that we are upset with other people, it also relates that we are no longer standing in an upright position ourselves. Once we are off-balance, other forms of disappointment may cause us to become even further out of sorts. Such elevated offense usually results in some form of ungodly actions potentially creating more problems and potential division.

Rule #2 literally becomes a partial fail-safe for Rule #1. If everyone in the Body of Christ learned Rule #2, then no matter who else violated Rule #1, no one would take it personally. Of course we would still have to deal with the curse issues.

Jesus had multitudes and their leaders repeatedly rise up against Him. The Cross wasn't the only time they persecuted or even tried to kill Him. They mocked Him, rejected Him, and even tried to throw Him off of a cliff! And at the Cross, He experienced the most torturous form of execution ever devised by man. But understand, He never went off into tirades. He didn't cry out: *"Father, just strike them dead."* Nor did He crawl off into a corner to have a *pity party*. Yet at times, we find ourselves saying, thinking, or doing those very things over minor issues. If someone cuts us off in traffic, our reaction may be to condemn them to Hell's eternal flames!

Pastors and other church leaders must frequently make decisions that may affect people's lives. Church members are looking to them for direction, for wisdom, and for comfort. And hopefully only occasionally, leaders are going to make mistakes. I myself have erred a few times in pastoring. I have given incorrect counsel. I have attempted to bring correction to innocent parties. I have found it necessary to apologize and ask forgiveness for errors made to the affected persons. My deepest desire is that when these mistakes are made, no lasting harm is done. My prayer is that we can all proceed forward into the glory without any lasting effect or negative consequences.

I as well, have been corrected by leadership when I was right. And when I would take the situations to God He would always say: *"Don't worry about it, just love them and refuse offense!"* At times, members allow themselves to be removed from their church over even small issues. However, God is often not as much concerned with who is right in a situation as He is with us being unoffendable and immovable

And so, it is mandatory that we refuse to be offended whenever we are criticized, accused, disappointed, or even corrected. We eventually are going to be let down by other people. Someone is going to make us a promise and fall short of it. Others are going to give way to offense themselves and direct their frustration toward us. They may even do something that impacts us financially. But if we refuse offense in the situations, no permanent damage will be wrought to church unity. We must refuse to take any type of criticism personally but must instead use such events as an opportunity to enter our prayer closets and turn the care over to God.

As we go through these types of situations with their accompanying emotional onslaughts and refuse to take offense, our love level potentially increases. Every time that we successfully overcome an attack, we stand to increase in our anointing. It's a Biblical principle. Psalm 18 promises us that we will be promoted when we come through an attack properly by trusting in God.

Through successful spiritual warfare our anointing increases.

> *Psa 18:18-20 –"They prevented me in the day of my calamity: but the LORD was my stay.* **He brought me forth also into a large place**; *he delivered me, because he delighted in me. The LORD rewarded me according to my righteousness; according to the cleanness of my hands hath he recompensed me."*

When we go through an opposing wall rather than repeatedly bounce off of it, our anointing will be enhanced. However, the obstacle that we do not overcome will rise to stand against us again. The battle that we don't win, we will have to fight again. But, the confrontations in which we are victorious promote us such that the next time we face a similar situation, we go through it with much less difficulty. The authority and anointing that we access elevates us above those levels of attack. Thus the enemy loses one more weapon he has used against our lives and calling.

Potential offense is the predominant challenge that we will face as revivalist Christians. We've got to get to the place emotionally where no one is able to rent space in our heads regardless of what they do against us. And when we do that, we are well on our way to walking in the power of God's love.

Rule 3 of Covenant Keeping: *A covenant Christian develops an attitude of service toward everyone in the body of Christ.* We must learn to look for opportunities to be a blessing to others without concern for how they may reward us in return. We must seek for opportunities to serve and bless because this becomes the fulfillment of our new divine nature. Whom can we help? Whom may we bless? For whom can we supply? For whom might we pray? This becomes the attitude of the covenant Christians who understand - if we will supply the needs of the Body of Christ then God will meet our needs in the fulfillment of His covenant to us. Remember, giving releases the love of God in our lives and servitude is a form of giving.

We have numerous verses that we can go to that reinforce the concept of servitude. In the attempt to produce a servant mentality within them, Jesus washed the disciples' feet and instructed them to do likewise. The disciples argued about which of them would be the most honored in Heaven, and Jesus informed them that they had it all backwards! He responded: *"And whosoever will be chief among you, let him be your servant."* This spells out clearly a summarization of Covenant Principle #3.

If we are going to fulfill our high calling, it is going to be because we have applied ourselves to walk in the highest levels of love. And this will be attained because we have become servants to all. We may no longer be limited by fear or by concern over guarding our social status. We can no longer believe that we are above a certain level of job. Nothing is beneath us anymore; but now through love, nothing is above us any longer as well!

As a side note: We have to be able to hear God specifically in whom we are to bless at any point in time. There will be times that we may be instructed of God not to come to someone's aid. It is not uncommon for *spiritual leeches* to enter the church. These parasites do not want to develop faith and love for themselves but instead attempt to drain our supply. In the parable of the ten virgins, five were wise and five were foolish. Paraphrasing, the five foolish said: *"Give us of your oil."* And the five wise responded: *"No, or we will deplete our own supply needed for our current assigned task."* There was an opportunity to serve, but it wasn't God's assigned role for them at that point. We've got to hear God regarding who we are to bless at any given time. God has called us to serve but not to cripple the slothful through enablement!

Rule 4 of Covenant Keeping: *A covenant Christian remains in touch with and obeys the Holy Spirit in all of their actions.* I told you this wasn't always easy. When we begin speaking of covenant laws or rules, a danger arises when people attempt to follow them legalistically. Rule 4 of Covenant Keeping states that we can't convert the first three rules to a law. The covenant rules are intended to be used as guidelines and not as laws.

There will be times that we will need to be discerning enough to identify and point out wolves in our midst. If we make Rule #1 a law, then we may be apt to confuse our wisdom with criticism. Although it is never appropriate to harbor offense, Rule #2 does not demand that we entrust ourselves to those who have proven themselves unworthy. And as we have already mentioned, Rule #3 does not require that we become caretakers for the slothful.

If we're going to walk in the love of God, we're going to have to let the Holy Spirit have free access and full authority over our lives. He is the one who will direct our steps. God has established the process to access and walk in His love in such a fashion that we cannot escape the necessity of advancing in our relationship with Him. To walk in supernatural love, we must become a person given fully over to the leading of the Holy Spirit because God is the dispenser of this love. God is love!

CHAPTER 8

GOD'S STAIRWAY TO AGAPE

MANDATORY STEPS TO LOVE

In this book, we examine from the Scriptures several areas of revelation and action necessary to step into the supernatural love of God. This chapter discusses the most intensive and personally demanding of these areas. We are about to learn of a series of progressive steps that the Holy Spirit will lead us through to maximize our capacity to manifest love. And since these are steps that build upon one another, I refer to our foundational bible passage for this revelation as God's **Stairway to Agape** or the **Stairway to Love**.

Before we can examine this stairway, it will be beneficial for us to understand in greater detail what our ability to walk in the fullness of love is going to entail. We discovered in the *Recipe for Love* from First Timothy 1:5 that three ingredients are required to walk in love. The second of these ingredients was a *good conscience* representing a mind renewed to the Word of God - in particular to the revelation of our new born-again righteous nature. Our Stairway to Agape provides us with additional detail to what is required in this renewal process. **The actual process of transforming our minds requires more than merely gaining revelation of our new heavenly identity. It also demands radical change in our attitudes, actions, and reactions.** Through the purifying operation that takes place as we progress up this Stairway to Love, God will totally transform us unto the manifestation of His glory. And there are no shortcuts around this qualifying process.

For God to be able to genuinely flow the fullness of Himself through our lives, it is necessary that all impurities are purged from our souls - including wrong motivations, pride, fleshly mindsets, and much more. Any areas of our thinking, speech, and actions that are not aligned 100% with the Word will act to slow the flow of love through us. The God-initiated lifestyle of proceeding up this stairway takes us through a lifelong cycle of change from *"faith to faith"* unto *"glory to glory."*

Before we get to our target verses detailing the individual steps of the Stairway to Love, we are going to look at the verses leading up to them:

> *2Pet 1:1 -"Simon Peter, a servant and an apostle of Jesus Christ, to them that have obtained **like precious faith** with us **through the righteousness of God** and our Savior Jesus Christ:"*

In the above verse, the Apostle Paul is speaking to believers who have developed their faith - and in particular, faith regarding their new righteous nature. And Peter refers to this faith as precious! Until we grow in faith regarding the new nature of love on the inside of us, it will be nearly impossible to display any high level of love on the outside. A Christian who does not believe in faith for more than someday attaining heaven will find it challenging to step into supernatural love. Let's go on and examine the verses that follow:

> *2Pet 1:2-3 –"**Grace and peace be multiplied unto you through the knowledge of God**, and of Jesus our Lord, According as His divine power hath given unto us all things that pertain unto life and godliness, through the knowledge of Him that hath called us to glory and virtue:"*

Grace is God's provision to fulfill the individual calls upon our lives. Each Christian has set aside for them a personalized grace package tailored to meet the demands of their God-given assignment. Through the knowledge of God and of this grace we can walk in total peace, understanding that all of our needs have already been met if we will receive them by faith. The more we know about God, and of course His Word, the more of His provision we will learn to access.

We see in verse three, that He has made available for us everything that we need to enjoy fullness of life! This includes healing, prosperity, family salvation, our marriages blessed, and our high callings fulfilled. And as well as all of this, He has called us to carry His glory and to display His virtue. God has called us to manifest His glory rather than to just hang on until Jesus comes back! He's called us to be victorious and shine as lights in this world! Keep in mind that the glory is God's love in concentrated form.

> *2Pet 1:4 –"Whereby are given unto us exceeding great and precious promises: that by these ye might be partakers of the divine nature, having escaped the corruption that is in the world through lust."*

Through God's grace and divine power, we as believers have been granted access to all of the promises of the Word of God. These are not ordinary promises to be taken for granted, but are *"exceeding great and precious promises."* God kept compounding the adjectives for these promises to let us know just how spectacular they are. These are the promises that grant us rights to divine health, wealth, peace, and love! And, we don't have to wait until we get to Heaven to receive of them - they are available for us today. The Word of God provides us more than just the offer to enter heaven when we die. God's promises make it possible to enjoy of Heavens' blessing today.

Verse four also lets us know that we are to be partakers of God's divine nature. However in that we are born again, we have already been imparted His divine righteousness. Our spirit man has been recreated righteous. This verse must then refer to more than the salvation experience alone. We find here that once saved, we now have rights to partake of all of the promises of God. Our divine nature qualifies us to access all that God has granted us through His promises. And the more that we come to know God, the more we discover and are able to receive of these blessings. The more that we know about our son-ship and comprehend our righteousness, then the more we can partake of His blessings in life. And the number one blessing that we are to partake of is His love.

But now let's look at this **Stairway to Love**:

> *2Pet 1:5-7 –"And beside this, giving all diligence, add to your faith virtue; and to virtue knowledge; And to knowledge temperance; and to temperance patience; and to patience godliness; And to godliness brotherly kindness; and to brotherly kindness charity [agape love]."*

Here we see a series of developmental steps - a progression of attributes that the Christian is to build into their lives with the end goal of manifesting the love of God. As we add one characteristic upon the other, we advance through a cycle that manifests this love in an ever increasing fashion. Keep in mind that the ability to walk in love demands a long term developmental process. It is not the result of a microwave, quick-fix activity. Someone may taste of God's love through the laying on of hands or other impartation experience but they will not carry it long-term through such methods alone.

To qualify to carry the love of God, we will need to give Him access to totally renovate us from the inside out. God must adjust the way that we think and act. He will highlight to us things that are holding us back from walking in His love. As we cooperate with these alterations, we will be able to have the love of God freely flow through us.

Before we examine this progression in more detail, I want to explore the verses following our stairway to view the passage in context.

> *2Pet 1:8-9 –"For if these things be in you, and abound, they make you that* **ye shall neither be barren nor unfruitful in the knowledge of our Lord Jesus Christ**. *But he that lacketh these things is blind, and cannot see afar off, and hath forgotten that he was purged from his old sins."*

Here it declares that as we cooperate with this personal progression and begin to manifest the love of God, we are going to discover to a full flourishing level just who God is. The Greek word used for *"knowledge"* here is *epignosin*. The more common word translated *knowledge* in the New Testament is *gnosis* - representing *general or even fragmentary knowledge* of the things of God. Our word has the prefix *epi* added to it meaning *over* or *above*. The word *epignosin* therefore refers to *above general knowledge* of the things of God. *Epignosin* instead points to a *precise and complete knowledge* of Him. Since God is love, *epignosin* would certainly include exposure to and comprehension of this most important attribute of Him.

As well, we see that a person who is not involved in this progression has forgotten that he has been made a new creation. He will attempt to walk in love through his own efforts rather than allow God to take him through this transformational process. But what really should gain our attention is the next verse:

> 2Pet 1:10 – *"Wherefore the rather, brethren, give diligence to make your calling and election sure: for **if ye do these things, ye shall never fall**:"*

If any phrase should ever stand out to us it would be *"ye shall never fall."* Every Christian should gravitate toward this passage, for we all want to do those things necessary to remain in right standing with God. And the *"things"* we are to do to stay in this exalted place with Him point to us remaining in His personal training program of love. If we target the continual ascension of the Stairway to Love – we shall never fall. God lets us know that if we will keep pursuing His love, then there is nothing that the enemy can do to take us out of His hands. Praise the Lord!

The Stairway elevates us through *faith, virtue, knowledge, temperance, patience, godliness, brotherly kindness* and *love* as a progression. And we don't only climb this stairway one time! Because *"faith worketh by love,"* once we access any level of the love of God, it energizes our faith to an even higher level. Because faith is the first step in our progression, this forms a cycle and we begin advancing through the process once again. Every time that we go through this cycle, we outwardly manifest more and more of the love of God.

STEP 1: FAITH

*" giving all diligence, **add to your faith** ..."*

Ingredient #1 in our stairway is *"faith."* The Greek word for *faith* is *pistei* meaning *divine persuasion*. Faith represents our ability and capacity to receive of God's supernatural power and promises. It allows us to connect the world we live in to the realm He lives in. **Faith enables us to receive *Third Heaven* power to resolve *First Heaven* circumstances.** We live in this first heaven realm, this world which operates by the understood laws of physics. However, God resides in the Third Heaven. Paul states in Second Corinthians:

> *2Cor 12:2 – "I knew a man in Christ above fourteen years ago, (whether in the body, I cannot tell; or whether out of the body, I cannot tell: God knoweth;) such a one caught up to the third heaven."*

The Third Heaven is where the throne of God sits and is where all the power of God originates. And faith is the tool or the conduit that we have been given to channel this power into our lives. There is no other tool or method available which we can use to access the power in the Third Heaven realm other than our faith.

In the Gospels, Jesus compares faith to a mustard seed:

> *Luke 17:6 –"And the Lord said, **If ye had faith as a grain of mustard seed**, ye might say unto this sycamine tree, Be thou plucked up by the root, and be thou planted in the sea; and it should obey you."*

We see here that a small amount of faith can accomplish a great deal. Understand that the amount of faith we possess will determine the amount of God's kingdom blessings and love we may access. Therefore, it becomes of vital importance for us to increase our faith. Jesus mentions the mustard seed again in Mark chapter 4:

> *Mark 4:30-32 –"And he said, Whereunto shall I liken the kingdom of God? or with what comparison shall we compare it?* **It is like a grain of mustard seed***, which, when it is sown in the earth, is less than all the seeds that be in the earth: But when it is sown,* **it growth up***, and becometh greater than all herbs, and shooteth out great branches; so that the fowls of the air may lodge under the shadow of it."*

When we were born-again, God made a down payment within us in the form of a *"measure of faith,"* the size of the mustard seed. As we develop our mustard seed faith, it will grow allowing us to manifest the fullness of the Kingdom of God - His love and glory upon us bearing witness of His majesty. However, faith development rarely takes place accidentally. Faith development is best advanced through intentional effort - for *"faith cometh by hearing and hearing."* As God progresses us up the Stairway of Love, He will direct us to build and utilize our faith every step of the way. Although we list our first ingredient as faith, it is interesting to note from our verse that the first thing that we must bring to the table in our pursuit of love is *"diligence."* It will be very difficult for a Christian who is inconsistent in their relationship with God to progress far into this process. Jesus stated that those *who hear and do His sayings build their house upon a rock*, not those who are up and down in their pursuit and obedience!

Faith allows us to receive of God's healing power through understanding of the stripes that Jesus took on our behalf. Faith lets us access supernatural provision and financial blessing via the promises of God to multiply our seed. And by the *"shield of faith"*, we can stand against all that will attempt to oppose us. And bringing to mind our *Recipe for Agape*, faith allows us to carry the power of God's love.

> 1Tim 1:5 – *"Now the end of the commandment is charity out of a pure heart, and of a good conscience, **and of faith unfeigned.**"*

Faith is the third ingredient in our previously covered recipe to access the love of God. And faith becomes the mandatory component to remain submitted to God's developmental process in climbing the remainder of the steps on our Stairway. It cannot be overemphasized that it requires great faith to allow God to deliver us from our prior identity and build within us His attitudes and reactions. Each step in our Stairway is going to place demands upon our lives to shift us from natural to supernatural thinking and living. Without faith, we will bail out of His accelerated training program. The Christian who understands and activates Biblical principles of faith will trust God to reward him for taking actions that at times stretch him to the breaking point. The one who does not will never advance far into the remainder of these qualities. He will truncate the process of stepping into the love of God. Therefore faith becomes the first step on our Stairway to God's ultimate prize - His love!

STEP 2: VIRTUE

*"... add to your faith **virtue**; ..."*

Virtue is the second attribute that God will attempt to develop in us as we move up the Stairway to Love. The Greek word translated *"virtue"* means *moral excellence.* When we first become saved, God will immediately start convicting us to clean up our lives. We may not even be aware that He is speaking to us but we will feel the need to stop lying, stealing, cheating, and carousing. He is building within us virtue. You may say: *"But God had me quit all of that before He ever said a word to me about growing in faith."* This is almost always the case, but remember, when we were born again God deposited in us an initial *"measure of faith"* to launch us into this process. If not for this down payment of faith within us, we would never be willing to let go of the things that virtue demands of us.

Also contained in the list of character flaws on which God will deal with us to produce virtue are pride, manipulation, arrogance, jealousy, and any other works of the flesh. **This process of building virtue into our lives does not save us but it does certainly make us more publicly presentable.** We have all heard the claims that the church is full of hypocrites, and sadly many of these accusations are true. However, those members of the local church who are saying one thing but doing another have never proceeded far in virtue development. At some point early on, they have rebelled against the conviction of the Holy Spirit attempting to deliver them from worldly mentalities and actions.

Integrity is a subset of virtue. We will be called to become a person of our word to the point that we will not be allowed to exaggerate or even slightly bend the truth. We will no longer be permitted to operate in a sloppy fashion.

It is somewhat humorous that baby Christians who discover that they can believe God for finances frequently declare: *"I believe I receive one million dollars!"* However, they have certainly not yet been far along in the development of virtue in their lives. God wants us wealthy. However, He does not want a whole bunch of cheating and lying *rich* Christians running around anymore than He does the wicked rich.

If you have been a Christian for very long then you should know by now that money is **not** the *"root of all evil!"* Scripture makes it clear that *"the LOVE of money is the root of all evil."* Money is not evil of itself - God even told Adam where to find gold and that the gold is *good*. Money merely amplifies the character of the one who possesses it. An evil man will use his funds for wicked purposes but a good man will use wealth to be a blessing. Therefore, God must develop character within us so that we can walk properly with the wealth that we receive.

However, most baby Christians who eagerly claim the million dollars do so because they do not want to be dependent upon God for their needs anymore. They want a large security fund set aside so that they don't have to use their faith any longer. For God to give them the wealth they desire would most likely cause them to exit the very lifestyle of living by faith that He is trying to get them to follow. Were the millions to manifest, in such cases it would probably result in most believers' downfall! Again, God wants us wealthy but He must first build virtue within our lives before He can entrust us with great financial riches.

Another subset of virtue where God is going to start dealing with us is in our tithing and giving. Before God ever dealt with me on faith for healing and prosperity, He dealt with me on tithing. Not having been raised in church, I knew nothing of church offerings. However upon even my earliest visits to church, when the bucket would pass by, God would instruct me of certain amounts to give. Some of the earliest tests that God ever challenged me to were in the area of sowing. And as I would be obedient, God would always bring me some form of confirmation or reward. Our tithes open the *"windows of heaven"* over our lives. These *windows* allow *heavenly light* to pass through providing us with illumination to the Word of God. Until we initiate this system of blessing, it will be difficult to receive adequate revelation from the Word to advance far up the Stairway to Love.

Manifesting virtue, which includes tithing and walking in integrity, requires faith. We must trust that God will work out a better solution for our challenges if we choose to tell the truth rather than use deception. So, Step 1 of *"faith"* is followed by step 2 of *"virtue"*.

STEP 3: KNOWLEDGE

*"and to virtue **knowledge:**"*

As we cooperate with the Holy Spirit to develop *"virtue"* in our lives, He then calls upon us to begin growing in spiritual *"knowledge."* We will be directed to His Word to learn of His Kingdom and of Him. To truly accelerate a Christian up this Stairway, He may create a thirst within them that draws them to spend hours daily in the Bible. **A foundation of the Word of God becomes the anchor point for all other Kingdom development in our lives.** We can never grow in love or in any other attribute of the Kingdom beyond our knowledge level of the Word. The Greek word used for *"knowledge"* in verse five is *gnosis*. As we mentioned earlier, *gnosis* represents *partial or fragmentary knowledge* of God. As we spend extensive amounts of time in God's Word, attend anointed church services, and listen to biblically accurate messages through the vast array of media forms available, we begin to piece together knowledge of God and of the principles of His kingdom.

It is paramount that a Christian connect to a church that is teaching truth, otherwise they build upon a faulty foundation. However, a problem arises in being able to identify those pastors that are properly interpreting the scriptures. There is so much disagreement being proclaimed, how do we know who to follow? The best answer involves many facets:

- We must spend much time in the Word to assure that what is taught is in context and is truth.
- We must genuinely pray and seek God - and learn to follow the leading of the Holy Spirit within our heart versus hearken to the voices in our head.
- We must FOLLOW THE POWER. If the church does not believe that the power of God is available for us today, it is disqualified. If they do not recognize the need for the believer to be baptized in the Holy Spirit with the evidence of speaking in tongues, they cannot take you where you need to go. And even if they are proclaiming that both exist but no miracle power is being displayed, then something is amiss. At this time, God is pouring out His healing and deliverance power as never before.

God desires to reveal Himself to us because when we are first saved we have little revelation of who He really is. Religious churches all over the world are proclaiming that *"God is good all the time."* Yet, they will then instruct from their pulpits that God puts sickness on us to teach us a lesson or that He wants us poor to keep us humble. Such teaching represents that they do not really have a revelation of God's goodness but are merely echoing a hollow statement. The epitome of such perverted doctrine is the declaration made when young children die - some ministers proclaim that God took them because *"He needed another angel in heaven"*. Jesus declared in John 10:

> *John 10:10 –"The thief (satan) cometh not, but for to steal, and to kill, and to destroy: I am come that they might have life, and that they might have it more abundantly."*

The devil is the killer, Jesus is the giver of life. To point to God as the one who killed a child is to openly confess that we do not know Him, especially in the form of *"a good God all of the time!"*

So God will begin revealing Himself to us. He's going to start showing us that He is a loving God and that He's interested in each of us personally. He will start unveiling His word to us. We have already brought forth that the Word of God is Jesus in print form. By revealing His word to us, He elevates us to higher and higher levels of knowing Him and higher and higher levels of understanding the principles of His kingdom.

As we continue to cycle through the Stairway to Love, we gain ever increasing *gnosis* of all things pertaining to God. As we piece together our puzzle parts of fragmentary knowledge, we begin to develop *epignosis*. Again, *Epignosis* as promised in verse eight, represents *full and complete knowledge* of God. The Bible tells us that as we mature in God, we should come to total knowledge of Him; the full and complete knowledge of who He is and of how His kingdom functions.

One of the most vital truths that God is going to reveal to us is that the Word represents His covenant commitment to us. God's Word is His bond; His promises to us are unbreakable. Many Christians will attempt to tell you, *"Oh, we can't understand the word of God!"*; *"His ways are not our ways!"* and *"His thoughts are not our thoughts!"*; *"Who can comprehend the mind of God?"* Well, we can receive revelation of all of this if we commit ourselves to the cycle of developing in God's love. And the more that we know Him, the more we will deepen in our relationship with Him and the more He can direct us into leading a victorious life.

STEP 4: TEMPERANCE

*"and to knowledge **temperance;**"*

"Temperance" is from the Greek word *enkrateian* meaning *self-control*. Once we have to some level renewed our minds by the Word, God will then draw us to begin invoking deeper personal change. The Holy Spirit will begin to shine His light upon how we react to challenges and pressure. He will deal with us in the area of self-control. We will experience conviction over temper tantrums and other fits of carnality. God desires to free us from fits of anger, gluttony, slothfulness and any other escape mechanisms.

God's intention is that *we cast all of our cares upon Him for He cares for us*. This means that when pressured, we trust in the Word of God to meet all of our needs. To escape pressure, the world turns to entertainment, shopping sprees, comfort food, and even exercise. For many, relief is pursued through drugs and alcohol. However, God's plan has always been for us to turn to the Word. His grace is sufficient for us to overcome any form of obstacle in our lives.

As we cooperate with God's promotional process toward love, He will reveal to us all of the escape mechanisms we use in life to flee pressure other than the Word. The enemy has spent all of our lives attempting to program us to think and react in a natural versus supernatural fashion. The devil has led us to build walls in our lives when we were hurt and to withdraw or even lash out when threatened.

I refer to the fleshly responses imbedded within us by the enemy as *Landmines of the Soul*. *Landmines* represent those areas of our lives where it is hazardous for others to tread. When challenged, pressured, stretched, corrected, and often just questioned, a hair trigger is set off resulting in an explosion of emotional release. Tears, outbursts, profanity, and extreme criticism may all suddenly erupt from the seemingly placid Christian. The believer with any sensitivity to the Holy Spirit whatsoever will be challenged by God to deal with these responses.

And the devil really knows how to use these explosions against us. After an episode, he will declare to us: *"And you thought you were saved."; "A Genuine Christian would never act that that."* and *"You should just quit, you'll never make it as a child of God."* And often, afterwards we may not even feel saved but we must not let the devil win. We must allow God to change us such that, instead of manifesting the lusts of the flesh we develop the fruit of the Spirit.

Know that those improper reactions that rise up from within us do not represent who we really are. Our real identity is embedded within our spirit man that was recreated righteous when we were born-again. However when we were saved, our soul wasn't transformed, only our spirit. Our souls will experience their own form of salvation as we renew our minds by the Word. By *soul salvation*, I am not referring to an action where our soul man is finally granted access to heaven. The term *salvation of the soul* in scripture involves the process over time, where the Word transforms our minds to think in alignment with the Bible. We thus become spiritually minded as the Word rewires our thinking.

The *mines* that go off when someone *steps on our toes* or touches on our *last nerve*, all point to areas of our thinking not yet transformed by scripture. These are leftover mindsets from our old life that we refer to as *dross*. *Dross* is defined as *waste matter* or *refuse* - thus it refers to *garbage thinking and programming* from our lives before we came into Kingdom understanding. When smelting or purifying metals, as the ore is heated to the melting point the impurities embedded with the metal all rise to the top. The refiner then scoops off the dross producing a purified product. From Proverbs:

> *Prov 25:4 – "Take away the dross from the silver, and there shall come forth a vessel for the finer. Take away the wicked from before the king, and his throne shall be established in righteousness."*

We are the kings that God wants to purify through the process of building into us temperance. Rather that condemn ourselves when dross rises to the top we should use the opportunity to skim those reactions out of our lives. We can target those areas of ungodly thought by intentionally speaking and meditating verses that renew our minds to respond otherwise. In doing so, we take the *"Sword of the Spirit"* - the Word of God, and circumcise out of our lives that which is not aligned with love. To not address these inappropriate reactions as they manifest allows them to settle back down within us only to arise at another inopportune time.

I told you this wasn't going to be automatic! God wants to delve deep within us and illuminate areas of thought not yet submitted to Him. He wants to assist us to address the anger fits, shopping sprees, eating binges, and other inappropriate escape mechanisms that we have relied on in the past.

STEP 5: PATIENCE

*"and to temperance **patience**;"*

Recall in verse five that we are to be people of diligence and diligent people are going to require *"patience"*. The Greek word for *"patience"* in this passage is *hypomonen* - meaning *endurance* or *remaining under*. This word for patience infers that we are consistent in our godly actions regardless of our circumstances. **Patience is really self-control over the long haul**. God will begin to develop patience within us so that circumstances cannot ruffle us whatsoever. The devil knows how to apply pressure to our lives. Patience allows us to walk in the fruit of the spirit for extended periods of time regardless of his efforts.

There are *familiar* demonic spirits assigned to each of us - probing to find our weak points. Have you ever found yourself falling for the same attack over and over again? My *Achilles Heel* would show up as people would repeatedly cut me off in traffic. They would do it abruptly, rudely, and with no turn signals such that it frequently stole my joy. My wife would say: *"People always pull in front of you."* – and they did! The devil made sure that they did because it allowed him to get *under my skin*. Once I was able to develop more patience in my life, the occasions where others would drive erratically around me ceased to set me off. Instead, I would pray for them. Once the enemy discovered it no longer affected me as before, the number of people pulling in front of me dropped dramatically. Again, the devil doesn't continue attacks that do not produce his desired results.

If we are people who cannot stand disorganization, the devil is going to make sure that there is clutter around us. If we are sticklers for being prompt, he will be sure to delay the other parties or even ourselves from our set appointments. Whatever the area might be, the devil will attempt to upset us. And patience is the fruit that allows us to live above the pressures of the enemy - above those little barbs he wants to use to disrupt our consistent walk of peace.

Another key function of patience is that it keeps our faith in operation unto manifestation of the promise. Once we release our faith for a promise of God in our life, in most cases the results are not visible immediately. The element of *time* is usually involved. Even when Jesus cursed the fig tree, though it became dried up at the roots no change was instantly evident to the natural eye. Whenever we speak the Word in a situation, faith may go to work right away at the root of the issue but it may be a while before we actually see any manifestation.

In chapter four, we brought out three steps to apply faith: Speaking, Acting, and Standing. Standing is the step that requires that we access patience. We must continue to speak and act in agreement with the Word of God regardless of what adverse symptoms and circumstances arise. Patience, often being the result of having experienced God's faithfulness in the past, enables us remain steadfast in our faith efforts. Without patience, we will begin to doubt that the Word will produce for us and we will begin to waver in our stand. And according to James chapter one, wavering will neutralize our faith from working. Faith - the first step of the Stairway to Love combined with patience - the fifth step, allow us to receive of God's blessings in our lives.

If we don't spend enough time involving ourselves in *spiritual exercises*, our patience will wear thin. To maintain our patience level requires time in prayer, the Word, worship, church, and praying in the spirit. The Word becomes the *"bread of life"* that fuels our inner man. If the spirit man becomes malnourished, even the most experienced of saints will revert to following God out of their own strength rather than via the anointing.

When we find ourselves growing irritable, frustrated, or angry, it should be a signal to us that our patience is waning and that we need time alone with God to replenish our spiritual tanks. At such times, we need to recognize that we are running on fumes and need to get with God! To fully accelerate ourselves into the love of God, we need our patience levels at their peak. And this brings us to the next step in our ascension up the Stairway.

STEP 6: GODLINESS

*"and to patience **godliness**;"*

So all of the initial activities – *faith, virtue, knowledge* and *temperance* all lead us into developing *patience*, which then enables us to live in some level of victory. But to keep step five energized requires step six - *"godliness"*. Often godliness is associated with the term *godlikeness* - inferring that we are to present ourselves in a godly fashion. And although this is true, the word *godliness* is translated from the Greek word *eusebeian* meaning *to venerate or pay homage to*. True godliness involves our genuine reverence for God and will take the form of piety or worship.

To walk in godliness means that we live or walk in a state of God awareness and we develop a lifestyle of worship. We who want to keep our fuel tanks filled and desire to walk in victory in life, must recognize when sour attitudes arise from within us. Upon this revelation, we need to immediately begin worshipping God. As we do, His presence comes on the scene refreshing and strengthening us unto renewed joy and patience.

Nothing can refuel us like the presence of God. And God has given us means by which we can freely and without limit access His presence.

Jas 4:8a –"Draw nigh to God, and he will draw nigh to you."

The Word promises us that if we will draw near to God, He will manifest His presence to us. And the primary way that we draw near to God is through praise and worship. We virtually have the ability to worship our way into His presence! David confirms this in Psalm 22:

> *Psa 22:3 – "But thou art holy, O thou that inhabitest the praises of Israel."*

As we praise God, His tangible presence visits us. This often works most effectively in our church gatherings where we corporately lift His name - giving us even another reason to not skip church. God wants to be with us on a full time basis, however He desires us to want His presence enough to seek Him first.

I want to relate one particular instance where the Lord directed me to activate this spiritual principle when I allowed the stress of the day to get to me. Early in ministry, I was filling out tax forms with a typewriter that kept striking double Y's. This was prior to the availability of electronic filing and tax preparation software, so every form had to be completed manually. Each form seemed to have a dozen carbon copies attached so if I made an error, it could not be easily corrected and I would have to start over.

I was going through form after form after form messing up stack after stack of W-2 blanks. Often as I was about to finish a copy, the typewriter would type Y's across the entire page. Built up frustration had me ready to pick up that typewriter and send it into outer space. Then, when on my final W-2, the typewriter stuck one more time and destroyed my last unused form. By this time it was late in the afternoon and everyone else had gone home. And I jumped up to storm home myself. As I exited my office door, God spoke to me and said: *"Worship Me."*

I responded: *"I don't want to worship right now; I'm not in the mood."*

"You need to worship Me right now." He firmly repeated!

I knew that He was right. My family didn't deserve for me to take home the platoon of demons currently tap dancing on my head, but I didn't want to do it. However, feigning obedience I went into the sanctuary and started to go through the motions of worship. *"I praise you God, I worship you,"* I muttered with no enthusiasm or genuine reverence whatsoever.

He interrupted this farce and said: *"That's not genuine worship."*

So I tried again more earnestly. *"Oh, Lord, I know that this isn't your fault! I love you Lord! I worship you, Lord!"* And after about fifteen minutes of real praise, having put my heart into it, God's presence filled the area! All of the demons left, my tank was refueled, and I had peace. Subsequently, I was able to go home without taking along a carload of unwelcome company. The next day I picked up more W-2 forms, returned to work and finished the task with no more problems. By drawing me into worship, God was able to release the anointing that I needed to overcome the frustration and resultant bad attitude.

Godliness creates within us a continual awareness of God and produces a lifestyle of worship. This worship ushers in His presence allowing us to overcome every form of demonic opposition. And all of this enables us to continue in our ascension up the Stairway of Love. Without godliness, we cannot access sufficient anointing to advance far into God's calling upon our lives.

STEP 7: BROTHERLY KINDNESS

*"and to godliness **brotherly kindness**;"*

This brings us to *"brotherly kindness"*. *"Brotherly kindness"* is from the Greek word *Philadelphia* which is a compound of the words *philos* - *loving friend*, and *adelphos* - *a brother*. *Philadelphia*, therefore refers to *the love of the brethren*.

Understand that for Christians, *brethren* represents our co-members within the church. *Philadelphia* primarily represents our deep consideration for one another as members of the family of God. It involves the covenant bonds that we are to develop within the body of Christ which motivate us to continually be a blessing. *Philadelphia* connects the knowledge that we are in a *church body covenant* from chapter seven with the recognition from chapter four that to step into the supernatural love of God requires a *seed*.

We covered in some detail how *philadelphia* becomes the seed step of faith that we must take to be able to manifest *agape* love!

When we operate in *philadelphia* targeting the anointing of love, it acts as a pivotal step to bring *agape* into our lives. Recall the prior event where my wife and I were at odds with each other and God told me to rub her back, apologize, and tell her that I loved her. Although it took all of the faith that I had, the actions of brotherly love taken released the anointing of *agape* and destroyed the enemy's efforts to divide us.

Brotherly kindness also involves our transition from being a self-serving individual to one that endeavors to become a servant to others - especially those within our church. For those who desire spiritual promotion, Jesus highlighted the need to develop a servants' heart in Matthew:

> *Mat 20:25-28 – "But Jesus called them unto him and said, Ye know that the princes of the Gentiles exercise dominion over them, and they that are great exercise authority upon then. But it shall not be so among you: but **whosoever will be great among you, let him be your minister**; And whosoever will be chief among you, let him be your servant: Even as the son of man came not to be ministered unto, but to minister, and to give his life a ransom for many."*

To genuinely move into supernatural love requires that we follow His example of laying down our soul for our friends. We have now learned that as we pour our lives into aiding those around us, we position ourselves to step into the greatest levels of God's love.

STEP 8: LOVE

*"and to brotherly kindness **charity** [agape love]."*

So as God develops all of these attributes in us, we progress up the stairway arriving at our goal to manifest the supernatural love of God. As we learned in chapter one, love fulfills all of the intentions of the Old and New Testaments - thus love becomes

God's highest call upon our lives. From chapter two, we discovered many of the amazing benefits that walking in love produces for our lives. Once we have partaken of this heavenly gift, we find that no other experiences of life can equally satisfy. Our initial trip up this Staircase will not likely result in us carrying the full-blown glory of God, however we will no doubt be walking in increased manifestation of the fruit of the spirit. Once we have had this initial taste of the goodness of God, we should be willing to make whatever changes are necessary to attain to our ultimate goal - to carry that glory!

The wonderful thing we find is that this Stairway to Love does not involve only a single progression through each of these steps, but God will draw us through this *cycle* repeatedly! Each time we advance forward, we step into more and more of His highest and most powerful anointing - His love.

THE STAIRMASTER

The Stairway is a cycle that God will continue taking us through to manifest more and more of His love unto the glory. If at any time of this growth process we get to the place where we decide that we no longer want to progress up this Stairway - at that point, we peak in our love development. If we refuse to cooperate with the Holy Spirit to make the changes we are assigned, we truncate our progress toward the glory.

It's easy to see that if we remain selfish and refuse to live to serve others, then we won't be able to develop in love. In the same way, to the level that we develop moral excellence, knowledge of God, self-control, patience, and become a worshipper, we establish how deep we will be able to extend our roots of faith into His *agape*.

And we can't just pick and choose for ourselves which steps we want to focus on or remain. We've got to let God deal with us on a daily basis regarding which attributes we need to develop. Every day we will face challenges; and every challenge we face is going to demand that we activate and at times stretch into some aspect of this cycle.

Some might be tempted to say: *"Well, not mine - My challenge is that I need the house payment paid."*

Well, that need will require faith because it demands supernatural manifestation of provision. It will involve knowledge of God and of His Word to comprehend that it is His will to meet this need. This also requires patience to enable us to stand in faith. These all become facets of whatever challenges we're facing. To become spiritual powerhouses, we must strive for mastery in all of these steps. **We must become** *Stair-Masters.*

If we will allow Him, God is going to take us through this cycle over and over again. Often He will be working with us in several different areas simultaneously. He may be dealing with us in patience regarding one area of challenge and knowledge in another - all working together to advance us up God's promotional ladder to love.

CYCLE I -

Now, let's explore some potential examples of how a Christian might progress through these cycles of the Stairway to Love.

With the new-born believer, the first area that they will most likely focus on is developing **faith** to know that they are saved. They were given a measure of faith to become saved, but now they will need to get into the Word to build their faith to remain convinced that a supernatural conversion has actually taken place.

When I was first saved, it took all of the faith that I had just to believe that I was changed! Daily, the devil would inform me that I was deluded to believe that I could really be saved. Doubt would then drive me back into the scriptures to cover repeatedly all of the verses that promised me salvation. It took me a year just to get victory over that. It seemed I would answer every altar call to make sure I was right with God. When I would have an evil thought, condemnation would make me feel the need to run to the altar again. Eventually my faith grew to the level that I knew at all times that I was saved.

Once we as new believers have built up some level of faith in our salvation, then God will challenge us to develop **virtue**. He will challenge us to no longer lie. He may convince us to no

196

longer pad an expense account or take home office products. God will convict us, that as Christians, we can no longer do these and many similar things.

Then God starts bringing us into deeper **knowledge** of Him and the Word. He will begin showing us just how great a price was paid for our salvation at The Cross. We will become aware of God's desire that all should be saved and even discover the promise of the Baptism of the Holy Spirit. The knowledge step becomes the foundation upon which all other steps rely.

Then God will begin to build **temperance** within us as new believers. He will initially convict us to stop cussing, quit throwing temper tantrums, and to stop screaming at the kids. Our friends and families will celebrate these victories with us. They will stand amazed and commend us on the remarkable transformation that we have experienced. We may have already been personally convinced of our salvation, but temperance displays it openly to all.

Next, we are led into **patience**. A person new to Christianity will usually begin to voice defeat at the first sign of opposition but God will teach us enough of patience to hopefully keep us in church. Our first step of patience will not be so dramatic as to obtain total victory in the words that we speak. Initially, our patience comprehension may just be to just *not quit* and to stay in the Word.

The first sign of **godliness** that we will experience may be that we are full of zeal for God, but lack knowledge. We will praise God when things go our way, yet complain when they do not. We will thank God for saving us but will not have yet learned to use worship as a weapon against darkness. The Lord desires that we maintain this initial zeal all the way through our Christian walk.

The first step that we as new believers take in **brotherly kindness** is to tell everybody that we meet about Jesus. And we're going to invite all of them to church. We will profusely testify to everyone what happened to us - but can demonstrate little to personally prove our internal transformation as a child of God.

And, our first step of **love** is that we will develop a love for God. And hopefully, we'll love other Christians. We look forward to being used in the church. We are excited at the opportunity to help meet another's needs.

I was naive when I was first saved. Not having been raised in church, I was convinced that all Christians were surely perfect. I thought that all Christians had right motives. I would pursue conversations with other church-goers at work only to find out that many still lived in the world as much as they did before they were saved! I thought: *"What's wrong?"* The answer was - either they had never really become born-again, or at some point they had bailed out of God's developmental program - the 'Stairway to Love'.

CYCLE II -

As we learn to hear and obey God, He will then begin to take us through the cycle again. However, each time through, the demand for changes to be made within us increases.

The first trip through, we developed **faith** to stay saved. Next, we build faith to be healed, faith for finances, and faith for the hand of God to move in our lives.

Regarding **virtue**, instead of just learning to not lie, cheat and steal, now we learn how to respect other people's feelings and walk in integrity.

In the second trip around, on top of the **knowledge** that God is a saving God, we will discover that God wants to be our supplier, rewarder, and protector. In fact, we will find that God wants to be involved in blessing every area of our lives.

Now, when we come to the step of **temperance**, instead of learning not to cuss, now we will learn not to blame other people for our mistakes, not to entertain pity parties, and not to eat everything in the refrigerator. We will be instructed not to go on shopping sprees thinking a new outfit will make us feel better about ourselves.

As for **patience**, where before we spoke defeat upon the first sign of opposition but stayed in church, now we remain calm when the phone bill is not paid within three days of the due date. We learn to be patient amid some circumstances that in the past would have crushed us. Our increased patience allows us to confront physical symptoms without altering our confessions of health.

With regard to **godliness**, where before we were full of zeal but lacked knowledge, now we learn to praise God when symptoms arise. Not that we are happy that we are experiencing the attacks, but we now know that praise becomes a key step for us to access victory. We learn to worship God whenever things are not going quite our way. We are developing in godliness.

As God takes us further into **brotherly kindness**, on top of inviting everyone that we meet to church, we insist on being used within the church. We become involved in children's church, church cleaning, maintenance, and even in doing visitations. We are usually willing to take on whatever the church needs. We identify ourselves with the church and become personally vested in its success.

With round two of stepping into **love**, instead of just loving God and other Christians, now we learn to love ourselves. We learn how to accept our mistakes and still recognize that we are made in the image of God. Increasing levels of the fruit of the spirit begin to show up in our lives and we may begin to operate in the Gifts of the Spirit.

By this point in the book, you should be aware that a Christian who attends a *sin-oriented* condemnation church will never step into elevated levels of the love of God. They will never progress beyond the disappointment they feel in their walk with God. They have been taught to view themselves as sinners and thus to hate themselves. Being convinced of their short-comings, they will never feel qualified to carry the supernatural power of God's love!

CYCLE III -

Let's go through this cycle a third time.

Where previously we developed **faith** to manifest God's promises, now we develop faith to minister and release the gifts and anointings that we have now learned to carry. I didn't say that we were yet called into ministry - that's up to God. However, we will learn to lay hands on people. We will operate in the Gifts of the Spirit. We will prophesy with authority. God is taking us into higher and higher levels of spiritual maturity as we continue again through this cycle.

When it comes to **virtue**, where in the second cycle we ceased from mistreating others, now we have developed total thought control. We learn to fulfill the directive of Philippians 4:8:

> *Phil 4:8 - "Finally, brethren, whatsoever things are true, whatsoever things are honest, whatsoever things are just, whatsoever things are pure, whatsoever things are lovely, whatsoever things are of good report; if there be any virtue, and if there be any praise, think on these things."*

We learn to monitor and categorize all our thoughts appropriately. We ask ourselves - *"Is this thought of God, is this of the devil, or is it birthed of ourselves?"* We then sort all of our thoughts in order to deal with them in the way that they need to be handled. If the thought is of God - it is received; and if not - it is cast down. Once skill is developed in the arena of controlling our thoughts, we are well on our way to possessing everything that God has promised us.

In the second cycle of knowledge, we found out that God is our supplier, rewarder, and protector. Step three in **knowledge** takes us deeper into discovering that God is a God of glory. We find that He is a finishing God.

> *Phil 1:6 – "Being confident of this very thing, that he which hath begun a good work in you will perform it until the day of Jesus Christ:"*

We become aware that we are to walk in His presence on a full time basis. As we begin piecing together all the other areas of revelation that God has given us, we reflect ever increasing levels of His image

Not only that, but once we fully realize that God is a good God - that He is a God of love, it allows us to advance into any challenge knowing that He's going to be there to help us through it. He's a finishing God - what He has called us to do, He will help us to complete if we don't quit.

The third cycle through **temperance** will involve much deeper introspection of what makes us tick. At this point, God will point out our hidden landmines of the soul and direct us to permanently eradicate them. Here we obtain total control over the flesh. We no longer turn to any prior pressure escape mechanisms. Now to some level, the flesh becomes a non-factor. The body becomes totally obedient to the purposes of our spirit. Hallelujah!

Christians usually speak of the warfare between our spirit and flesh described in Galatians as being permanently ongoing and somewhat unwinnable:

> *Gal 5:17 - "For the flesh lusteth against the Spirit, and the Spirit against the flesh: and these are contrary the one to the other: so that ye cannot do the things that ye would."*

As long as there is a battle within our soul between our spirit man and our flesh, it limits the amount of God's will that we are able to fulfill. But the truth is, this conflict was never meant to last forever. Through the process of renewing our minds to the Word of God, we gain greater and greater ascendency over the flesh until it becomes our servant. It is intended that the flesh become an obedient vessel to the will of our spirit man versus the flesh repeatedly dictating our actions and overturning our plans. Therefore, as we spend extensive time gaining Biblical knowledge, it advances us in temperance.

In cycle three of **patience**, where before we learned to be calm when the phone bill wasn't paid on time, now we are *joyful* in the midst of multiple, seemingly impossible major situations. What would those be? Potentially at one time, we may be attacked with a physical condition that seems untreatable; financial challenges that arise greater than the sum of our assets; the kids begin to run with the devil; and our spouse threatens to leave. Understand that this would be a very extreme case, however the Christian who has advanced far into patience speaks the Word, turns it all over to God, and worships Him.

Certainly, we declare that none of these things are going to happen to us. But do know that there will be times when we will be faced with impossible situations – dead situations. Jesus tells us in John:

> *John 12:24 - "Except a corn of wheat fall into the ground and die, it abideth alone: but if it die, it bringeth forth much fruit."*

There are going to be assignments that God has called us to accomplish that will at times appear dead in the water. Often when we sow a seed, it will seem as if nothing is happening or circumstances may even grow worse. Per what Jesus here declared, before we see full manifestation of fruit in our situations conditions may first undergo a *death phase*. Here it will appear that our best faith efforts have failed. Our efforts will appear to have fallen short. But if we stay with it and remain patient, resurrection life power will hit our seed and a full turnaround of our circumstances will take place.

As we truly step further into the realm of patience, we will have peace because we realize that we're going to witness full restoration of all that the enemy has stolen. We will maintain joy in the midst of all challenges. We will refuse to surrender, quit, fly off the handle, get frustrated, or whine and cry.

As we move into our third cycle of **godliness**, where before we learned to praise God when symptoms arose, now we will enthusiastically worship God in dead situations. We'll learn how to be content in our walk of faith. Paul said in Philippians:

> *Phil 4:11 - "Not that I speak in respect of want: for I have learned, in whatsoever state I am, therewith to be content."*

In other words, it didn't matter if Paul was in jail or out, he was going to be a worshipper of God. It didn't matter if he was rich or poor - he was content.

When we get into high levels of godliness, the circumstances that we experience do not dictate our level of worship or impact our relationship with God. Circumstances will not hinder our ability to manifest more and more of His love.

With regard to **brotherly kindness**, in cycle two, we started to assist in the church. In cycle three, we now discover and enter into our own personal calling. We are now going to live for the Kingdom of God on a full time basis. Our life is no longer our own. Whatever the call, we will continually walk in brotherly kindness regardless of how we feel. We will no longer need to seek out others to bless - for our anointing will draw multitudes who want to receive of us.

Understand, when God calls us to do something, it's going to be beyond what we can do of ourselves. It's going to be above our own strength, wisdom, financial resources, and skill. God's callings always require faith to complete them.

Whether our calling is in full time ministry or not, we will be required to remain steadfast in it whether we feel like it or not. We will learn to evangelize even on our worst days. We will learn how to stand in faith for family members and friends that we may not desire to stand for anymore. We will have to bless and encourage others when we ourselves feel like we would rather run and hide.

When we ascended to love in cycle one, we learned to love God and others. In cycle two, we learned to love ourselves. In cycle three, we are supernaturally enabled to love our enemies. We walk in the love of God amidst persecution and opposition. And as we progress through cycle three, we become equipped to carry God's glory.

* * * * * * * * * * * *

Please understand that the examples given here of proceeding up this Stairway to Love for three cycles ARE completely ambiguous. This version was developed for instructional purposes only. We may go through some of these steps numerous times - some certainly more than others. We may have passed one level only to require development at that step again should we regress. No two Christian's progress up this Staircase will be the same.

To continue stepping through these cycles requires that we maintain a strong relationship with God. This allows the Holy Spirit to delve down deeply inside of us and show us our inner motives or nonbiblical thought processes. This means that our prayers must go beyond, *"Now I lay me down to sleep... ."* This means our prayer life becomes more than, *"Oh, God, I need this, this, and this... ."* Though God wants to supply our every need,

He as well wants to establish us in a relationship where He is allowed to transform us. He wants to take us through a purifying process that will require our full cooperation. This deep, interactive relationship with God is mandatory to manifest His love.

When we spend time developing ourselves spiritually, we position ourselves to become a conduit of His love. As we spend time in God's word, develop a life of prayer, and allow God to repeatedly cycle us through the Stairway to Love, we step into the fullness of who God has created us to become. We subsequently manifest the full fruit of the spirit. We will automatically walk in all of the attributes listed in First Corinthians 13:4-8 and we will usher in the glory of the Father.

Whatever the demand is upon our lives, we now have inside of us the ability to access victory for every situation. What is it that made us able? What is it that empowered us to walk with such capability? We allowed God to meddle on the inside of us. We developed a lifestyle of progressing up this Stairway. To the level that we allow God to develop us internally, we become a processor of the love of God such that we can manifest whatever we need as we need it.

Yet, most Christians won't let God get personal with them - to clear out their dark inner gunk so that they can become spiritually mature, clear, shining prisms of light. Instead they walk around hypocritical and powerless - operating out of the flesh instead of the supernatural power of the love of God.

CHAPTER 9

ABIDING IN LOVE

CONNECTED TO THE VINE

Throughout this book, we have pointed out the need to have an established prayer life to be able to manifest the supernatural love of God. In this chapter, we examine in more depth the need for God to become our intimate friend. Jesus spoke of our need to *"abide"* in Him in John chapter 15. We want to take a close look at these verses of scripture:

> *John 15:1-2 – "**I am the true vine** and my father is the husbandman. Every branch in me that beareth not fruit he taketh away: and **every branch that beareth fruit, he purgeth it, that it may bring forth more fruit.**"*

Here Jesus compares Himself to a *"vine"* that we are to connect to in an abiding fashion. This abiding relationship involves ongoing intimate interaction - even as a marriage of our lives and His. The product of this connection to Him is for us to bear forth fruit - and fruit production represents the end goal of a tree. The tree works all through the growing season, absorbing nutrients, water, and sunlight with the end purpose of bearing fruit with the seed contained therein. Likewise, as we are connected to Jesus as the vine, spiritual nutrients will be transmitted to us.

Fruit for the Christian may take many forms. We may refer to any manifestation that we receive by faith as fruit - whether healing, finances, or any other form of blessing. As we are able to lead others to Jesus, we consider this to be the *fruit of our labors*. But in the context of this book, and I believe as the primary intention of this passage, *"fruit"* represents the *fruit of the spirit* which is love. We must be engrafted to Jesus as the vine in order to manifest the love of God.

However in verse two, we discover that if we want to remain connected to the vine, then we must advance toward walking in this fruit of supernatural love. In chapter one, we covered First Corinthians 13:1-3, where we found that all of our best efforts to be a good Christian profit us nothing if we do not produce this fruit. As the branch cannot bear fruit of itself, God's love cannot flow through us unless we remain engrafted to Him. In our chapter on the *Stairway to Agape* we found just how intensive God's purging process can become to enable us to maximize our fruit production.

In the next verse, we see again God's primary tool to invoke this purging process:

> *John 15:3 –"**Now ye are clean through the word** which I have spoken unto you."*

The Word of God transforms us! All of our old worldly mindsets must be renewed for us to walk in love. These include our own personal self-reliance and dependence upon the world system. The Christian genuinely fused to Jesus the vine can rarely read or study the Word of God without the Spirit of God unveiling some area of needed change for their lives. Reading further:

> *John 15:4-5 –"Abide in me, and I in you, **As the branch cannot bear fruit if itself, except it abide in the vine; no more can ye, except ye abide in me.** I am the vine, ye are the branches: He that abideth in me, and I in him**, the same bringeth forth much fruit**: for without me ye can do nothing."*

Many may say that to *"abide"* in Jesus merely means that we belong to a church. However, to truly abide involves a strong connection to the Word and an ongoing lifestyle where we allow the Word to transform us. Without the Holy Spirit actively leading us in life, we will never accomplish anything for the Kingdom of God. But through cooperation with Him in His efforts to take us from *glory to glory*, we can produce *"much fruit"*. God designed us to have supernatural love overflow from our lives. However, few even recognize that this is possible! In the next verse we see the consequences of rejecting God's transformational process:

> *John 15:6 – "**If a man abide not in me, he is cast forth as a branch, and is withered; and men gather them and cast them into the fire, and they are burned.**"*

What a serious statement. Those who do not bear fruit (in our example - love) are severed from Jesus and His life-giving flow. Numbers of Christians daily experience *burnout*. This almost certainly is the result of attempting to serve God out of their own strength and resources. We were never meant to fulfill a call out of our own abilities. Those branches that are cast forth and burned most likely represent Christians who fail to let the Word transform them and are trying to live holy of themselves. Such efforts are doomed to failure! How dangerous it is for us to not pursue a deep relationship with the Lord! The next verse reveals to us an additional benefit of abiding in Jesus:

> *John 15:7 – "If ye abide in me, and my words abide in you, **ye shall ask what ye will, and it shall be done unto you.**"*

Wow, not only does abiding in Him enable us to walk in love, but it also empowers us to live by faith! **As we allow the Word of God to purge us, we see multiple spiritual principles invoked that activate our faith.**

> *Rom 10:17 – "So then faith cometh by hearing, and hearing by the word of God."*

Time spent reading and meditating the Word of God produces the *"hearing and hearing"* which builds our faith. But also:

> *Gal 5:6 – "For in Jesus Christ neither circumcision availeth any thing, nor uncircumcision: **but faith which worketh by love.**"*

Here we see that our faith is energized by the love that abiding in Jesus produces for us. Abiding in Jesus and the Word acts as the common denominator to link our faith to the love of God. In our

Stairway to Love, we saw this link as a vital step to remain in God's love developing system. Once we reached the top of the Staircase, we restarted again with a new level of energized faith to advance into higher levels of God's glory! Returning back to our passage in John:

> *John 15:8 – "**Herein is my father glorified, that ye bear much fruit; so shall ye be my disciples**."*

What a statement! God is glorified when we produce much love. In other words, God is glorified as we manifest the essence of His divine nature. And until we agree to let God change us from the inside out, we cannot truly consider ourselves to be His disciples. God's primary assignment for the end-time church is to unveil His glory to the world. Without abiding in Him, this becomes an impossibility. And now we find that the next verse validates all of what we have just covered:

> *John 15:9 – "**As the Father hath loved me, so have I loved you**: continue ye in my love."*

Now we see it clearly. To produce fruit for God is to walk in His love! And our connection to Jesus the vine (including all of the corrections that He will make in our lives), centers around love. Jesus loves us with the same level of love that the Father has for Him. It is not acceptable to God that we get saved but continue to struggle in life as before. He wants to raise us up in His supernatural love where oppression, lack, and sickness cannot touch us. Only then are we truly able to display His goodness. However, we must continue to follow His instructions!

OBEDIENT BRANCHES

> *John 15:10 – "**If ye keep my commandments, ye shall abide in my love;** even as I have kept my Father's commandments, and abide in His love."*

To continue to abide in Jesus and to walk in love, it is mandatory that we allow Him to be Lord over our lives. Where Jesus here says that we are to obey His commandments, He is not referring to the Old Testament law. He fulfilled the Law such that we no longer are led by a set of commandments *engraven in stone*. We have been born again thus enabling the Holy Spirit to dwell within us and lead us into all truth. The commandments we now follow are the directives given to us by the Spirit of God. Understand however, nothing that the Spirit of the Lord will ever instruct us to do will violate the Word.

As New Testament Christians, we are to learn to be Spirit-led. To be Spirit-led, at times refers to us following the leading of The Holy Spirit and at other times it refers to being led of our own reborn spirit-man within us. Both end up being relatively synonymous since our spirit and the Holy Spirit are in communion with one another. It is the Holy Spirit that will lead us up God's Stairway to Love. It is the same Holy Spirit that will convict us when we miss the mark. **For someone to declare that they love God and yet not follow His leading is a clear indication that they have been deceived.** We see Jesus state this in the previous chapter of John:

> *John 14:23-24 –"Jesus answered and said unto him,* ***If a man love me, he will keep my words****: and my Father will love him, and we will come and make our abode with him. He that loveth me not keepeth not my sayings: and the word which ye hear is not mine, but the Father's which sent me."*

Our level of obedience to Jesus indicates our love for Him and thus establishes the level we may abide with Him. The level that we abide with Him will determine the level of supernatural love that we may manifest. As walking in love indicates the maturity of the believer, so does being led of the Spirit of God. We find this in Romans:

> *Rom 8:14 –"For as many as are led by the Spirit of God, they are the sons of God."*

The Greek word here translated *"sons"* is *huioi*. *Huioi* represents more than just sons by birth - it represents *mature sons*. The *huioi* are those *sons who have grown up, have full rights to all that their father possesses, and are ready to take over the family business.* Since both walking in love and being led of the spirit indicate spiritual maturity, then to be fully led of the Spirit of God infers that we are also walking in love.

The Spirit of God will never instruct us to do anything that violates the Word. As well, love fulfills all of the intentions of the Word. Therefore, all that the Holy Spirit directs us to do is designed to lead us into love! If we faithfully follow His leading, we will always produce actions of love and eventually will end up manifesting His glory. When we walk in love, our outer actions will match our inner nature and we will be truly fulfilled. The result of living a fulfilled life (being in the center of God's will for us) is *joy*. We see this in the next verse:

> *John 15:11 – "**These things have I spoken unto you.** That my joy might remain in you, and **that your joy might be full.**"*

So many worldly-minded Christians are afraid to follow God fully with their lives. They are concerned that once they commit themselves to follow God with all of their hearts, they no longer will have any fun in life. How ridiculous this must sound to God. His greatest pleasure is that we enter into His joy. In the **Parable of the Talents** in Matthew chapter 25, He rewarded those who utilized their gifting to *"enter thou into the joy of the Lord"*. Only by committing ourselves to follow His every whim can we ever know fullness of joy. By attempting to find *happiness* on our own, we will inevitably end up disappointed. Again know that we are not to target obeying a written list of commandments, but instead are to set our sights on walking in love as is verified in the next verse:

> *John 15:12 – "**This is my commandment, That ye love one another, as I have loved you.**"*

Our commandment is to allow God to transform us such that we can walk in the same level of love that Jesus has for us. Wow! As impossible as this seems, it is God's plan for us. However, we will not get there without God performing an entire *makeover* on, in, and through us! Only true disciples stay in the transformational process long enough for this to take place. My hope is that through the teachings of this book, you will be motivated to become one of those determined disciples! We have already addressed the next verse in our chapter on *The Seed of Love*, but let's review it again:

> *John 15:13 – "Greater love has no man than this, that a man lay down his life for his friends."*

We discovered that the Greek word here used for *"life"* is p*suche,* actually meaning the *soul.* And this is not a definition of the greatest level of love, but the pathway to it. If we want to attain to the highest levels of the love of God, we must be willing to lay aside our plans and desires on behalf of those with whom we are in covenant. We must be willing to battle through rejection and fear to move into the glory of God. Many are mistaken to believe that we must pour out our lives to everyone that we meet. However according to the next verse, there is a specific category of people that we are to especially bless:

> *John 15:14 – "Ye are my friends, if ye do whatsoever I command you."*

Jesus lists His friends as those that obey Him. We have already found out that those who obey Him and bear much fruit are described as His disciples. They are those who have lain down their lives for Him. They are the believers who have stepped fully into their covenant roles. They are the ones best positioned to receive of God's highest levels of blessing. **Disciples also become the ones on whose behalf, we are to lay down our souls.** As we truly become participants of a body of disciples who are sold out to God, we become the end-time **Bride of Christ** that will overflow with His glory! By becoming one that lays down our souls for the brethren, we qualify to become a *"friend"* of Jesus:

> *John 15:15 – "Henceforth I call you not servants; for the servant knoweth not what his lord doeth: but I have called you friends; for all things that I have heard of my Father I have made known unto you."*

The disciple is not one who is merely performing good deeds on behalf of his Christianity. He is instead walking in a deep, abiding relationship with Jesus. He has become a friend of God and has been instructed in the *ways* of the Lord. The disciples have moved into the lifestyle of being totally Spirit-led - doing only those things which they are instructed. Since they as branches are grafted to the vine, the very essence of God's love may flow through them. As they have lain down their souls on behalf of their calling, they have become fully positioned to walk in love. In the final two verses of this passage that we are going to cover, Jesus reiterates that His commandment for our lives is to love one another:

> *John 15:16 –"Ye have not chosen me, but I have chosen you, and* **ordained you, that ye should go and bring forth fruit**, *and that your fruit should remain: that whatsoever ye shall ask of the Father in my name, he may give it you."*

We have been ordained to bring forth the continual fruit of love. As we do so, it enables us to walk in such a level of faith that all of our prayer requests are answered. There is such a strong tie between love and faith that not only does love energize our faith, but under loves' influence, faith for what we proclaim becomes nearly automatic. Because we are so aware of the Father's love for us, we become convinced that He will answer our petitions.

One aspect of this verse may act as a stumbling block to some Christians; *"Ye have not chosen me, but I have chosen you."* Responses may vary between, *"He has not chosen me to be a disciple."* to *"Because He chose me to be saved, I will now be able to walk in love regardless of my level of obedience to Him."* Both are incorrect. It is the Father's will that all be saved and that none perish, yet we know that many will not receive Him. We must choose to invite Jesus to be our Lord and Savior. We see also that our ability to step into full discipleship is based on our decisions to allow Him to lead us and even to purge us.

So why does this say: *"I have chosen you?"* The answer lies in that, at this point, Jesus is addressing His disciples who have already followed Him faithfully and proven their willingness to be used. They have been chosen because they had demonstrated obedience to Him and His words. Undoubtedly, like the *rich young ruler*, many were most likely summoned who did not follow His ministry.

We don't choose the day of our promotion. We stretch into our initial callings awaiting the Lord to deem us faithful and prepared disciples ready to fill higher appointments. Know as well, that just because we are called does not guarantee that we will finish our course. Much internal and thus external change will be required. As spoken by Jesus in Matthew:

> *Mat 22:14 –"For many are called, but few are chosen."*

We must choose to follow Jesus with all of our heart. As we do so, He will *choose* us to carry His glory.

John affirms again the tie between abiding in God and walking in love in First John:

> *1John 4:16 –"And we have known and believed the love that God hath to us. God is love; and* **he that dwelleth in love dwelleth in God***, and God in him."*

We may manifest no more of the love of God than the depth of our relationship with Him permits.

KNOWING LOVE

> *1John 4:7-8 –"Beloved, let us love one another: for love is of God; and every one that loveth is born of God, and knoweth God. He that loveth not knoweth not God; for God is love."*

We have already learned from this scripture passage that it is impossible for anyone to carry the love of God unless they are born-again. We must be *"born of God."* Now we want to examine a second stipulation of this passage to walk in love - that we *"knoweth God!"* In fact, we are going to find that there is another cycle involving love that is to be operating in the life of the believer: **The Love–Knowledge Cycle.**

This *Love-Knowledge Cycle* establishes two limiting parameters that determine the depth of our love walk:

One: We will never be able to walk in supernatural love beyond our genuine knowledge of God.

Two: The more that we experience the genuine supernatural love of God, the more we will have unveiled before us the intimate knowledge of who He really is. The overwhelming experience of basking in His love allows us to taste and know of His goodness.

Knowing that *God is love*, how could we possibly believe that we could manifest this most powerful force in the universe without intimate knowledge of Him? **God is not going to dole out His love - the essence of His very nature, to those with no deep desire to follow Him in a heart to heart fashion.** Only by targeting to know of God through study of the Word and involving ourselves in prayer will He unveil Himself to us as the fullness of love. And only by tasting of that love will we have verified to us how magnificent He truly is.

We see that Jesus emphasized forcibly the need to know Him:

> *Mat 7:21-23 –"Not every one that saith unto me, Lord, Lord, shall enter into the kingdom of heaven; but he that doeth the will of my father which is in heaven. Many will say to me in that day, Lord, Lord, have we not prophesied in thy name? and in thy name have cast out devils? And in thy name done many wonderful works? And then will I profess unto them,* **I never knew you***: depart from me, ye that work iniquity."*

Jesus here ties doing God's will with knowing Him. Those who develop in relationship with the Lord will be moved to obey what He instructs. And of course, His will for us is to walk in love. **Many who are caught up trying to merely perform good works for God without coming to know and obey him may be in for an awakening at some point.** Jesus did not even validate the *wonderful works* that they claimed to complete.

Paul also expressed that his greatest desire was to know God:

> *Phil 3:8 - "Yea doubtless, and **I count all things but loss for the excellency of the knowledge of Christ Jesus my Lord**: for whom I have suffered the loss of all things, and do count them but dung, that I may win Christ,"*

And again, two verses later:

> *Phil 3:10 - "**That I may know him**, and the power of his resurrection, and the fellowship of his sufferings, being made conformable unto his death;"*

Paul declares in no uncertain terms that nothing mattered in life to him above knowing Jesus. Regardless of the persecution or whatever other price he might have to pay, he was determined to advance in his knowledge of God. Paul infers a tie between love and knowledge elsewhere in scripture:

> *Phil 1:9-11 – "And this I pray, **that your love may abound yet more and more in knowledge** and in judgement; That ye may approve things that are excellent; that ye may be sincere and without offense till the day of Christ: **Being filled with the fruits of righteousness**, which are by Jesus Christ, unto the glory and praise of God."*

Other translations state that *"your love should overflow in knowledge and discernment."* Verse nine may be viewed from either perspective of our Love-Knowledge Cycle:

One: The more that we move into the love of God, the more we will develop knowledge of Him and of proper discernment of good versus evil. Nothing opens our eyes to the root cause of all wickedness as does experiencing the tangible love of Jesus. **Being encompassed with supernatural love makes one keenly aware of the demonic forces manipulating the lives of those still caught in the world's clutches.**

Two: As we develop full and complete knowledge (*epignosis*) of God, the more our love will overflow. It is not an accident that knowledge is one of the steps we must take on the Stairway to Love. Scripture relates in First John:

> *1John 3:2 – "Beloved, now are we the sons of God, and it doth not yet appear what we shall be: but we know that, when he shall appear, we shall be like him; for we shall see him as he is."*

This powerful verse assures us that if we are born-again then we have already been made *"sons of God."* Yet, just because we are saved does not mean that we have comprehension of or have stepped into the fullness of who God has made us. However when we *see Him as He is*, we shall be transformed to be like Him. Since Jesus is the epitome of love; therefore the more knowledge of Him we gain, the more of His image of love we reflect. We have already mentioned the *mirror* of the Word from Second Corinthians but let's look at it again from this new perspective:

> *2Cor 3:18 – "But we all, with open face beholding as in a glass the glory of the Lord, are changed into the same image from glory to glory, even as by the Spirit of the Lord."*

Again, the glass represents God's Word. Since Jesus is *the Word made flesh*, then as we spend time in God's Word we should see Jesus. As we see Him, we gain knowledge of Him and are transformed into the same glorious image of Our Savior. Knowledge of Him causes our love to *abound yet more and more*! We don't have to wait until we die to carry the image of love. We can carry it today as we come to know Him. John the Beloved also spoke of the tie between the knowledge of God and love:

> *1John 2:3-6 – "And hereby we do know that we know him, if we keep his commandments. He that saith, I know him and keepeth not his commandments, is a liar, and the truth is not in him.* **But whoso keepeth his word, in him verily is the love of God perfected**: *hereby know we that we are in him. He that saith he abideth in him ought himself also so to walk, even as he walked."*

Those who genuinely know Jesus obey Him. How could we not fully follow the God of love? **To not obey Him is proof that**

one does not actually know God. But here we see that **the love of God is perfected in someone who first knows Him and then subsequently obeys Him**. Without obedience, we can never step into the love of God. Our walk of love becomes the evidence that we are truly abiding in Him as discussed earlier in this chapter.

A NOTE ON HYPER-GRACE

A destructive wave of teaching is currently sweeping the world. Though it appears new and fresh, this lie has been around from the beginning. This new fad is labeled by many as **Hyper-Grace**. The core focus of this teaching declares to its adherents that to walk in the fullness of Christianity, once born-again all that is required of them is to know that God loves them. By merely believing that God loves them, they too will be able to freely love all those around them. No development is necessary; no process of purging is required. In fact, even their obedience to God becomes a relative non-factor.

Hyper-Grace declares that once we are saved, God will never convict us of sin again. This doctrine states that now that we are his children made righteous through The Cross, God can no longer even witness any sin in our lives. The mantra for this message is: *"It is finished"* - as declared by Jesus at Calvary. Any efforts that one might make to stretch into the Kingdom of God or develop any spiritual discipline is labeled as *works*. There is no longer any need to fast, pray long hours, or tithe. These all become labeled as religious works rather than the actions of someone wanting to fuel their spirit man, crucify their flesh, and go from glory to glory.

Instead of allowing God to correct them of any ungodly actions or mindsets and thus move up the Stairway to Love, instead they harden their hearts to the convicting power of the Holy Spirit. Confusing the conviction that God brings with the condemnation of the devil, they forfeit their ability to be led of the Spirit - especially in any areas that might stretch them. Because they have been able to harden their hearts to the leading of God to deal with sin or needed change, they confuse their lack of conviction with walking in the *peace of God*. The love that they claim to walk in is from a placebo effect of convincing themselves that they are *right* with God and that He loves them regardless.

Although their teachers will boldly proclaim that they are not providing their followers with a **license to sin**, the capacity to shun the convicting voice of the Holy Spirit has that same effect. Any efforts of God to correct them or to chastise the flesh are instantly labeled as works, religion, or condemnation. Such actions veer dangerously close to *blaspheming the Holy Spirit* - attributing the actions of the Spirit of God to satan.

We have discovered in this book that much work is required to manifest the genuine supernatural love of God. We must allow God to delve deep within us to enact great personal change. The Christian genuinely desirous of walking in supernatural love does not look at the conviction of God as a barrier to peace in their lives. They welcome all conviction as God's means to accelerate them up His ladder to manifest *perfect love*. Without ongoing conviction, no impetus will motivate us to our finish line. Those fully ensnared by the hyper-grace doctrine can have little genuine hope of moving into God's last day glory.

REVELATION BY LOVE

For the end-time church to fulfill God's plan for us to manifest His glory, we as its member's must receive revelation knowledge from the Word as has no prior generation. This is related to us in the vision from Habakkuk toward which every revivalist Christian is to be running:

> *Hab 2:14 –"For the earth shall be **filled with the knowledge** of the glory of the Lord, as the waters cover the sea."*

Fullness of knowledge of the Word must precede the glory! **God is performing His *finishing work* on the church through the full unveiling of His Word in these end-times.** Paul referred to the knowledge of glory in Second Corinthians:

> *2Cor 4:6 –"For God, who commanded the light to shine out of darkness, hath shined in our hearts, **to give the light***

of the knowledge of the glory of God *in the face of Jesus Christ."*

Throughout church history, God has always released new revelation of His Word to produce maturing growth spurts in the Body of Christ. Each time such revelation was released, The Church experienced major, often worldwide revival. Revelation always precedes revival, and here we see that God has *shined into our hearts* revelation knowledge of His glory. The Church is in the process of stepping into the greatest revival the world has ever witnessed. We are about to manifest the end-time glory of God as we overflow in the anointing of His love. This revival will require the *meat* of the Word to be poured forth as never before.

As this end-time revival will usher in His glory, the *meat* that we will partake of is *the revelation of the supernatural nature of love and how we may step into it.* In fact, the true meat of the Word is the message of love. Since Jesus is the *Word made flesh* and He as God is also love, then love is the flesh (meat) of the Word. Love sums up the entire content and comprehension of both the Old and New Testaments. Therefore God is pouring out revelation of Himself and of His love as toward no prior generation.

> *John 14:21 –"He that hath my commandments, and keepeth them, he it is that loveth me: and he that loveth me shall be loved of my Father, and I will love him and will manifest myself to him."*

Jesus is unveiling Himself through the mirror of His Word to those who will establish themselves in a love relationship with Him. And as we have mentioned, as we gain knowledge of Him we are positioned to move into His love. If we can gain revelation of and consequently begin to walk in love, all other revelation will follow. Paul states in First Corinthians:

> *1Cor 2:7-10 –"But we speak the wisdom of God in a mystery, even the hidden wisdom, which God ordained before the world unto our glory: Which none of the princes of this world knew: for had they known it, they would not*

> *have crucified the Lord of glory. But as it is written, Eye hath not seen, nor ear heard, neither have entered into the heart of man, the things with God hath prepared for them that love him. But God hath revealed them unto us by his Spirit: for the Spirit searcheth all things, yea, the deep things of God."*

The mysteries of the Word are ordained to be revealed to us to take us into His glory. This deep revelation is laid up for those who are moving into His love. Just as God will shine His light deep within us to allow us to be purged of anything that hinders the flow of love, He is also imparting to us the deep truths of the Word to freely activate this love unto the glory. This process is related to us in Psalm 97:

> *Psa 97:10-11 – "Ye that love the Lord, hate evil: he preserveth the souls of his saints; he delivereth them out of the hand of the wicked.* **Light is sown for the righteous**, *and gladness for the upright in heart."*

As we move into love, we will despise any form of evil - especially that which would attempt to cling to us. Subsequently, God preserves our souls as we cooperate in His purging process. Light (revelation) is sown to us to illuminate the path to higher levels of this love and eventual glory. In the chapter on *Rooted in Love*, our main passage referenced was from Ephesians chapter three. Looking at it further, we see again the tie between love and the revelation of Christ:

> *Eph 3:17-19 – "That Christ may dwell in your hearts by faith; that ye, being rooted and grounded in love, May be able to comprehend with all saints what is the breadth, and length, and depth, and height; and to know the love of Christ, which passeth knowledge, that ye might be filled with all the fullness of God."*

As we endeavor to extend our *roots of faith* into the love of God, we are positioned to gain full and comprehensive knowledge of Christ and of His love. Notice as well that this passage refers to *"with all saints."* This represents that His love is to be poured out to a corporate body, all seeking the same finish line of His glory.

This multidimensional, multifaceted, glorious love though birthed through knowledge will surpass even our greatest expectations. It will allow us to be *"filled with all the fullness of God"* - a love so overwhelmingly glorious that, no matter how prepared we think that we are, our natural minds will not be fully able to comprehend it.

The next verses bring this out:

> *Eph 3:20-21 –"Now unto him that is able to do exceeding abundantly above all that we ask of think, according to the power that worketh in us, Unto him be glory in the church by Christ Jesus throughout all ages, world without end. Amen."*

God's glory is going to exceed our wildest expectations. However, it will not manifest upon those with no expectation.

A step that the believer needs to take to accelerate their growth into love is to pray much in tongues. Per First Corinthians 14, when we speak in tongues we are speaking *"mysteries"* unto God. As we sow forth the mysteries of The Kingdom, we receive back a harvest of revelation knowledge. God reintroduced an outpouring of the *Baptism of the Holy Spirit* to His church at Azusa Street over one hundred years ago. This was necessary to allow the Body of Christ to accelerate into the knowledge of Him that will culminate in the manifestation of the glory in these now last-days.

Praying in the Spirit allows us to overflow in scriptural knowledge and thus move fully into His love. Without extensive time praying in tongues, it becomes difficult if not impossible to receive the revelation necessary to manifest the glory. God has given His church this power tool of tongues to finish the work assigned to them.

God is now pouring out understanding as never before. He is bringing us all that we need to be fully adorned as the Glorious Bride of Christ.

CHAPTER 10

PERFECT LOVE

As we progress in our endeavor to walk in the supernatural love of God, the closer that we approach to walking in His glory, the more change will be invoked and even demanded in our lives. In this chapter on *Perfect Love*, we will look at some of the finishing work necessary to step into God's fullness. Those who genuinely desire to display the fullness of the stature of Christ are willing to make whatever modifications are required of them to do so. Let's begin at a point we covered in the last chapter:

BOLD LOVE

1John 4:16-17 –"And we have known and believed the love that God hath to us. God is love; and he that dwelleth in love dwelleth in God, and God in Him. **Herein is our love made perfect we may have boldness** *in the day of judgement; because as he is, so are we in this world."*

As we learn to abide in a deep intimate relationship with God, He brings us to the place where we are, as Jesus, doing only those things that we see the Father do. At this point, our ability to walk in His love is perfected and subsequently his love overflows in our lives. Through the recognition of, *as He is – so are we,* great "*boldness*" arises from within us. The revelation of our righteousness and thus our right standing with God gives us boldness to approach the Throne of Grace.

As well, because dwelling in love brings such tangible awareness of the presence of God, we have great boldness in every area of life and ministry knowing that He has our backs! Once love has overtaken our lives, no longer will we shrink back from even the slightest ministry opportunity.

However we have learned that anytime we want to step into an anointing or a promise of God by faith, action must usually be first initiated by us. Remember from James:

> *Jas 2:17 – "Even so faith, if it hath not works, is dead, being alone."*

Therefore if we want supernatural love to overtake our lives, it may be necessary that we learn to boldly step into actions that this love would inspire. How may one who is too timid to worship God without embarrassment move into the love of God? Or how may another who is too ashamed to testify of the goodness of God expect to manifest this evangelistic anointing? We must be willing to charge beyond any roadblocks of the *fear of man* to break through into this highest of empowerments. We must know who we are and understand what has been made available to us.

> *Prov 28:1 – "The wicked flee when no man pursueth:* ***but the righteous are bold as a lion."***

We must become as bold as lions recognizing that the very nature of the **Lion of Judah** abides within us and that He stands with us. I recognize that some people are just naturally bolder than others - those who can easily speak publically or who live with total abandonment from the fear of making a public spectacle. In no way am I stating that we have to become so outgoing. However, we must be willing to develop enough gumption to proclaim the Word, lay hands on the sick, or even confront wickedness as the Lord would desire to lead us.

For a Christian to step into new levels of the love of God, they must be able to blast through prior comfort zones. Many have confessed a lack of boldness over themselves their entire lives declaring: *"I don't like to make a scene."* or *"I'm not a people person."* Understand that once supernatural love comes upon you, you will make a scene everywhere you go. As well, this same love will make you a people person. Faith actions for love will involve going beyond our pre-established mindsets of who we think we are or what we imagine we can do.

Those who want to carry love may be required to muster courage to speak boldly to those who would oppose the Gospel. As the disciples prayed in the early days of the church:

> *Acts 4:29-31 –"And now, Lord, behold their threatenings: and grant unto thy servants, that with all boldness they may speak thy word, By stretching forth thine hand to heal; and that signs and wonders may be done by the name of thy holy child Jesus. And when they had prayed, the place was shaken where they were assembled together; and they were all filled with the Holy Ghost, and **they spake the word of God with boldness.**"*

Apparently God is moved when His children become determined to represent Him unashamedly! As the disciples recognized the need to minister the Word with boldness, the power of God filled them and boldness automatically resulted. Equally, when the love of God comes upon us we WILL minister boldly. However, we will need to be determined to step into boldness by faith before this infilling fully manifests.

In Ephesians 3:14-20, we examined Paul's prayer that those in Ephesus would be *"rooted and grounded in love"* and that they might *"know the love of Christ which passeth knowledge."* This passage is preceded by Eph 3:12-13 which states:

> *Eph 3:12-13 –"In whom we have boldness and access with confidence by the faith of him. Wherefore I desire that ye faint not at my tribulations for you, which is your glory."*

Here, possibly the most powerful prayer in scripture regarding love is introduced by the declaration that regardless of probable persecution, we are to have boldness. Boldness displays openly that we fully believe that the Word is true.

In chapter five, I shared of an event that took place many years back where while street witnessing the supernatural love of God came upon me. Know first of all, that I am not an evangelist nor does evangelism come easily to me. My primary gifting is that of a teacher, and being somewhat of a geek I always struggled a bit in initiating conversations with strangers. While some people 'have never met a stranger', I avoided conversations with those I did not personally know.

However, I had a heart to serve God and knew from scripture that we were all to evangelize. So on several occasions, I went witnessing on the streets with others more gifted in this arena. For me to walk up and share the Gospel with anyone demanded all of the faith and boldness that I could muster.

And then one Friday night, the supernatural love of God descended upon me and I effortlessly was able to lead five people to Jesus in 45 minutes. Had I never made myself go *boldly* past my natural inclinations, I would never have experienced that glorious event. In fact, it was an experience that altered the course of my life. God showed me that He had a love anointing that could empower me to soar far above my natural abilities. This event continued to fuel my fire to experience the genuine love of God and to discover how we can intentionally access it.

Paul alludes to the tie between love and boldness in Second Timothy:

> *2Tim 1:7 – "For God has not given us the spirit of fear; but of power, and of love, and of a sound mind."*

In the King James Version, it reads as if Paul is letting us know that fear opposes our ability to walk in God's power, love, and mental soundness. And this interpretation would be acceptable as we shall discuss shortly. However, the word translated *"fear"* in this verse is the Greek word *deilias* which is better rendered as *timidity*. To any level that we give way to timidity, we hinder the flow of God's power and love to our lives! Knowing that timidity is the opposite of boldness, we can see the need to overcome various fears to walk in love.

There are numerous areas where the enemy may have established roadblocks in our lives to hinder us from stepping into love. And many of them can only be breached by determined boldness! As mentioned:

We need to be bold to witness, testify, or to pray publicly.

We need to be bold in worship - unashamed to raise our hands or to dance before Him.

We need to be bold to lay hands on others for healing and to prophecy.

We need to be bold to stand for holiness and be willing to confront sin.

We need to be bold to bless our enemies and to forgive those who have hurt us.

Once we set ourselves to boldly go beyond the limits set for us by public opinion, tradition, our own view of our personal capabilities, or even fear, we position ourselves to move into perfected love. We must let nothing hinder us. We must be willing to step out. God has our backs!

ADDRESSING FEAR

*1John 4:18 – "**There is no fear in love; but perfect love casteth out fear**: because fear hath torment. He that feareth is not made perfect in love."*

As with timidity, every form of fear that would arise against us must be recognized and properly dealt with. Here it is clearly stated that love cannot be perfected in the presence of fear. **Perfect love will cast out fear. However to step into love will require that we exercise our faith to confront fear issues in advance of love's manifestation.**

We have already emphasized that to be led of the Spirit equates to walking in love. The Holy Spirit will never instruct us to do anything outside of the Word. And since love fulfills all of the intentions of God's Word, then to be led of the Spirit of God is to automatically walk in love. We found in Romans 8:14 that those who are led of the Spirit are the mature sons of God! However let's proceed from there to include the next verse:

*Rom 8:14-15 – "For as many as are led by the Spirit of God, they are the sons (huioi: mature sons) of God. **For ye have not received the spirit of bondage again to fear**; but ye have received the Spirit of adoption, whereby we cry, Abba, Father."*

Here, walking with fear is contrasted to being Spirit-led and thus is opposed to walking in love. The bondage that fear produces paralyzes us from stepping into the glorious liberty of *agape*. Thus to step into perfect love, we must identify and eradicate fear from our lives as if it were a cancer to the Body of Christ. By recognizing that we have been adopted into the family of God and that Father God is now watching over us, we may boldly say: *"Whom shall I fear?"*

Fear acts as the enemies' primary weapon against the children of God. Fear will always be launched against us in the attempt to get us to hesitate or even disobey His assignments. Through fear, we question whether God will come through for us, whether man will persecute us, or even if friends will reject us. Even when casting out demonic spirits, the first level of defense that the confronted entities will emit is fear. I am confident that every evil spirit in operation uses fear in some form as their primary tool of entry.

Fear is the opposite of faith. After the disciples awoke Jesus to rebuke the storm, He chided them, *"Why are ye so fearful, O ye of little faith?"* When Joshua was to take the Promised Land, God said *"be not afraid, neither be dismayed."* When Jairus received word that his daughter had died, Jesus exhorted, *"Fear not, believe only, and she shall be made whole."* Because, supernatural love may only be accessed by faith, we can comprehend why *"He that feareth is not made perfect in love."*

Therefore to walk in love, it becomes vital to confront areas of fear in our lives - because fear represents doubt of God and of His word. We must be willing to search out our thoughts and reactions to sniff out the existence and operation of even subtle fears.

Common fears most people might identify with may be of *snakes, bugs, spiders, germs, dark, heights, airplanes, dogs, and on and on.* Know that the devil will use these fears against us at every opportunity. How can we lay hands on the sick if we are afraid of germs? How can we fulfill a worldwide ministry calling if we are afraid to fly? And rest assured, whichever other fears that we embrace will be used against us in some form at the most inopportune times. If we are afraid of snakes, eventually the enemy will assure that one is spotted at the place you are to go to pray for someone.

But fear goes far beyond the feeling of terror one might entertain with regard to creepy crawlers and other phobia. Fear can reside in the deepest hidden connections within our mind. Hindering fear can take the form of *fear of rejection, perfectionism, legalism, fear of lack, fear of failure, fear of pain, fear of public speaking, and of course fear of death.*

Unaddressed fear may:

1. **Rewire our thinking such that it inhibits the flow of genuine love in our lives. Interactions with others that should birth love from within us are instead avoided due to previous mindsets of rejection.**
2. **Prevent us from stepping into God-given opportunities to release love where we are instead paralyzed by fear of man.**
3. **And more seriously, fear may open doors to demonic activity that hinders us in even more detrimental ways.**

Because fear is the opposing force to faith, it works to open holes in our *Shield of Faith*. Wherever we doubt (a form of fear) a promise of God, it negates our ability to receive of that promise. Many people question God's goodness based upon the trials of Job. However even with Job, fear provided the open door through which satan was able to attack him - for he declared:

*Job 3:25 –"**For the thing which I greatly feared is come upon me**, and that which I was afraid of is come unto me."*

Job had been making daily sacrifices in fear of disaster striking his household evidently tied to the apparent continual carousing of his children. Even though God declared him to be a perfect man who hated evil, perhaps Job did not view himself as such. Such fear produced through entertaining a sin mentality is possibly the avenue by which satan was able to attack him. Regardless of whether you receive this explanation or not, without doubt fear opens doors to give the devil access to spoil our lives and even keep us from walking in the supernatural love of God.

There is also a need to refuse to entertain fear when God is moving supernaturally among us. So many Christians are afraid to go to churches where the genuine power of God is being displayed. They make statements like: *"That's the church where they lay hands on people and they fall down."; "They speak in tongues."* or *"They believe in casting out demons."* These all point to fear being used to limit the people of God from experiencing His goodness.

Jesus upon calling His first disciples, instructed them to go beyond the fear of the supernatural if they were to fulfill their callings! After ministering, Jesus told Peter to launch out in the deep to receive an abundant reward. In doing so, they were able to net so many fish that their boats began to sink. The soon-to-be disciples shaken by this event were instructed of Jesus to go beyond their initial fear:

> *Luke 5:8-10 –"When Simon Peter saw it, he fell down at Jesus' knees, saying, Depart from me; for I am a sinful man, O Lord. For he was astonished, and all that were with him, at the draught of the fishes which they had taken: And so was also James, and John, the sons of Zebedee, which were partners with Simon,* ***And Jesus said unto Simon, Fear not;*** *from henceforth thou shalt catch men."*

To move into the love of God, it becomes imperative that we overcome any fear of the supernatural, whether of God or of the devil. The power of love is well able to overcome every scheme and manifestation of darkness. It was Moses who had to overcome his initial fear of God's supernatural manifestation (remember the burning bush). Yet it was he who was able to ascend Mount Sinai to experience the personal manifestation of God's glory. The multitudes however, were afraid to approach the mountain and required that Moses put a veil over his face lest they gaze upon this glory. Those who fear exposure to the supernatural will never be enabled to carry the love of the Father.

At this point, it will be valuable for us to define an area of fear repeatedly referred to in scripture: **The Fear of God**. We as Christians are instructed to overcome the fears of the world yet we are implored to embrace the fear of God. Without some level of understanding of this term it becomes difficult if not impossible to make the changes necessary to develop in love. This phrase carries different implications based upon whether or not we are truly following God.

For the sinner, the fear of God represents a fearful (fear-filled) anticipation of coming judgment. For the Christian who has been repeatedly instructed that he is still a sinner or that he is *falling short of the glory*, this fear indicates a hesitation or apprehension to draw near to God. However for a Christian who recognizes that they have been recreated the righteousness of God, the fear of God refers to an awesome reverence for God and for His kingdom.

For the Christian sold out to fulfill the plan of God for their life, the fear of God represents to them an overwhelming concern and even a dread to not be in God's perfect will. This fear is not tied to a concern of God's judgment coming upon them, for they work continually to live above sin. Their fear is induced by the recognition that only in God's perfect will can they experience the full measure of His love and power.

The fear of the Lord is actually one of His greatest blessings for those seeking the full force of God's love to be released in their lives. The revivalist Christian invites God's convicting voice to keep them on the *straight and narrow* rather than harden their hearts to it - calling it *condemnation*. The fear of God becomes His greatest promotional tool to elevate us above the temptations of the world and to draw us to strive for spiritual perfection. The fear of God is birthed out of His love for us! We see this in Second Corinthians:

> *2Cor 7:1 – "Having therefore these promises, dearly beloved, **let us cleanse ourselves from all filthiness** of the flesh and spirit, **perfecting holiness** in the fear of God."*

"Holiness" for the Christian represents *right living*, whereas in most cases *righteousness* refers to our *new nature* and *right standing* with God. Once we are saved we are made righteous, but now God expects us to learn and endeavor to live holy. And holiness to God does not refer to what we wear or how we fix our hair. Holiness to God is reflected by the level that we rise above the sinful mindsets and actions of our past. True holiness is an indication of the amount of God's love in which we walk and dwell. The fear of God motivates us to live a holy life! Per Hebrews, the fear of God becomes our impetus to serve Him in an acceptable fashion:

> *Heb 12:28-29 – "Wherefore we receiving a kingdom which cannot be moved, let us have grace, whereby **we may serve God acceptably with reverence and godly fear**: For our God is a consuming fire."*

Reverence for the things of God and fear of spending even a day dwelling outside of His will and presence move us to live fully for Him without restraint. **One potential area of hindrance to walking in God's will and thus His love is the FEAR OF MAN**. This fear may subtly take the form of a need for acceptance by friends, family, or coworkers. It may have access to us through a root of rejection. Or we may merely fear out and out persecution. However, Jesus instructed us to allow the fear of God to override the fear of man. Regarding the wicked, Jesus commanded:

> *Matt 10:26-28 – "**Fear them not therefore**: for there is nothing covered, that shall not be revealed; and hid, that shall not be known, What I tell you in darkness, that speak ye in light: and what ye hear in the ear, that preach ye upon the housetops. **And fear not them which kill the body, but are not able to kill the soul**: but rather fear him which is able to destroy both soul and body in hell."*

The fear of man would hinder us from proclaiming the good news and love of God. However, the fear of God will spur us beyond such temporal concerns! The fear of God is a protective mechanism to keep us positioned to remain anointed. Many who would consider themselves Christians yet oppose this fear are discussed in detail in the book of Jude:

*Jude 1:12 –"**These are spots in your feasts of charity (love)**, when they feast with you, **feeding themselves without fear (the fear of God)**: clouds they are without water, carried about of winds; trees **whose fruit withereth, without fruit, twice dead, plucked up by the roots**;"*

We understand that as trees of righteousness, we are to manifest the fruit of the spirit which is love. Yet, we find in this passage that those without the fear of God keeping them above corruption cannot manifest this fruit. However, many Christians confusing the conviction of the Holy Spirit with the condemnation of the devil have seared their conscience to the fear of God.

Fear is declared by John to produce torment. Where faith proclaims: *"No weapon formed against us shall prosper,"* fear decries: *"but it won't work for you."* Obviously fear is the result of ungodly thought processes or strongholds that pose a barrier to our advancement into the things of God. The ultimate damage that unaddressed fear can produce in the life of an on-fire Christian is where the fear or rejection will transform them from a *God-pleaser* to a *people-pleaser.*

Therefore, fears must be confronted by the revivalist Christian to progress into the love of God - especially when identified as being initiated by demonic spirits. If the fear of something tends to paralyze us and terror grips our soul, then there is a likelihood that the demonic is involved. This is more than merely the *fight or flight* adrenaline rush that we experience in sudden close calls or from loud noises that awaken us. Instead, we must confront unreasonable fears that limit our liberty to flow unchecked in the direction that God assigns us.

When embedded fears are unveiled in our lives, we must find and confess scriptures to displace those fears. We must command the spirits of fear to leave and then act in a fashion to counter fear's threats. Faith acted upon will deliver us.

Some may say: *"I don't want to be free of these fears. I don't want to like snakes and bugs."* Know that there is a difference between fear and dislike. We may not want to own a pet snake, but we must not let the concern that there might be snakes (nonlethal) in an area keep us from going there - especially if God directed us to that place. Confronting fear of snakes, bugs, and spiders probably will not alter our efforts to access the love of God to a great deal, however the fear of man and the fear of rejection most likely will.

REJECTING THE WORLD

1John 2:15 –"Love not the world, neither the things that are in the world. If any man love the world, the love of the Father is not in him."

It is amazing how we can often skim over bible passages and think that we fully comprehend the meaning of the verses. Our traditional interpretation of the above verse is something like this: *"It is impossible to sin like the world sins and experience the love of God."* And without doubt, this is true. However, to move into *perfect love*, this passage carries much greater implications.

True *love of the world* does not refer only to sin, but to all forms of entertainment, activities, possessions, or even responsibilities that we place ahead of our desire to seek, know, and serve God. The *Love of the World* and the *Love of God* stand in perfect opposition to one another - whichever is dominant in our lives will dictate our capacity to flow in love.

When the genuine supernatural love of God manifests upon us, attraction and involvement in the distractions of the world will fall off of us automatically. However to step into the love of God by faith, it will be necessary to eliminate many time-consuming, non-productive activities not tied to developing ourselves for God's kingdom. To move into the full level of His love, God will guide us into *fasting* specific activities in our lives which He may deem that we care for more than for Him! Just as fasting food forces our souls to become more Kingdom alert and aware, as we fast the World's escape activities they will diminish in their hold upon us. Our souls, seeking rest, will then gravitate to the Word of God for fulfillment.

So many Christians have placed the world at a higher priority in their lives than God and His Word. Many often view spiritual development activities such as prayer, Word time, church attendance, etc. as *work* that we must do to please God. Yet they want to reward themselves with the entertainment activities of the World. In no way does God want the world's entertainment industry to be our source of rest or joy above the level that we find our rest in Him. Those who have truly ever tasted of the love of God will witness that nothing the world has to offer can compare.

A short list of possible areas of worldly addiction or just over involvement may include but not be limited to:

Television, Sports, Movies, Shopping, Hobbies, Sleep, Trips/Vacations, Novels, Computer Games, Facebook, or even the News. None of these may be bad of themselves but they will be damaging to us spiritually if they choke out all of our time for God. And of even greater concern is when we derive more enjoyment from these than from watching God move in our lives and in the lives of those around us. Reading the following verses we find:

> *1John 2:16-17 –" For all that is in the world, the **lust of the flesh**, and the **lust of the eyes**, and the **pride of life**, is not of the Father, but is of the world. And the world passeth away, and the lust thereof: but he that doeth the will of God abideth forever."*

The things of the world will pass away but what we invest our time in spiritually stands to produce eternal results.

Of the three areas of worldly involvement listed, *"the lust of the flesh"* most closely describes those activities that we would most often consider as sin. Unquestionably, if one is involved in thievery, fornication, homosexuality, killing, etc. they are not qualified to carry the love of God. But other forms of the lust of the flesh may include bondage to comfort food and sexual addiction - possibly even within the constraints of marriage. To be able to step into the full love of God may require a price to be paid that many are not willing to expend.

The second reference to loving the world, *"the lust of the eyes"* is as well usually glossed over. The lust of the eyes is usually tied to looking at a woman or a man with sexual desire. However, the eyes operate as a primary gateway to all that we imagine or consider. I know people who are totally addicted to television - watching pretend programs of make-believe lives often more than eight hours per day. The demonically birthed sitcoms, movies, and even news programs cramming men's minds full of images, ungodly actions, and subsequent thoughts make it impossible to move deeply into the realm of faith and supernatural power.

Through the lust of the eyes, the enemy would attempt to muddle down our understanding of truth and holiness and instead draw us into a lifestyle of living in a fantasy world. Even many who endeavor to *see the world* and travel profusely may miss out on life's greatest adventure - that is, to see Jesus manifested in our lives.

In many cases, our affinity for the activities and entertainment of the world may take the form of idolatry. We usually think of idolatry in terms of worshipping some little statue on the shelf. For most people today including non-Christians, the concept of worshipping some man-made icon seems preposterous. However, idolatry represents anything that we value, enjoy, or worship greater than our desire to draw near to God! How we spend our time demonstrates before God where our heart truly lies. The entire list of activities that were just iterated all may take the form of an idol in our lives.

Potential idols can be recognized by examining our own thoughts. By determining what we continually look forward to doing, we may be able to identify idols. This is especially true if God cannot interrupt us during any of these activities.

By examining what we are always drawn to speak about we may be able to pinpoint areas of misplaced worship in our lives. Understand, these areas may not be something that will keep the believer from heaven - but for those endeavoring to attain to the ultimate heights of God's Kingdom, it may be necessary to lay them down. Whatever most dominates our thoughts, speech, and actions, if not tied to the Kingdom of God, stands to be a potential idol.

The two main idols that were in my life were *fishing* and *The University of Tennessee football program*. There was a season of my life that I ate, drank and chased after both of these with all that

I had. From the time that I was young, I lived to fish. I invested all of the funds I could muster to purchase fishing tackle and read profusely on the subject. Any opportunity that I had for decades, I went fishing. It dominated my life; but no more. God supernaturally delivered me from the addiction to fishing and instead redirected my focus upon Him. Now, no longer can the thought of holding a slimy fish displace my desire to seek after God. Some may think that they would not want to make such an exchange, but once the shift is made you'll wonder what took you so long. I will mention more of Tennessee football in a bit.

The third phrase tied to loving the world is *"the pride of life."* The pride of life deals with those activities and areas of involvement where our egos become inflated. At times this may even relate to pride in our spiritual accomplishments. Through the attempt to satiate the pride of life, men may invest their entire lives' efforts to impress those about them. Some may want to restore old vehicles, make the perfect quilt, or be the best at whatever field of endeavor that they undertake. Even in my desire to fish, it was important to show off my catch to gain accolades from my peers. Again, none of these activities are sinful of themselves but the problem arises in what motivates us to pursue them.

Pride is the motivating force of the world, whereas love is to be the motivating force of the Christian. To launch into love will require at some point that we forcefully confront pride in our lives. Pride is addressed as a key hindrance to our spiritual promotion in First Peter:

> *1Pet 5:5-6 "Likewise ye younger, submit yourselves unto the elder. Yea, all of you be subject one to another, and be clothed with humility: for* **God resisteth the proud**, *and giveth grace to the humble. Humble yourselves therefore under the mighty hand of God, that he may exalt you in due time."*

Not only is pride tied to our inability to receive spiritual promotion, but this gives us a bit of a hint as to why this is true. Those who walk in high levels of pride find it difficult to submit to

God's divine authority structure within His church! Because no pastor can effectively speak into their lives, those in pride are more than likely going to end up off track and in deception. In fact even now, if you are getting upset at this statement you are most likely one of those walking in spiritual pride.

Another term for the *"pride of life"* is *self-reliance.* Many atheists are declaring: *"There is no God."* Yet, those Christians who are caught up in the world system are declaring through their actions: *"I don't need God."* How preposterous it is for us to shun the God who is *"upholding all things by the Word of His power."* Without God's hand of power and stability upon this creation, all would dissolve into oblivion.

Christians who are caught up in pride attempt to serve God out of their own strength and ability rather than access the anointing of the Kingdom. One aspect of self-dependence is reflected when believers, through ignorance, attempt to be loving Christians without manifesting the supernatural power of *agape* to do so. Not that God would be displeased with any effort that we make to reflect His love, but how limited those attempts are without the anointing of love to make those efforts productive.

Reflecting back to my addiction to Tennessee football, much of my involvement in this area was tied to pride. Being a graduate of this university, I didn't just cheer for the team merely for the joy of the game. I identified myself with this school. They became *my team*, although in no fashion did I ever play for them. In fact, I had so tied my soul to this worldly event, that if Tennessee won - I won; and if they lost - I lost.

Sometimes a loss could impact my emotional state for days. Not to mention, at some points in the games I could become dangerously close to compromising my Christianity. I would look forward all week to the upcoming games, which is remarkable since so often I didn't really enjoy them. The games for me weren't about the joy of the competition. My soulish connection to a stupid ball game became for me a competition that determined whether 'I' was winning or losing at life.

It is no wonder that when I was first saved, God began to deal with me regarding this soul-tie. Soon after I was born-again, I was seeking God with all of my heart - at least that part not tied to fishing or football. In my pursuit of Him, during prayer I declared: *"God, I want to know your voice."* And a still small voice whispered back: *"I want you to give up Tennessee football."* After I had effectively cast this down, I said again: *"I want to hear your voice."* And again I received the same response: *"I need you to give up Tennessee football."* This actually continued for about two weeks until after again making my same petition, God responded a bit more firmly averring: *"If you want to hear anything other than give up Tennessee football, then you'd better give up Tennessee football."*

It would be ten years before I would be permitted to follow the team again - but only then after demonstrating that it no longer had an emotional hold upon me. Now, as with fishing, I could care less if I ever watched another game. God is a miracle worker indeed. It was necessary that I be set free from such pride of life to continue ascending into the love of God. How could I fully experience the goodness of an infinite loving God with such misplaced devotion in my life?

An additional area of concern, even where Christians do sever their commitments to the world and attempt to sell out to God, lies in the threat of *spiritual* pride. This occurs when we become proud of our spirituality and becomes a very dangerous place indeed. Initially, the experienced minister may begin to feel elevated above those without his demonstrated resume of commitment and accomplishments. People for them then become pawns to use rather that the targets for God's love.

However, a much greater danger exists when a minister becomes so busy that he leaves off his prayer life and is no longer hearing God effectively. Because he may know how to access the gifts of the spirit it will appear as if his ministry is thriving. He may become deceived, believing that he knows how God would respond in each situation. He no longer follows Him but instead establishes his own agenda. He has now become self-reliant in spiritual pride versus God-reliant as in his past.

The result is that the man of God may still put on a good show. But because he is not staying connected to God in prayer, his spiritual tanks are becoming depleted. Without the strengthening power of God on his life and since he has probably already compromised the convicting voice of the Holy Spirit, he is positioned to become prey to temptation. What a tragedy it is for an individual to invest so much effort in seeking the power of God only to end up in deception as the pride of life takes its toll.

To develop in love, God has established a critical trimming process which we must be willing to undergo:

> *Deut 30:6 –"And the Lord the **God will circumcise thine heart**, and the heart of thy seed, **to love the Lord thy God with all thine heart**, and with all they soul, that thou mayest live."*

To move into perfect love, we must examine our lives to determine where we place our focus. Those things that overly occupy our time and attention - whether entertainment, activities, work, or even friends must be laid at the feet of Jesus. We must then make the proper adjustment within to eradicate pride and then await his permission to see what we may again take back up.

CHAPTER 11

THE TRUTH OF LOVE

WHAT IS TRUTH?

Psa 138:2 – "I will worship toward thy holy temple, and praise thy name for thy lovingkindness and for thy truth: for thou hast magnified thy word above all thy name."

Of all the attributes that are used to describe the nature of God, *"love"* and *"truth"* stand above all of the rest. Our Creator - who is love, is also the foundation of all truth that exists. And He has elevated His Word - which declares to us the truth, above His very name. His promises to us and His covenants with us remain unbreakable.

To be a people who are built up in God's image, we must become determined to both walk in the truth of God's Word and manifest His supernatural love. These two attributes become inseparable, for one cannot exist without the other. When one walks in love, they automatically fulfill all of the intentions of the Word. Conversely, to fulfill all of the directives of the Word would result in us walking in love.

Truth and love become the primary building blocks which God is using to raise up His last-day church - a bride transformed by the Word and filled with His love. As simple as this may seem, it is amazing how easy it is for men to deviate from this building process. Rather than center on the Word, ministers focus on church growth programs, public surveys, and user friendly efforts. **The Christian mentality of today is more oriented to *sympathize* and *empathize* than to elevate those hurting to victory by the Word.** Instead of teaching to walk in genuine love (which involves radical transformation as the Holy Spirit is allowed to stretch us), hirelings look to make the services *easy* and *convenient*. The dangers of frightening off members outweighs the genuine concern to build the church by faith.

God's growth program is for minsters to teach the *truth* and instruct to walk in *love*. The Spirit of God may at times direct a pastor to become involved in miscellaneous outreach activities to target bringing people to the church. However, the number one emphasis must be to train the glorious church to live by faith and flow in the anointings. The end-time church will not be erected by man-made means, but by cooperating with God as He directs His bride to operate in truth and flow in love.

We have already defined *truth* as the *Word of God*. However for us as Christians endeavoring to walk in this truth, further clarification will prove helpful. In a time when the truths of the Word are being challenged as never before, it is more important than ever for us to gain a firm understanding of what truth actually represents. As perplexing as the concept may seem, we also need to comprehend the difference between the *truth* and *facts*.

Whereas *facts* represent the hard concrete evidence and activities witnessed taking place in the first and second heavenly realms. **The *truth* refers to the promises, principles, and power of the Third Heaven.** Third Heaven truth contains power to override the facts of the First and Second Heavens. Restated, we can be victorious over any physical or mental challenge we face by accessing the power of the Kingdom of Heaven through applying truth. Truth is of higher authority and power than facts. Facts may be temporal but truth is eternal.

Those who have not learned to live by faith have been limited to living by the facts or circumstances that all men encounter. Even though God has provided us with *"exceeding, great, and precious promises"* which allow us to overcome all obstacles, if we are unaware of this then we will continue to live in defeat. Truth has the potential to deliver us from all earthly bondages and limitations. Jesus referred to the power of the truth in John's Gospel:

> *John 8:32 – "And ye shall know the truth, and the truth shall make you free."*

It is only the truth that we "*know*" that can make us free. Until we know and understand the power of the Word, it's liberating potential remains beyond us. As spiritually minded Christians, we realize that God is real and that His kingdom is far more substantial and reliable than the world in which we live. The natural universe is far less tangible and fixed than men have imagined. Even now, quantum scientists are discovering the limitations of this realm and are recognizing infinite power emanating from others. For this reason, I define *"truth"* as **Fully Unveiled Reality**.

Only the Kingdom of God - based out of the Third Heaven forms for the believer *true reality*. To genuinely walk in truth requires the revelation of this kingdom. The Word of God acts as a portal for us to view the true realities of all that surround us. Through time spent meditating the Word, faith is developed which allows us to access the power of God's Kingdom. All of the enemy's lies based on momentary facts may be overridden by the application of truth.

LOVING TRUTH

Because truth is unveiled reality and the foundation of all reality is God, then all truth that we obtain will result in a deeper understanding of God and of His love. We must allow the Word to convert our minds to a truth-based, heavenly-positioned viewpoint from a fact-based earthly limited mentality. As we do so, all limits are removed from us and nothing exists out of the realm of possibility if it aligns with the Word.

This renewing of our minds to truth is also critical to being empowered to walk in supernatural love. We see the tie made between receiving truth and having the capacity to walk in love made by Peter:

> *1Pet 1:22 –* **"*Seeing ye have purified your souls in obeying the truth*** *through the Spirit unto unfeigned love of*

*the brethren, **see that ye love one another** with a pure heart fervently:"*

As our souls are reprogrammed by the Word of God, we are thus equipped to step into the supernatural love of God. When we cooperate with the Holy Spirit as He instructs us from the Word, individual *nuggets* of truth become established within our thinking. As we spend even more extensive time in study and meditation, these nuggets of truth begin to link together to produce *understanding* of the Kingdom. And as we gain more and more understanding of God's Kingdom, our lives begin to conform more and more to the image of Christ. We thus subsequently walk in higher and higher levels of the love of God.

In this fashion, truth establishes within us interconnecting links to form a containment system to house love. Much in the same way that a basket is woven together to carry fruit, truth is interwoven within our souls to carry the fruit of the Spirit - supernatural love. The genuine love of God may only flow through a conduit framed by truth. And only as we seek and honor truth may we grow in love.

By honoring truth in an uncompromising fashion, we walk in *integrity*. **Therefore, Integrity becomes our *personal application of truth*.** As we mentioned in our *Stairway to Love*, a step toward love that we must develop is virtue which includes walking in integrity. Again, we see that a person lacking integrity cannot manifest the fullness of the love of God. God will not anoint in love, those not grounded and walking in truth.

When the Old Testament Tabernacle was constructed, specific design instructions had to be followed precisely. God even chose out the men to head up the project. Once completed exactly as God had assigned, His glory filled the building. The Tabernacle could not be constructed to man's specifications but had to be finished totally according to God's Word. To some fashion, the erection of the Tabernacle became a *truth building project*.

As Christians, we are the New Testament versions of the Tabernacle. God no longer dwells in buildings made by men's hands but instead dwells within us. For the Holy Spirit to dwell within us, we need only be born-again. Through this miracle event, God builds within us a new nature qualified for Him to inhabit. However, only by renewing our minds to the truths of God's Word may the fullness of His love be channeled to flow through us. Truth becomes the pipeline which carries love from within us to without, thus producing all of the desired results of this supernatural force.

As God's glory could not fill a halfway completed Tabernacle or Temple, neither will His end-time glory fill halfway committed Christians. We must be sold out to the Word of Truth. Men of God fail through compromising truth. When faced with overwhelming pressure or persecution, those without a comprehension of truth will quit. For those committed to truth, no other options in life are available other than to fulfill the assignment that God has placed upon their lives. To do anything else would represent living a lie.

I was saved because of a divine recognition of truth. Whereas many people get saved because their life is falling apart and they finally reach out for the savior, my salvation was not produced by such. In July of 1984, I thought my life was nearly perfect. I had an excellent job, I had just purchased my first home, and was recently married to the most beautiful woman in the world. Being raised outside of church, I felt no need for a God. However, in an attempt to explore the possibility that God was real, my wife and I agreed to attend various church services with different friends.

In one case, we attended with an acquaintance of my wife who was *charismatic*. The service had no sooner started when a guest minister called us out through the gift of the *Word of Knowledge*. As he began to describe us in detail, we both knew that God was speaking to us. At that very moment in time, I had to choose between what I thought I understood from my past and what God was supernaturally revealing to me as truth. As I pondered the decision of how to respond to this situation, I considered many of the ramifications committing to God would require. I knew enough about Christianity to comprehend that I would have to give up my partying ways. In a moment, after weighing all of my future plans against what was being revealed to me at that precise time, I chose to go with revealed truth. How could I have chosen to live a life that denied the creator of the universe once His reality had been revealed? That night, both my wife and I gave our lives to Jesus through recognition of truth.

We come to church for the truth and because of truth. Truth becomes of greater importance to the revivalist than their own personal reputation - they may be besmirched but the truth will stand. These are the vessels committed to truth which God will fill to overflowing. **God is saturating His end-time saints with truth as with no prior church generation to enable them to manifest the glory as none have before.** As the Christian commits to truth, God can pour through him the fullness of His love. As churches corporately commit to truth, God will saturate them in the fullness of His glory.

Looking back at Ephesians:

> *Eph 4:11-13 –"And he gave some, apostles; and some, prophets and some, evangelists; and some, pastors and teachers; For the perfecting of the saints, for the work of the ministry, for the edifying of the body of Christ: Till we all come in the unity of the faith, and of the knowledge of the Son of God, unto a perfect man, unto the measure of the stature of the fulness of Christ."*

God has instituted the five-fold ministry to instruct the body the truths of the Word. The Word enables our faith to be fully developed as we gain full and complete knowledge of the Son of God. As love flows through the conduits of our lives that truth has created, unity of the saints is produced bringing us into perfection. Such love allows us to grow up *"unto the measure of the stature of the fullness of Christ."* Truth and love develop the body of Christ in conjunction with one another. Reading further:

> *Eph 4:14 –"That we henceforth be no more children, tossed to and fro, and carried about with every wind of doctrine, by the sleight of men, and cunning craftiness, whereby they lie in wait to deceive;"*

Until we ascend in advanced faith-building knowledge and supernaturally unifying love, we remain as children in God's eyes.

And as children, we continue to be prey for the powers of darkness. From this it is evident that true church spirituality is not indicated by the numerical size of the congregation, but by the amount of truth and love in which they are established. God's view of church maturity and success is far different than that of men.

We spin our wheels if we are trying to work for God without pursuing *both* truth and love. **A minister that is attempting to teach truth without love will become condemning.** While desiring to instruct the full content of God's Word, without centering on the power of love his messages become legalistic.

Those endeavoring to lead the body into love without teaching the full truth of the Word of God produce *flaky* **followers.** *Flakes* are often those who have become convinced that they can manifest the love of God through their own mere efforts. They believe that to walk in love, it is sufficient just to recognize that *God is a God of love* - yet they never allow the Holy Spirit to produce true internal change. Rather than fast, pray, and study, they convince themselves that they are walking in love because they have chosen to perform good deeds. Walking in the supernatural power of love demands much more than merely trying to be nice.

Pastors who compromise truth to keep a congregation comfortable or to maintain a position extinguish the possibility that genuine love will overtake their gatherings. All too frequently, even charismatic churches are no longer proclaiming publically the Baptism of the Holy Spirit or laying hands on the sick. Ministers who quench any moving of the Spirit on behalf of maintaining church respectability sacrifice love for the sake of man-made church growth. How can God release His glory into such a setting?

Any efforts to unify Christianity by requiring *compromise of the Word* from the participants are attempting to produce a unity of lies rather than of faith. Since so many Christians have refused to embrace the full revelation of the Word, God can only actually unite those Christians and churches who do so. As *gross darkness* continues to fill the earth, God's glory is prophesied to produce the greatest revival the world has ever seen. Certainly at that time, multitudes will sell out for God and be able to come into the unity of faith.

Too many Christians remain in dead churches for fear of ridicule for attending a church moving in miracle power. These can never activate the necessary truth to manifest end-time love. So often, people who will not relocate to an on-fire church because their whole family goes to the *other* church, state through their decision that they value their family's approval more than God's. Again, it does matter where you go to church. Jesus spoke of this refusal to fully follow Him:

> *Mark 10:29-30 – "And Jesus answered and said, Verily I say unto you, There is no man that hath left house, or brethren, or sisters, or father, or mother, or wife, or children, or lands, for my sake, and the gospel's, But he shall receive an hundredfold now in this time, houses, and brethren, and sisters, and mothers, and children, and lands, with persecutions; and in the world to come eternal life."*

Many believe that this passage only applies to those who allow fear of family and possible ramifications to prevent them from becoming born-again. However, being born-again does not qualify you to receive the hundredfold. Only fully selling out to God and His plans position the believer for such reward. The full fruit of love may only flow through those totally given over to the leading of God. If God makes something real to us or shows us the path that leads to His power then we must take it. No mere soul-ties should hinder us from it.

Returning to our passage in Ephesians:

> *Eph 4:15-16 – "But speaking the truth in love, may grow up into him in all things, which is the head, even Christ: From whom the whole body fitly joined together and compacted by that which every joint supplieth, according to the effectual working in the measure of every part, maketh increase of the body unto the edifying of itself in love."*

Once we are filled with love, we may effectively speak the truth - motivated and empowered by this attractive force. Truth and love permit the body of Christ to be fitly pressed together without the members bailing out. This unification process, instigated through truth and love, cause the church to experience genuine God-initiated growth. God is going to produce His mega-church in these last days, but it will come via a people who proclaim and live out the full counsel of the Word rather than attempt to produce growth through compromise.

It is the Holy Spirit who will draw people to our churches. Since Jesus referred to the Holy Spirit as *"The Spirit of Truth,"* then rest assured that this same Spirit will direct His followers to churches unabashedly proclaiming truth. Choosing truth becomes a deciding factor which enables us to remain free of deception.

> *2Thes 2:10 – "And with all deceivableness of unrighteousness in them that perish; because they received not the love of the truth, that they might be saved"*

To compromise truth is to roll the dice with our salvation. Once deception has been entertained, the once illuminated Christian potentially loses their ability to continue walking in light. Truth must be guarded at all cost. Without an established containment system of truth being developed within us, love cannot be effectively carried regardless of one's level of church attendance. Should this person have hands laid on them and a high measure of love be transmitted to them, it will most likely leak out before they reach home.

Truth plugs all of the holes in our lives enabling us to function as vessels of love. Recognition of truth permits the blood to wash away all prior hurt from our lives that normally would have separated us from love. Truth allows us to see others in the body of Christ as righteous and thus worthy to receive of our love and blessing. Truth empowers us to go beyond the fear of man and to boldly proclaim that we are ambassadors of His love. Truth is not optional for the revivalist targeting running toward the glory. Truth keeps us living a lifestyle targeted toward blessing others.

> *1John 3:18* – *"My little children, let us not love in word, neither in tongue; but in deed and in truth."*

THE "ALTERNATE" RECIPE FOR LOVE

In First Timothy we discovered *God's Recipe for Love*, which lists the three primary ingredients to develop the love of God in our lives.

> *1Tim 1:5* – *"Now the end of the commandment is charity out of **a pure heart**, and of **a good conscience**, and of **faith** unfeigned."*

A similar version of this recipe is listed in Ephesians:

> *Eph 5:9* – *"For the fruit of the Spirit is in all **goodness** and **righteousness** and **truth**;"*

Knowing that the *"fruit of the Spirit"* is love, we are now provided with an alternate list of components for our recipe. Where our original recipe consisted of **"a pure heart,"** **"a good conscience,"** and **"faith,"** our new recipe refers to **"goodness,"** **righteousness,"** and **"truth."** Understanding that the Word of God is inerrant, we should be able to equate these two lists.

Recalling from our teaching on the initial Recipe of Love, the first ingredient listed, *"a pure heart"* becomes an easy match. A pure heart refers to our new righteous nature that we receive when we are born-again corresponding to *"righteousness"* as listed in the second recipe.

The second ingredient of our initial recipe was *"a good conscience."* A good conscience is the result of allowing our minds to be renewed to the Word of God. As the Word transforms our thinking, we are able to speak and act in alignment with our new righteous nature. The Word delivers us from all soulish clutter that would hinder the flow of love from the inside of us to the outside. This becomes an obvious tie to *"truth."* As our conscience becomes permeated by the truths of the Word, it no longer restricts love's flow from our lives. When we were saved, God reprogrammed truth and love into our reborn spirit nature. As we spend time in the Word, we discover the miracle that took place at that exact moment in time and are liberated to walk in the fullness of both.

The third ingredient in our original recipe was *"faith"*; specifically the ability to believe, speak, and act in expectation of love flowing through us. The third ingredient of our alternate recipe is *"goodness."* The Greek word for *"goodness"* in this verse is *agathosyne* defined as *uprightness of heart and life* demonstrated through kindness and benevolence. The *syne* suffix denotes *a goodness that proceeds from God showing itself in moral excellence.* Both *"faith"* and *"goodness"* are listed in Galatians as individual fruit of the spirit. Whereas, faith in our recipe indicates our belief that love will flow through us; goodness points to our corresponding actions.

Paul ties *"goodness"* and *"faith"* to the glory in Second Thessalonians:

> *2Thes 1:11-12 -"Wherefore also we pray always for you, that our God would count you worthy of this calling and fulfil all the good pleasure of **his goodness, and the work of faith** with power: That the name of our Lord Jesus Christ may be glorified in you, and ye in him., according to the grace of our God and the Lord Jesus Christ."*

Enabled by His supernatural power, we are to demonstrate God's goodness through faith - which results in our display of His glory. After the Exodus from Egypt, Moses besought the Lord to show him His glory. God's response gives us further insight to the role of goodness in manifesting the supernatural love of God.

> *Exo 33:18-19 –"**And he (Moses) said, I beseech thee, shew me thy glory. And he (God) said, I will make all my goodness pass before thee**, and I will proclaim the name of the Lord before thee; and I will be gracious to whom I will be gracious, and will shew mercy on whom I will shew mercy."*

God equated His *"glory"* with His *"goodness"*. This goodness which results in being *"gracious"* and showing *"mercy"* directly ties to the actions of faith we learned of in our chapter on God's Recipe for Love.

As discovered, we cannot manifest the supernatural love of God outside of our determination to be renewed by and walk in truth. In our Alternate Recipe for Love, it is of no surprise that *"truth"* is listed as a key ingredient.

CHAPTER 12

FORGIVING LOVE

THE LOVE LIMITER

There are innumerable books written on the subject of forgiveness and in no way is this chapter meant to represent an exhaustive study of the subject. However, in our study of love it is imperative that we spend some time on this topic. Possibly no other area can effectively contaminate our souls and thus block up the channels of our love as refusing to forgive. Hate absolutely shuts down loves flow from within us. Repeatedly, the need to forgive is emphasized throughout the New Testament.

> *1John 4:19-20 – "We love him, because he first loved us. If a man say, I love God, and hateth his brother, he is a liar:* **for he that loveth not his brother whom he hath seen, how can he love God whom he hath not seen?"**

Recognizing that hate is a result of being unable to forgive, it is evidenced here that love is truncated in the life of the unforgiving. *"Brother,"* most likely refers to a co-member of the church as discussed previously. To hold hate toward anyone, especially a brother within the church, indicates that we not only do not have love for them but also are lying if we declare that we love God. If we truly loved God, we would obey His commandment to forgive.

As fear is the opposing force to faith, an unforgiving attitude is the greatest obstruction to the flow of the supernatural love of God. To refuse to forgive is to take upon us the mentality of darkness - that of the father of lies himself. When we think of *darkness*, we usually think of the absence of light. However, the darkness that the enemy brings produces a spiritual blindness which prevents the lost and even those spiritually compromised from being able to see the light. Those spiritually blind can sit under the ministration of the glorious Gospel and still not be able to comprehend it. Paul spoke of this type of blindness:

> *2Cor 4:3-4 –"But if our gospel be hid, it is hid to them that are lost: In whom **the god of this world hath blinded the minds of them which believe not**, lest the light of the glorious gospel of Christ, who is the image of God, should shine unto them."*

Satan's greatest weapon against truth is spiritual darkness, but he needs man to provide him an avenue to manifest it. Man, being unable to forgive and instead manifesting hate potentially gives him this access. We see this declared in First John:

> *1John 2:9-11 –"**He that saith he is in light, and hateth his brother, is in darkness even until now. He that loveth his brother abideth in the light**, and there is none occasion of stumbling in him. But he that hateth his brother is in darkness, and walketh in darkness, and knoweth not wither he goeth, because that darkness hath blinded his eyes."*

Hate results in deception while love releases revelation. I find it interesting that John, as the Apostle of Love, was given the vision we refer to as *"The Revelation."* For satan to get men caught up in spiritual darkness, all that he has to do is to get them offended and refusing to forgive. This knowledge, if truly comprehended, should fully motivate the Christian to refuse any form of offense. It should become inconceivable that we would hold to hate.

We found earlier from Second Peter 1:10 that those who develop in love will never fall. Likewise, we see here that those who reject hate will never stumble. From this it should be obvious to us our need to walk in total forgiveness of those we believe may have wronged us - for our very salvation lies at stake! As well, we can ascertain from this passage that to walk in love, to dwell in light, and to be led of the Spirit are all synonymous with one another. The Holy Spirit will always lead us into the light which will result in us walking in love.

The end-time glory of God is opposed by *gross darkness* and the refusal to forgive becomes an entry point for this darkness. Even now, the enemy is doing all that he can to stir up unresolved hatred in this nation and throughout the world. Satan cannot merely release a cloud of demonically induced thick darkness without some opening permitting him to do so. Chances are very strong that hate becomes the portal through which gross darkness has entry.

In our chapter on *Abiding in Love* we found that Jesus - as the vine, purges those branches that begin to bear fruit. This thus allows us to produce *"much"* fruit. Our willingness and ability to forgive become the main areas that God will address in our lives to purge out all obstructions to love's flow. John emphasizes the power that hate holds to choke out love in an eye-opening fashion in First John 3:

> *1John 3:14-16 – "We know that we have passed from death unto life, because we love the brethren.* **He that loveth not his brother abideth in death.** *Whosoever hateth his brother is a murderer: and ye know that no murderer hath eternal life abiding in him. Hereby perceive we the love of God, because he laid down his life for us: and we ought to lay down our lives for the brethren."*

Wow, John here declares that having love for those in our church body is the evidence that we have passed from death unto life. However, to carry hate is to abide in death and to allow murder to reside within us. Jesus declared that the man who looks upon a woman to lust after her has already committed adultery in his heart. Apparently, to hold hate in our heart toward another is to have committed murder within as well. Again, how important it is for us to aggressively deal with offense in our lives.

In the above passage, we are told to lay down our lives for the brethren to enable us to reflect the same type of love that Jesus demonstrated to us. As with John 15:13, the Greek word translated *"lives"* is *psuche* meaning the *soul.* To walk in great love, we must be willing to lay aside all offense even to the point of blessing our enemies. We have discussed the need to renew our minds to the Word of God to walk in love. However, the area of our psyche where it repeatedly seems most difficult to maintain victory is in forgiving those who have wronged us and refusing offense.

The enemy knows the debilitating effect that hate produces in our lives. Therefore he will continue to stir up memories of *what others have done to us* to keep us in bondage. This combined with the emotional baggage that comes with being betrayed, rejected, mocked, or taken advantage of, often requires intentional, repeated effort to forgive. Even the disciples struggled with this topic but Jesus was firm in His answer.

> *Mat 18:21-22 –"Then came Peter to him, and said, Lord,* **how oft shall my brother sin against me, and I forgive him?** *Till seven times? Jesus saith unto him, I say not unto thee, Until seven times: but,* **Until seventy times seven.***"*

Surely Peter felt quite spiritual in his stated willingness to forgive *"seven times."* However, Jesus let him know that he was not even close to exhausting the depths of God's mercy when he told him *"seventy times seven"* or 490 times. But, before we begin counting our own efforts to demonstrate mercy, we need to know what Peter and the others comprehended and what Jesus actually meant when He stated this.

"Seventy times seven" is a reference from the book of Daniel referring to the number of weeks of years until the return of the Messiah (excluding the two thousand years of the *Time of the Gentiles*). To the disciples, *seventy times seven* meant until the end of the age! Therefore, there is no time limit or upper number count where we are now entitled to carry offense.

Jesus follows up this answer with the parable of a servant who had been forgiven a great debt but was not willing to forgive those who owed him. The summation of the story is related in verse 34:

> *Mat 18:34-35 –"And the lord was wroth, and delivered him to the tormentors, till he should pay all that was due unto*

him. So likewise shall my heavenly Father do also unto you, if ye from your hearts forgive not every one his brother their trespasses."

To be delivered to the *"tormentors"* is far too high a price to pay for the temporal self-righteous fulfillment of holding on to offense. The supernatural power of love is an anointing which will deliver us from all offense and strife. We must *choose* to forgive those about us to step into this divine empowerment which is able to complete the offense delivering process. To hold on to past hurts hinders love and keeps us in bondage to hate. The choice to forgive coupled with the release of God's love, releases the power to permanently free us from animosity's clutches.

FORGIVENESS SEED

We are repeatedly commanded to forgive in the New Testament. And in most cases, this admonition is tied to our right to be forgiven ourselves. Apparently the action of forgiveness acts as a seed in our life to keep us in right standing with God - as we sow forgiveness, we reap likewise. We see this principle verified in the passage we just read above - where those who do not forgive from the heart are turned over to the *"tormentors."* Jesus imbeds the results of forgiving others in what we refer to as *The Lord's Prayer*:

> Mat 6:12-15 – *"And forgive us our debts, as we forgive our debtors. And lead us not into temptation, but deliver us from evil: For thine is the kingdom, and the power, and the glory, forever. Amen. For if ye forgive men their trespasses, your heavenly Father will also forgive you:* ***But if ye forgive not men their trespasses, neither will your Father forgive your trespasses."***

Jesus lets us know that we should review our willingness to forgive others on a daily basis. This focus on forgiveness should even be included as an integral facet of our prayer lives. Our ability to come before God with clean hands is tied to this activity.

When the Lord's Prayer is normally quoted, each line of

petition is usually compartmentalized separate from the others. *"Thy will be done," "Give us this day our daily bread,"* and *"Forgive us our debts"* are most often envisioned apart from one another. However, when we come to *"And lead us not into temptation, but deliver us from evil: For thine is the kingdom, and the power, and the glory, forever,"* we find in Matthew that it is sandwiched between verses dealing with forgiveness. As mentioned, refusing to forgive opens the door to demonically inspired darkness and leaves us susceptible to temptation. Forgiveness, which opens the channels for love to flow through us, positions us for the power and glory of God as well.

It is interesting to note that for those who forgive, their *"father"* referred to in verse 14 is *"heavenly Father."* However, for the unforgiving, when referring to their *"Father,"* the adjective *"heavenly"* is omitted. Perhaps once someone refuses to forgive, they exchange their fatherhood from the heavenly to the fallen. Jesus even told the wicked leaders that they were *of their father the devil.* I propose that once one opts not to forgive, they reestablish satan as the head of their life.

Jesus inferred to forgiveness as a type of seed in a passage we regularly use in offering teachings.

> *Luke 6:37-38 –"Judge not, and ye shall not be judged: condemn not, and ye shall not be condemned:* ***forgive, and ye shall be forgiven****: Give, and it shall be given unto you; good measure, pressed down, and shaken together, and running over, shall men give into your bosom. For with the same measure that ye mete withal, it shall be measured to you again."*

In these verses, refusing to forgive is put into the same category as judgment and condemnation. With regard to our brothers in Christ, to refuse to forgive them is to declare that the blood of Christ is effective in our lives but ineffective in theirs. Apparently the opposite is actually true. Again, we see that our ability to remain in right standing with God is tied to our capacity to forgive.

As well, all of the actions listed in this passage are equally meant to be something that we *"mete"* out. Therefore, we have a right to receive forgiveness poured back to us *"pressed down, shaken together, and running over"* - not just from God but from men as well. The forgiving Christian receives a supernatural shielding that causes men to overlook their missteps. All of us, at one time or another, will say or do something that will be misconstrued and hurt someone's feelings. It is good to know that we have available the Holy Spirit's cooperation to counsel them to forgive us as we have forgiven others.

Jesus also connected the power of our faith to remove mountains to the need that we forgive.

> *Mark 11:23-25 – "For verily I say unto you, That whosoever shall say unto this mountain, Be thou removed, and be thou cast into the sea; and shall not doubt in his heart, but shall believe that those things which he saith shall come to pass; he shall have whatsoever he saith. Therefore I say unto you, What things soever ye desire, when ye pray, believe that ye receive them, and ye shall have them.* **And when ye stand praying, forgive, if ye have aught against any: that your Father also which is in heaven may forgive you your trespasses.** *"*

Where there is a lack of forgiveness in our lives, we forfeit our righteousness and thus our rights to have our prayers answered. This provides additional understanding as to why *"faith worketh by love."* Without love, forgiveness is compromised and faith is neutralized. Where so many Christians struggle to forgive those who have harmed them in the past, under the influence of supernatural love this becomes automatic.

Paul provides some understanding of just how important it is to God for us to forgive in Ephesians:

> *Eph 4:30-32 – "And grieve not the holy Spirit of God, whereby ye are sealed unto the day of redemption. Let all bitterness, and wrath, and anger, and clamour, and evil speaking, be put away from you, with all malice: And be ye kind one to another, tenderhearted,* **forgiving one another, even as God for Christ's sake hath forgiven you.** *"*

"Bitterness," "wrath," "clamor," and *"evil speaking"* are often the result of someone not answering the Holy Spirit's call to forgive. Such rebellious responses to the draw of the Spirit grieves him and threatens to harden our hearts to the voice of His loving guidance. We are commanded to *"put away"* from us such mindsets. Often much concentrated effort may be required to overcome these assaults against our love walk. The Christian determined to manifest supernatural love must be vigilant to guard against the subtle intrusions of offense.

FORGIVENESS INTERCESSION

As just discussed, the act of forgiving carries with it some of the qualities of seed - forgiveness begets being forgiven. As well, forgiveness enacts some level of intercessory power to allow God to bring others into His kingdom. To demonstrate this from the Word, it becomes necessary to look at a few scriptures to lay a foundation for this concept. Jesus let us know that Christians have been given the power to *"bind"* or to *"loose."* He relates to his disciples in Matthew:

> *Mat 16:19 –"And I will give unto thee the keys of the kingdom of heaven: and whatsoever thou shalt bind on earth shall be bound in heaven: and whatsoever thou shalt loose on earth shall be loosed in heaven."*

We have been given the authority to bind or loose *whatsoevers* on earth. This extends to every area of our operation on earth - with the exception that we are unable to bind or loose other people. We have no authority to violate the free-will decisions of others. However, we may be able to exercise authority over that which stands to affect them - including their own sins.

On the day of His resurrection, Jesus made an amazing statement just after He breathed on the disciples and they became born-again. Jesus declared:

> *John 20:23 –"Whosesoever sins ye remit, they are remitted unto them; and whosesoever sins ye retain, they are retained."*

We understand, that as we lead new converts to Jesus, we have the right to declare that their sins are forgiven them. Such is the delight of every Christian who cherishes the honor of bringing a new believer into the Kingdom of God. But Jesus also decreed that we have the authority to retain people's sins. As ambassadors of Christ, we apparently have the ability *through refusing to forgive* to cause people's sins to be retained. Such is the power of unforgiveness. We see this need to forgive and thus not retain sins demonstrated at The Cross.

> *Luke 23:33-34 –"And when they were come to the place, which is called Calvary, there they crucified him, and the malefactors, one on the right hand, and the other on the left.* **Then said Jesus, Father, forgive them; for they know not what they do.** *And they parted his raiment, and cast lots."*

Jesus, at The Cross opted to forgive mankind - and I shudder to think of what might be had He not. Potentially, the entire work of Calvary including the sufferings of Jesus might have been for naught had our savior not chosen to forgive us. He had to go through not just the pain of physical torment but also the pain of rejection as well. Through all of this, Jesus had to remain determined to refuse offense in order to provide the way of salvation to all.

And Jesus decreed that we have the same authority to forgive or retain sins. We see Stephen act on this spiritual principle in the same fashion as Jesus had already demonstrated.

> *Acts 7:59-60 –"And they stoned* **Stephen**, *calling upon God, and saying Lord Jesus, receive my spirit. And he kneeled down, and* **cried with a loud voice, Lord, lay not this sin to their charge**. *And when he had said this, he fell asleep."*

Stephen, a disciple who was with Jesus for most of His earthly ministry comprehended his Lord's instructions to forgive and not to retain men's sins. How much more in these end-times when God wants to bring in His last-days harvest, is it vital that his disciples reject offense and refuse to keep account of the transgressions of others? Being able to forgive allows the love of God to flow at maximum potential - not just from us but also from the Throne of Grace - thus winning multitudes to the Kingdom.

How can we as God's end-time representatives expect to bring in His harvest if we personally hold offense toward the lost? Paul assigns us the role of *Ministers of Reconciliation* in Second Corinthians.

> *2Cor 5:18-19 – "And all things are of God, who hath reconciled us to himself by Jesus Christ, and hath given to us the ministry of reconciliation; To wit, that God was in Christ, reconciling the world unto himself,* **not imputing their trespasses unto them***; and hath committed unto us the word of reconciliation."*

As Jesus took care not to impute the world's sins against them, we must be equally quick to forgive. The power of forgiveness enables us to not retain men's sins against them, thus allowing the evangelistic anointing of love to penetrate their hearts to bring salvation. Peter proclaimed the power inherent in love that enables us to forgive others their faults:

> *1Pet 4:8 – "And above all things have fervent charity (supernatural love) among yourselves: for charity shall cover the multitude of sins."*

Love motivates us to overlook the transgressions of others and even carries within it the supernatural power to make this easy. By viewing others through a heart overflowing with the love of God, we find it nearly impossible to hold a grudge or to entertain offense.

BLESSING OUR ENEMIES

Radical steps of reconciliation may at times be necessary to assure that we keep our hearts free from love restricting contamination and not continue to hold the sins of others against them. One of those radical steps may take place in the event that the Holy Spirit instructs us to *bless our enemies*.

Jesus taught of this in Luke:

> *Luke 6:27-28 – "But I say unto you which hear, Love your enemies, do good to them which hate you, Bless them that curse you, and pray for them which despitefully use you."*

Very little can run so contrary to our natural way of thinking as to *bless those that curse us*. However, the principles of the Kingdom of God were never meant to parallel the mindsets of the World but to overcome them. Understanding that a key requirement to flow in love is to keep our hearts free of all animosity should give us further insight as to why we might be instructed to perform such an illogical act.

When we have been slandered, betrayed, or mistreated, it is one thing to voice forgiveness but another to forcefully step into deliverance from the hurt. **By blessing and praying for those who have injured us, we are putting action to our faith that we are rising above the strife and pain of the situation.** Subsequently, a supernatural door is opened for God to move in and resolve the anger and rejection.

Blessing our enemies becomes an ultimate act of *laying down your soul*. This step is designed to release supernatural love into our lives where the devil meant to sow hatred. Jesus declared:

> *Mat 6:21 – "For where your treasure is, there will your heart be also."*

Something occurs, either when we bless someone or genuinely pray for them that enables our heart to be delivered from resentment. Know also that blessing those that rise up against us will have an impact upon them as well. Paul spoke of this in Romans:

> *Rom 12:19-21 – "Dearly beloved, avenge not yourselves, but rather give place unto wrath: for it is written, Vengeance is mine; I will repay, saith the Lord. Therefore if thine enemy hunger, feed him; if he thirst, give him drink: for in so doing thou shalt heap coals of fire on his head. Be not overcome of evil, but overcome evil with good."*

The act of blessing our enemies is not as much for their sakes as it is for ours. This radical action of faith works to reach down deep within us and eradicate that which would block love's flow through us. Blessing His enemies is the very act that Jesus performed at Calvary allowing love to flow to the World.

To walk in the supernatural power of love, it is mandatory that we refuse any mindsets or actions that are oriented toward avenging ourselves against our enemies. The Christian truly walking in love may at times desire to be vindicated, but never avenged. It is vital that we keep our hearts free of anger and hatred toward others. That Paul states: *"Be not overcome of evil"* is proof that the act of blessing our enemies is more for our benefit than for theirs. However, deliverance on their part may result as well.

The meaning of the phrase *"coals of fire on his head"* has been of much debate over the years. Suffice it to say, these coals are not intended to act as a form of punishment or torture but certainly are meant to work for their deliverance from evil.

Most Bible commentaries concur that the *"coals of fire"* refer to the shame our adversaries will experience when, after rising up against us, we in return bless them. This interpretation seems to be confirmed through Peter's comments regarding blessing our enemies:

> *1Pet 3:9 –"Not rendering evil for evil, or railing for railing: but contrariwise blessing; knowing that ye are thereunto called, that ye should inherit a blessing."*

> *1Pet 3:16 –"Having a good conscience; that, whereas they speak evil of you, as of evildoers,* **they may be ashamed** *that falsely accuse your good conversation in Christ."*

Peter seems to indicate that the *"coals of fire"* represent the presence of shame. And in my initial studies of these passages, I came to the same conclusion. However, the more that I learned of the nature of God, this explanation seemed perhaps limited. God's propensity is to deliver people from bondage through His anointing rather through psychological manipulation. To bless our enemies so that they will feel guilty for treating us wrongly doesn't match His character. I believe that there is more to this reference of *"coals of fire"* than this!

The answer lies in our newfound revelation of the supernatural power of love. We have discovered that to step into the power of love, we must put action to our faith by becoming a blessing to others. As we lay down our souls by blessing those who have come against us, we act to release the love of God into the relationship. The atmosphere of love that manifests upon our adversaries and upon us, destroys the very root of offense both are experiencing.

The *"coals of fire"* do not merely indicate the presence of shame, but of supernatural conviction initiated through the effect of love. We do not take steps to heap coals of fire on our enemy's head as a form of vengeance but instead as a step toward restoration.

THE PROCESS OF FORGIVING

There are few more challenging commands issued from God than to forgive those who have injured us. For this reason, I want to interject a short discussion of the steps that one may take to genuinely and effectively forgive.

Whom to Forgive -

Peter asked the question: *"How many times must we forgive?"* But the initial question that arises is likely to be: *"Whom must I forgive."* Is there anyone that we are allowed to hate or merely resent? Are there different levels of forgiveness in which we may function?

The relationships where we must focus our most vital efforts of restoration are those where we are in a covenant. This would include our marriage and the church body to which we belong. We must endeavor to forgive all people, however because these are covenants, our efforts to forgive here must extend beyond that of other more casual relationships.

Where offense or separation takes place within our covenants, it is not merely enough to forgive. Every effort must be taken to bring restoration of the relationships as well.

No division should ever be allowed to continue unaddressed within our marriages or church involvement. No relationship may endure long if offense is permitted to fester unabated. Paul addressed such issues with the church at Corinth, referring to their disputes as evidence that they were still baby Christians. He even rebuked them for taking one another to the world's courts to resolve their disputes:

> *1Cor 6:7 – "Now therefore there is utterly a fault among you, because ye go to law one with another. Why do ye not rather take wrong? Why do ye not rather suffer yourselves to be defrauded? Nay, ye do wrong, and defraud, and that your brethren."*

Jesus declared that *a kingdom divided against itself cannot stand.* A church that experiences unchecked division will never be able to manifest the end-time glory of God. A Christian that does not deal with offense toward those in his church body but instead entertains strife will eventually turn against those around him. At such times, either God or the pastor will most likely help him to relocate elsewhere. To stay in the position where God has assigned us, it is vital to walk in total forgiveness toward those around us.

Regarding relationships outside of our marriage or church where there is no covenant, even though we are required to forgive, restoration may not be necessary. For those persons we consider friends, considerable effort might be made to maintain or reestablish those friendships. However, should our efforts be rejected or if the others have proven themselves untrustworthy, such friendships may be discontinued.

The primary emphasis of forgiving others where we have no covenant is not so much to maintain the relationships, but instead is to keep our hearts clear of any form of offense. As discovered, all such offense may not just act to clog up the pipelines of love from our lives but may act to limit our access to the mercy of God. No grudge or chip we choose to carry on our shoulder is worth that cost.

Scripture declares that *"all that will live godly in Christ Jesus shall suffer persecution."* In no way will we ever have everyone like us. In fact, the more that we begin to manifest the power of the Kingdom of God, the more the enemy will stir up mockers against us. Our best efforts should be to continually examine our hearts to assure no resentment arises from within us. As we guard ourselves against all love obstructing attitudes, the very anointing that our critics are opposing may wash over their own souls and win them to the Kingdom. Keep in mind that we hate the sin but not the sinner. Direct all blame toward the devil!

Steps to Forgive -

The steps that we take toward forgiveness may differ depending upon the situation. Know that the surest means to forgiving effectively involves prayer and the leading of the Holy Spirit. However, because the enemy works so aggressively to keep us from stepping into full forgiveness, a set of potential steps that may be taken are listed below. Not every case of forgiving may follow these steps, but this at least gives us an outline to begin.

1. **Recognize the need to forgive:** We must be alert for ill feelings toward others and be sensitive to the existence of strife. We must be on guard to notice if others have separated from us. Often we may have offended someone else without knowing it. We should monitor our conversations for critical words - for they may point to what is in our heart.
2. **Speak forth to God and ourselves that we forgive them:** Our spoken words are the means by which we release our faith and authority. By vocalizing our forgiveness, we are making a statement of faith that we will harbor no animosity toward the offending person. As well, we are declaring that we reject the pain, strife, and division that resulted.
3. **Pray for the grace of God to supernaturally set us free of the hurt:** Once we have released our faith to forgive, we then have the right for the anointing of love to deliver us from the pain of rejection and abuse. We should expect this power to come upon us to provide total deliverance in our lives.

4. **Pray for those being forgiven:** Heart-felt prayer for someone goes a long way to eradicate and replace feelings of hurt with those of genuine concern for them. Once we have voiced forgiveness, those persons we are now praying for have been loosed from the condemnation we would have ordinarily spoken against them. They are now positioned for God to move in their lives to bring salvation and restoration.
5. **If necessary, go to them and apologize:** Many conflicts are the result of misunderstandings. Even if we feel that we are the innocent party, an apology may break down the walls erected by offense. Often the one positioning themselves for greatest spiritual promotion is not the one who was right in the first place, but instead is the one willing to apologize.
6. **Cast down negative emotions and thoughts**: In all future interactions with the person we have forgiven, it will be necessary to cast down any negative thoughts or emotions that may arise. We must refuse to share with others our past disappointments regarding the person, and if they are saved, instead speak of them as righteous. The new image that we speak and envision will override the damaged memories of the past.
7. **Quit rehearsing the offense:** Those memories that we constantly rehearse become reinforced within us. The devil knowing this, constantly tries to bring back to mind the wrongs that we have experienced in the past. Once he gets us to meditate upon our prior disappointments, he then declares: *"You said that you forgave them but apparently you haven't."* If satan can't get us into hate, he will draw us into self-condemnation. It is vital for the revivalist to quickly take authority over such thoughts and cast them down. We cannot afford to dwell on and keep reliving the emotional baggage of the past.
8. **Bless our enemies if directed:** Blessing our enemies is not something to be treated as a law for every situation where someone has risen against us. Blessing our enemies is a

seed that we sow as the Holy Spirit directs. Again, the primary purpose is usually to keep our hearts free of the sludge of animosity. The less it bothers us that someone persecutes or slanders us, potentially the less often we will find ourselves instructed of God to take such steps.

As we learn to embrace the act of forgiving, the devil has lost one of his most effective weapons to keep us separated from God's love.

FORGIVING VERSUS ENABLING

To forgive someone does not mean that we must entrust them at the same level that we may have prior to the offense. To forgive indicates that we are willing to hold no animosity or grudges against them. It does not however mean that they are guaranteed to recover the same position of confidentiality, responsibility, or close friendship that they formerly possessed. Without a word from God to do so, only a fool would keep someone as their church treasurer who had been caught embezzling in the past. They may be forgiven the wrong but the trust level is possibly irreversibly damaged. When someone has repeatedly betrayed or abused us, we must forgive them but we are equally foolish to continue to position ourselves for repeated mistreatment.

Many Christians have been instructed that to genuinely forgive is to *forgive and forget*. To some level this is true - we should *forgive* the transgression and *forget* the pain of the event. **However, to allow someone to continually mistreat or take advantage of us without making adjustments to the relationship transforms us into *enablers*.** The enabler has a confused concept of love which positions them to become another's punching bag. Too often, actions of enablement are confused as forgiveness.

A business owner can forgive someone and still fire them from a position or a job. A pastor can forgive a wolf and still ask them to leave their church. Paul didn't hate the young man living in sin from the Corinthian church that he commanded removed from the church covering. In fact, the actions that Paul took were motivated by love and resulted in the man's restoration in the fellowship.

An abused spouse can forgive their mate and still divorce them. If they have violated the marriage covenant in a fashion that scripturally provides grounds for divorce, it may be necessary to do so. The Bible tells us that we *become one* with those whom we have sexual relations. If your spouse has been cheating, it is your choice whether you want to deal with all of the demonic entities that they are potentially bringing to your home. As well, God never meant for you to forgive someone to the point that you are willing to catch the STD's that their illicit actions have brought them.

As a side note: Adultery is not the only grounds that exist for divorce or separation. Abandonment and repeated mental or physical abuse also may qualify. Such actions violate the committed marriage vows decreed.

Forgiving Christians must draw the line between forgiving others versus enabling them in their destructive lifestyles. We must love ourselves enough not to allow ourselves to be repeatedly abused.

One final area towards which Christians need to learn to exercise forgiveness is for themselves. Christians who tend to be the most on-fire are often the most condemning toward their own mistakes. So often, we beat ourselves up for the slightest missteps. I'm not referring to sin, but for small things such as falling asleep in prayer, breaking a fast earlier than we committed, or even having a moment of frustration that resulted in grumbling. Nobody seems to be able to beat us up as well as we bludgeon ourselves. To advance in love, we must be willing to forgive ourselves just as God forgives us and continue to move forward spiritually. As is often said, we must *admit it, quit it, and forget it*. The blood of Christ was shed to give us this right.

> *1John 1:9 – "If we confess our sins, he is faithful and just to forgive us our sins, and to cleanse us from all unrighteousness."*

CHAPTER 13

THE END OF LOVE

*"Hear counsel, and receive instructions, that thou mayest be wise in thy latter **end**." - Proverbs 19:20*

By *The End of Love*, we are not insinuating of a time period where love will cease to exist. Instead, we are referring to the **end** of this book as well as to the **end** results that walking in love will produce in our lives.

This book has offered a glimpse of what is to come as we step into God's outpoured love and glory by faith in these end-times. Those who shine with the glory as indicated in Isaiah 60 will be those who intentionally clothe themselves with this force.

ALL IN

We have learned of:

- **The Need for Love,**
- **The Supernatural Results of Love,**
- **God's Stairway to Agape,**
- **The Recipe of Love,**
- **The Fruit of the Spirit,**
- **The Love – Knowledge Cycle,**
- **The Covenant – Love Cycle,**
  and much more.

It is my desire that the contents of this book have motivated you to overcome all distractions, prior roadblocks, and lack of understanding to enable you to pursue the love of God with all of your heart, mind, soul, and strength.

It should be apparent by now that walking in the supernatural love of God involves more than a part time, halfway spiritual effort. It cannot be manifested merely by gaining the understanding that God loves us but requires an *all-in* effort to allow the Holy Spirit to transform us.

As a form of summarizing much of what is contained in this text, a checklist has been assembled itemizing many of the topics contained herein. This checklist may be used to track your progress in manifesting God's highest anointing – His supernatural love.

Of course, merely checking items off of a list does not guarantee that we will see the results of love manifested in our lives. Hopefully however, as we frequently review this list it will bring to mind areas in our walk with God that we may need to target or at least shore-up. Each point ends with the chapter reference where each facet is explained in more detail.

A LOVE CHECKLIST

___ **Born-Again**
By being born-again we exchange our fallen sin nature within for the nature of God. Because *"God is love,"* through this miracle event love becomes imprinted to the core of who we are.
CHAPTER 3

___ **Convinced of our Righteousness**
Once we are born-again, we are recreated righteous. Once saved, to walk in love it becomes imperative that we discover that we have been delivered of our prior sin nature. Only then can we overcome the condemnation that would block the flow of love from us.
CHAPTER 3

___ **Led of the Spirit**
To fulfill the call of God upon our lives, we must be led of the Spirit of God. Because God's high call for every believer is to walk in love, then everything that the Holy Spirit directs us to do will be targeted to get us functioning in that love. To resist the leading of the Spirit is to reject personally advancing into love's flow.
CHAPTER 1

___ **Building Faith for Love**
Because love is a supernatural force, it can only be accessed through intentional efforts of faith. Since faith is best developed through focused effort, it is vital that we set aside time to target building our faith for the love of God.
CHAPTER 4

____ **Confessing Love**
Faith is released through *voicing* the promises of God given to us. Therefore it is important that we declare His promises over our lives to fill us with this love.
CHAPTER 4

____ **Corresponding Actions of Love**
Faith without corresponding action remains dormant. We must step out in faith into the actions that love would normally produce and resist those improper responses that love would counter.
CHAPTER 4

____ **Laying Down your Soul**
We must be willing to lay aside our own personal desires to take up the assignment that God has for us. We will need to press through every form of opposition that would try to separate us from our brothers in Christ.
CHAPTER 4

____ **Fruit of the Spirit**
All of the fruit of the Spirit listed in Galatians 5 are all outward manifestations of our inner nature of love. We must be willing to examine our lives for the absence of this fruit to motivate ourselves to press further into the power of love.
CHAPTER 5

____ **Unmoved by Emotions**
The mature Christian learns to use their emotions to determine who is dominating the atmosphere around them. If what they are feeling is affecting their attitudes negatively it is obviously not aligned with that which love produces. They subsequently take active steps to usher in the presence of God.
CHAPTER 5

____ **Casting Down Imaginations**
To live by faith, it is mandatory that the believer takes authority over and casts down any thoughts that do not

align with the Word of God. To manifest supernatural love, we must refuse to entertain thoughts that might produce division in the body if not checked. Criticism and offense have no place in the life of the revivalist.
CHAPTER 7

_____ **Deactivation of Soul Landmines**
The enemy has been working our entire lives to place landmines in our souls. The demonically inspired mental programs have hair triggers that when touched cause us to explode in unfathomable ways. To move into love, we must be willing to allow God to point out these hazardous mindsets and then work with Him to remove them from our lives.
CHAPTER 8

_____ **United to a Church**
We are commanded to be united to a church body that is moving forward with God's end-time vision. It is unlikely that many spiritual *lone rangers* will manifest the last-day glory.
CHAPTER 7

_____ **Divine Order**
Because the anointing flows from the *Head* down to the remainder of the body, it is vital that we be submitted to *anointed and appointed* church leadership. To resist divine order within the church potentially may strip away the prayer canopy of covering that God desires in place over our lives.
CHAPTER 7

_____ **Transitioned to a Life of Sowing**
It is impossible to be a tightwad and manifest the love of God to any high level. Because genuine love always results in giving into the lives of others, those who refuse to become radical sowers are living a lifestyle opposed to this love. Those truly flowing in the love of God *live to give*.
CHAPTER 4

____ **Servant to the Body of Christ**
It is not enough to bestow of our goods and finances to step into love. We must also put on the attitude of a servant. Jesus, the epitome of love, laid down his life as a servant to those around Him and encouraged His followers to do likewise. The love of God cannot flow through a self-focused, self-serving individual.
CHAPTER 4

____ **Refusing to Quit**
In that *"love never fails,"* we must be determined not to fail as well. Quitting cannot be an option in our pursuit of love. All of hell will be released to try to stop us from manifesting this highest of anointings. To quit is to let them win. However, if we will be obedient to follow God and continue our development efforts, satan cannot stop us.
CHAPTER 5

____ **Understanding and Honoring Covenant**
Covenant understanding and commitment act as a flywheel to the actions of love in our life. The covenant individual will choose to release actions of love regardless of their current emotional status. These love actions keep our relationships intact until love again blooms.
CHAPTER 7

____ **Refusing Offense**
Offense is the number one reason that people leave the revivalist churches that God has called them to attend. The enemy is quite adept at pointing out things that may rub us the wrong way to get us emotionally off-balance. Once off-balance, a fall from our love walk will almost surely follow. To maintain our ability to advance into love demands that we become unoffendable.
CHAPTER 7

____ **Acting as a Peacemaker**
When an atmosphere of strife arises within any of our relationships, sharp words and hurt feelings are sure to

follow. The Christian who is targeting walking in love learns to recognize the enemy's efforts to divide. Instead of responding in a defensive fashion or lashing out towards those about him, the alert Christian acts as a peacemaker despite how he may currently feel. By doing so, he creates an environment where love may flourish versus animosity.
CHAPTER 4

____ **Abiding in Christ**

Jesus made it clear that if we are to walk in love, it is mandatory that we abide in Him. To abide indicates a deep and continual relationship with Him where He is able to lead us into the fullness of His love and power. One of the most effective tactics of the enemy to neutralize love from manifesting in our lives is to try to get us so busy that we neglect our time with God. Just as we could never save ourselves by our own efforts, neither can we manifest supernatural love without His ongoing involvement.
CHAPTER 9

____ **Knowing God**

The Apostle John declared that to walk in love we must both be born-again AND know God. Knowing God is a direct result of abiding in Him. However, it is vital for us to understand that we can neither abide in Him nor know Him beyond our knowledge of and time in the Word of God. Time in prayer must be matched by time in God's Word. Otherwise, the believer is likely to be blown off course by deceiving spirits. The Word keeps us on track.
CHAPTER 9

____ **Bold Steps**

To step into supernatural love, it will be necessary to overcome excess timidity and the fear of man. No person will be able to step into the actions necessary to manifest supernatural love if they are afraid of what people might think or if they do not want to make a scene. Love is bold to step out and pray for others. Love is willing to confront evil.

CHAPTER 10

_____ **Casting Down Fear**

The Apostle John declared that *"He that feareth is not made perfect in love."* Therefore, it is imperative that we eradicate fear from our lives. This includes: Fear of Man, Fear of Failure, Fear of Rejection, and any other fears that might hinder our callings. How might someone transition their lives to become a radical sower if they live with a Fear of Lack?

CHAPTER 10

_____ **Rejecting the World**

John also declared: *"If any man love the world, the love of the father is not in him."* To walk in supernatural love, it becomes necessary to disconnect from our adoration of and devotion to the world and its temptations. What we love the most, if not God, becomes an idol in our lives and demands our time and attention. To walk in love requires that God becomes our number one focus.

CHAPTER 10

_____ **Choosing Truth**

God's Word is the truth. To become disciples who truly walk in love requires that our lives become conformed to the Word. As well, we must become believers who refuse to compromise the truths of the Word. However, we also must become people of unquestioned integrity. Those who are willing to bend the truth or even outright lie come under the influence of the father of lies - the devil.

CHAPTER 11

_____ **Forgiving**

Nothing so clogs up the pipelines of the love of God within us as refusing to forgive those we perceive have wronged us. Scripture makes it clear that we cannot say that we love God if we despise our brother. Aggressive steps must be

taken to search out and eradicate any attitudes within us where we have chosen not to forgive.
CHAPTER 12

_____ **Blessing our Enemies**
We are instructed to bless our enemies, not as much for their benefit as for ours. It works to cleanse us of animosity and hatred thus aiding us in our ability to forgive. It also acts as a step of faith that we can take to see supernatural love manifest and damaged relationships become restored.
CHAPTER 12

STAIR STEPS TO LOVE

See **CHAPTER 8** for an explanation of each.

_____ **Faith**
_____ **Virtue**
_____ **Knowledge**
_____ **Temperance**
_____ **Patience**
_____ **Godliness**
_____ **Brotherly Kindness**

God is even now awakening those who truly grasp the opportunity given us to walk in supernatural love. Once aware, the pursuit of this love becomes the central focus of the remainder of their lives. The choice is ours to make. Let's go for the glory!

ABOUT THE AUTHOR

Jack Shoup is founder and senior pastor of Grace Fellowship of Georgetown located in Georgetown, Kentucky.

He is a graduate of The University of Tennessee in mechanical engineering and has an MBA from Xavier University. Beginning in 1977, Jack spent 14 years with IBM Corp. and another 2 years with Lexmark Corp. working in both engineering, business office, and management positions.

Jack and his wife Patty were both saved the same evening soon after they were wed in 1984. From that moment, Jack was imparted an insatiable hunger for the Word of God. He was called into full-time ministry in 1993 and has served as Pastor of Outreach Ministries, as an Assistant Pastor, and since 2001, as a senior pastor.

Jack is called of God to search out the Scriptures and to impart, through his teaching, in-depth understanding of the spiritual principles that govern the Kingdom of God. His primary area of instruction has focused much on the love of God and on the covenant that believer's enter into as members of the Body of Christ.

After 25 years of concentrated scriptural study on the supernatural love of God, he knew that it was time to consolidate much of his revelation of love into a book.

Jack and Patty have two daughters, Amy and Lori, both grown and pursuing their own careers.

www.ingramcontent.com/pod-product-compliance
Lightning Source LLC
Chambersburg PA
CBHW071600080526
44588CB00010B/970